Gathering the Desert

Also by Gary Paul Nabhan

The Desert Smells Like Rain:
A Naturalist in Papago Indian Country

Gathering the Desert

GARY PAUL NABHAN

Illustrations by

PAUL MIROCHA

THE UNIVERSITY OF ARIZONA PRESS

Tucson & London

About the Author

GARY PAUL NABHAN is the associate director of the Desert Botanical Gardens in Phoenix. He is also president and cofounder of Native Seeds/SEARCH, a nonprofit agricultural-conservation organization that maintains seed banks of indigenous Southwestern plants, among its other services. An ethnobotanist and conservationist, Nabhan received his Ph.D. from the University of Arizona in 1983. He is the author of *The Desert Smells Like Rain: A Naturalist in Papago Indian Country* and of numerous popular technical articles.

About the Illustrator

PAUL MIROCHA graduated from the University of Minnesota with an interdepartmental degree in fine arts and biology. He has pursued an interest in relating art and natural science in his own drawing and photography, as well as through his work as a scientific illustrator and graphic designer for the Office of Arid Lands Studies at the University of Arizona in Tucson.

Fifth printing 1993

THE UNIVERSITY OF ARIZONA PRESS

Manufactured in the U.S.A.
♾ This book is printed on acid-free, archival-quality paper.

This book was set in 11/14 Compugraphic 8400 Berkeley Old Style.

Library of Congress Cataloging-in-Publication Data
Nabhan, Gary Paul.
Gathering the desert.

Bibliography: p.
1. Desert flora—Sonoran Desert. 2. Ethnobotany—Sonoran Desert. 3. Indians of North America—Sonoran Desert—Ethnobotany. 4. Botany, Economic—Sonoran Desert. I. Title.
QK211.N33   1985   581.6'1'097217   85-13933
ISBN 0-8165-0935-2
ISBN 0-8165-1014-8 (pbk.)

Contents

Acknowledgments

FRIENDS frequently get one another in trouble by attempting to do things together that neither in his right mind would try to do alone. In the spring of 1983, while bouncing down a road in the Pinacate lava fields of northwestern Mexico, the two of us somehow talked ourselves into collaborating on a project for which neither of us really had time. Both of us had recently become fathers, were getting little sleep (but still more than our wives), and we had diapers on our mind more than the creation of books. We were on our way to climb Pinacate Peak, which rose steep and black in the distance, and we planned to carry Anna (at fifteen months and twenty-six pounds) and Dustin (at thirteen months) on our backs. We made it—although Paul swore he'd retire as a pack animal—and it was worth the effort. As lava crunched under our weight, the kids bounced around, upsetting our balance and exclaiming "fower!" upon seeing the penstemon and brittlebush that surrounded us. This primal excitement of discovery and meeting is at heart what stimulated our work on this book. So, against our better judgment, we ignored the laws of physics and made the arguable assumption that it would be possible to be good fathers, good husbands, and good at sketching plants all at the same time.

We thank our wives, Karen Reichhardt and Kay Mirocha, and our children, Anna Crystal Mirocha, Dustin Corvus Nabhan, and Laura Rose Nabhan, for their encouragement when it seemed we were trying to work forty-hour days. Kay's eye as an artist and editor and Karen's skills as a field botanist contributed greatly to the quality of this work. This book is dedicated to our children, for the values we have learned from them, and in the hope that these plants will still be the subject of stories, passed orally from generation to generation, when they are as old and as foolish as we are.

Just as we were supported and tolerated by our families throughout this work, the Old Pueblo community of biologists, anthropologists, and artists served as our sounding boards and guides. There is an old tradition of creative collaboration in Sonoran Desert ethnobotany in Tucson, going back at least as far as the friendships of Edward and Rosamond Spicer with Howard Scott Gentry and Alfred Whiting, or back further to Robert Forbes, Carl Lumholtz, and the Tumamoc Hill gang at the turn of the century. We thank the many Tucsonans who shared their original discoveries, experiences, and knowledge with us: Tony Burgess, Charles Miksicek, Richard Felger, Steve Buchmann, Thomas Van Devender, Janice Bowers, Don Sayner, Ofelia Zepeda, Danny Lopez, Charles Lowe, James Griffith, Peter Warshall, Kevin Dahl, Bernard Fontana, Julian Hayden, Ray Turner, Margarita Kay, Wade Sherbrooke, Joe Scheerens, James Berry, Rodney Engard, Thomas Sheridan, Carl Olson, Susie Fish, Floyd Werner, Yar Petryszyn, and Lendell Cockrum. We also thank our colleagues at the Office of Arid Lands Studies, especially William McGinnies and Charles Hutchinson for discussion, and Ken Foster and Jack Johnson for allowing us the flexibility to work on this project. Native Seeds/SEARCH staff, including Karen Reichhardt, Mahina Drees, Barney Burns, Cindy Baker, and Esther Moore, also provided constant advice and interpretation of these plants.

Fortunately, Sonoran Desert plant experts are not all concentrated in Tucson. We are extremely grateful for the help given to us by Vorsila Bohrer of Portales, Anita Alvarez de Williams in Mexicali, Sally Pablo and Ruth Giff in Komatke, Delores Lewis of Big Fields, Laura Kermen on the Papago Reservation, Amadeo Rea of San Diego, Donna Howell of Terlingua, Ruth Greenhouse and Howard Scott Gentry at the Desert Botanical Garden, Laura Merrick and Conrad Bahre in Davis, Rich Pratt at Purdue, the Romero family in Puerto Peñasco, the Durazo family of the Río Bavispe, Eric and Anna Mellink of Caborca, the Cruz family of Cucurpe, and the Noriega family, the Murrieta family, and Rafael Aguirre of Hermosillo. Paul also wishes to thank long-time friend and artist Joe Byrne for his comments on the drawings, and to apologize to Albrecht Dürer for the chile drawing, and Gary is grateful to Lebanese cousin Valerie Burger for having moved to Nogales in time to help edit the manuscript.

There is no way to acknowledge all the Native American people—including Pima, Papago, Cocopa, Yaqui, Mayo, Seri, Cahuilla, Warihio, Tarahumara, and Hopi—who passed on the stories, skills, and observations that make our desert plant heritage so rich. Their wisdom and wit form the heart of this book.

Many segments of these essays are outgrowths of fieldwork done by Nabhan and colleagues over the last several years. Gary wishes to acknowledge support of technical research on ethnobotany and plant genetic resources from the National Science Foundation (BNS–8317190), the C.S. Fund, the Wenner-Gren Foundation, the Coleman Fund, the Tides Foundation, the U.S. Man and the Biosphere Program, the Tinker Foundation, and the USDA Agricultural Research Service.

Finally, we'd like to admit that a few characters in these sketches are
fictionalized, to protect related real characters from being
kidded for making such wonderfully hilarious or
spicy comments about plants. You figure
out which ones they are.
We'll never tell.

Gathering the Desert

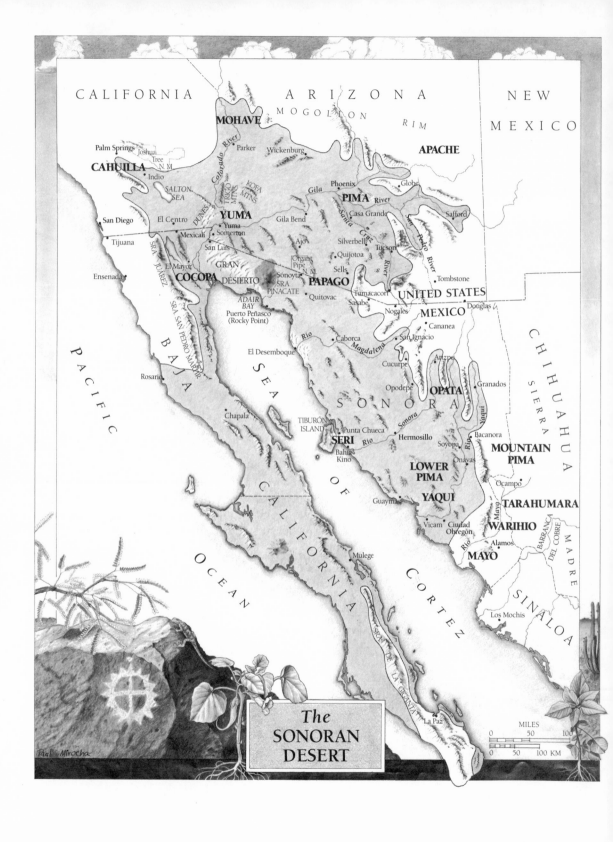

The
SONORAN
DESERT

ALONG the rivers of eastern Sonora, Mexico, the Opata Indians have been assimilated into "melting pot" *mestizo* culture for nearly two and a half centuries. Yet as we wandered down the streets of Granados on the Río Bavispe, an elderly man with a somewhat spooky voice was telling us dozens of Opata names for desert plants that he himself continued to use. There we were, two trained botanists, and Don Manuel, who knew more kinds of plants in these parts than we did, on a walking tour of his village's gardens. At the same time, we were seeking some bootleg mescal that we could take back with us across the border.

Don Manuel escorted us into the backyard of some of his relatives. We sidestepped turkeys and took a look at a colorful dooryard garden full of greens, flowers, chiltepines, pomegranates, and Mexican oregano bushes. A gray-haired but spry woman wiped her hands on her apron and greeted us, gesturing for us to enter the shade of a mesquite-branch ramada that served as a summer kitchen. After the perfunctory small talk about the hot June weather we'd been having, Don Manuel asked the lady of the house if her husband kept any home-brewed *mescal bacanora* on reserve.

"It's only nine in the morning!" she scolded. "Why don't you men start the day off with something more filling?" Before we could explain that we weren't asking for a drink on the spot, a smile broke across her mock-angry face. She told us that her husband could probably sell us a little mescal as soon as he returned from gathering organpipe cactus fruit, but that she could offer us something in the meantime to quench our thirst. We were welcome to taste some *atole de pechita* that had just been made, if we didn't mind a drink made of mesquite pods pounded on a crude old *batea,* a hand-carved mesquite wood metate.

Sweet, like carob or chocolate pudding in flavor and texture, the mesquite-pod atole was a special treat for my botanist friend, who had known that the pods were an important ancient food, but had no idea how they were customarily prepared. The woman explained her processing and cooking technique, while refilling our bowls for an additional taste.

"Well, that sounds so simple to prepare," I said. Thinking aloud, I asked, "I wonder why more people don't continue to make it," recalling that even the Yavapai, Pima, and Yaqui, who once ate mesquite as their mainstay, seldom eat it on a regular basis any more.

"It is easy to make," she said, shaking her head sadly. "It's good for you too. But I can tell you why most people here don't use the *pechita* any more. They're Lazies. They think food must come only from the CONASUPO, the V-H, El Gigante, and other big supermarkets. They'd rather waste their time driving to the costly stores in the cities to buy tasteless food than use what is right here around them...."

It is easy to dismiss such remarks as typical of any oldtimer unsettled by the younger generation's enthrallment with the trappings of the material world. Yet these comments are from a woman who is perfectly willing to draw upon the benefits of twentieth-century medical care, transportation, and electronic communications. She is not some romantic back-to-the-land advocate in search of a natural lifestyle; she speaks as a hard-working woman whose family has lived in the same desert valley for generations. She has no philosophical bias for "Indian ways" as opposed to "White Man's ways." In short, she feels there is no reason to give up mesquite gathering or other traditional practices which made good sense just because she accepts some things that are "modern."

From our vantage point, an additional concern emerges. Within the last three generations, changes in how and where we get most of our food and medicine may be as dramatic as any other economic change that has occurred in history or prehistory. There are both beneficial and detrimental effects on our health that have resulted from technological advances influencing food production, processing, and distribution during this century. Regardless of your opinion as to whether our diets are generally better or worse than those of desert dwellers a century ago, it can't be denied that their diets were significantly different from ours.

Overall, the changes in Sonoran Desert plant use during the last few centuries have been truly radical. One objective of the sketches that follow is to help us gain perspective on the dynamics of desert dwellers' use of plants for food and other purposes, as they have shifted through time. Reductions in the diversity, distribution, and abundance of plant resources, alterations in land-use patterns, harvesting pressures and dietary preferences, and even changes in animal populations all come into play. As a region of focus, the Sonoran Desert of Arizona, southeastern California, Baja California, and Sonora, demonstrates most patterns of plant/human interactions that can be found on this planet. A few of these sketches reach beyond the geographic limits of the Sonoran Desert proper, but nearly all scenes described take place within two days' walk of saguaro cactus, the indicator plant for this binational desert.

For ninety-nine percent of the time that humans have inhabited the Sonoran Desert, life was inconceivable without plants such as the ones in the following sketches. Certain key species—mesquite, fan palms, agaves, and columnar cacti— could each be called "the staff of life" to one or more cultures which lived within their range. Other important species might not provide such a variety of useful products, or are only seasonally available, but were nonetheless revered. Sandfood, for instance, is an obscure parasite on the roots of shrubs in the sand seas of the Gran Desierto. It reaches above ground to flower for less than six weeks each year, and today is so rarely seen that it has been considered an endangered-species candidate in the United States. Yet this succulent food was so esteemed that its reputation extended hundreds of miles beyond its natural range. Those who lived within grasp of it were nicknamed "the Sand Root Crushers."

Whether superabundant and storable, or as rare and perishable as manna, these plants helped shape and succor cultures within the Sonoran Desert. They served as calories, cures, and characters in tribal legends. Native Americans learned that certain chemicals in these plants—ones which had probably evolved as defenses against predators and pests, or as attractants to pollinators and seed dispersers—produced consistent results in pleasing the palate or easing pain. Thus desert peoples became dependent upon plant products which had co-evolved with birds, bats, rodents, or ungulates over hundreds of thousands of years. A few of these plant species have had their evolutionary destinies further altered by those who gathered, saved, and selected their seeds, thereby domesticating them. Devil's claw and Sonoran panicgrass are two endemic domesticates of the Sonoran Desert region, and they indicate that native farmers did more than simply accept a package of predomesticated plants wholesale from Mesoamerica. In fact, the

Sonoran Desert is the center of varietal diversity for tepary beans and cushaw squashes, two crops which have undergone as much significant evolution in this region as in the Mesoamerican area to the south.

In emphasizing the mutualistic relationships which have developed between native plants and Sonoran cultures, we may be accused of promulgating a kind of environmental or culinary determinism, or believing that Native Americans have always lived in a static balance with nature. To the contrary, what interests us most is the diversity of historic responses that individuals and cultures have had to the set of potential plant resources in the region. Why do certain people seem to be attracted to selected plants more than others? When were particular wild resources brought into cultivation and why? What are the reasons that some of these plants have fallen from use while others have not? Which plants are more vulnerable to overexploitation or to habitat degradation? When a useful plant does diminish in abundance, how do people respond?

Out of the 2500 vascular plants in the Sonoran Desert, why are we paying such an inordinate amount of attention to the twelve that follow? There are over 425 wild edible species in the Sonoran Desert flora, and roughly twenty-five crop species have been cultivated since prehistoric times. Why dwell upon so few?

Though somewhat arbitrary, our choice of these particular plants is based on considerations that reach beyond mere utilitarian criteria. Each exemplifies either a symbolic or an ecological relationship which Sonoran Desert dwellers had with numerous plants. A literary challenge was involved as well. Can our sketches express the character of plants, in the way that people sense the spirit of certain animals?

Coyote. Raven. Bear. Eagle. Snake. Anyone familiar with Native American legends or with contemporary Western American literature has a feeling for who these characters are, over and above their specific zoological features. Each is known for a particular *anima* in American folklore. It is less often acknowledged that certain plants have characteristics so distinctive that they have become personae in Native American folklore. For instance, among the Yoeme (Yaqui and Mayo) and O'odham (Papago and Pima), jimsonweed or sacred datura is recognized as a dangerous object, but has also played a role in shamanistic curing and song. People may ritualistically bring powerful plants offerings and place taboos on harvesting their products during certain times or at given places. They load meaning into individual plants that may be genetically aberrant or environmentally deformed. When a human community encourages its members to know the characters of select plants so intimately, it is also making its own cultural identity known.

Today, plants are used symbolically in ways which sometimes link people with their homeland and past, serving as a conservative element to slow change. Peter Farb and George Armelagos have observed that

> ...the surest way of discovering a family's ethnic origins is to look into its kitchen. Long after dress, manners, and speech have become indistinguishable from those of the majority, the old food habits continue as the last vestiges of the previous culture.

We recognize that these indigenous foods and medicines make up but a small portion of what even the most traditional desert family now put in their mouths. They are vestiges from a time when these plants made vital contributions to the health of desert-dwelling cultures. But because so many Native Americans and Mexican-Americans in the American Southwest now suffer from diabetes and other nutrition-related diseases, the demise of native plants in their diets has been tentatively related to the upswing of the incidence of certain diseases.

It has been suggested that certain native foodstuffs are high in dietary fiber and have other properties that make them useful in controlling the severity of diabetes and other health problems. There is some interest today in revitalizing the remnant traditions of indigenous foods and medicines to help Native Americans suffering from alcoholism, malnutrition, and diet-influenced ailments. Nicholas Hildyard's perspective bears consideration:

> If there is a solution to the world hunger problem, it surely does not lie in destroying cultures but rather in reestablishing them. Indeed, the great irony is that nutritionists are needed in precisely those societies whose culture has broken down.

For such reasons, we hope that folk botany—the traditional scientific knowledge of plants held as part of the heritage of various cultures—is more than historical trivia. We doubt that future generations can afford to ignore the valuable products derived from plants such as mesquite. Food production in North American deserts is now based on humid-adapted crops that consume twenty to thirty percent more water when grown in arid environments than they do when cultivated in the more mesic zones where they originated. This is extra water that we do not have.

Yet we do not want to imply that all wild desert plants brought into modern agricultural settings would necessarily use less irrigation water than conventional crops. Plants such as agaves and creosote bush, which are water-efficient in their natural habitats under unreliable rainfall regimes, do not usually make such good use of supplemental water when they are irrigated at regular intervals. Nevertheless, by evaluating native desert plants as potential economic resources, and comparing them with conventional crops, we stand to learn something about the tradeoffs between short-term productivity and long-term persistence in unpredictable environments.

We hope that these sketches will encourage arid-land dwellers to feel more at home with the desert's bounty, a richness that cannot be understood simply in utilitarian terms. Even if you were never to eat a carob-like mesquite pod, or treat a cold with creosote-leaf tea, these plants have something to offer. It may be just the music heard when standing beneath a spring-flowering mesquite canopy, alive
with five thousand solitary bees, or the smell of a creosote bush
releasing fifty volatile oils to the ozone-charged air during a
summer storm. Even if you don't gather the desert,
let it gather a feeling in you. Even if you
don't swallow it as medicine,
meditate upon it:
the desert can
cure.

WINTER

Earth Maker took from his breast the soil and began to flatten it like a tortilla in the palm of his hand. From it the first green thing grew: the creosote bush.
He gathered the gumlike lac from the scale insect on its branches and, pounding out shapes while singing, he formed the mountains.

The Creosote Bush Is Our Drugstore

L
ONG ago, darkness just lay there. No earth, moon, or stars had yet been finished.

The old people of the desert—certain Papago and Pima elders—remember such darkness whenever wintertime comes. They recall hearing of when there wasn't anything.

As darkness washed up against itself, a spirit grew inside it: Earth Maker. Earth Maker took from his breast the soil stuck to it, and he began to flatten this soil like a tortilla in the palm of his hand. He shaped this mound of earth, and from it, the first thing grew: the greasewood. From its branches, the first animal came. It was a tiny, scaly insect that could use the resin of greasewood to produce its own covering of lac. Earth Maker gathered this gumlike lac. He began to sing. Pounding out various shapes while singing, he formed the mountains. They hardened like shellac, making a hard crust for the earth. The space which brushed against their edges became the sky.

The plant called greasewood by the Papago is known in botany books as creosote bush, since scientists prefer not to confuse it with two other Southwestern "greasewoods," *Sarcobatus* and *Atriplex*. Whatever common name is preferred, *Larrea tridentata* goes back a long time. Paleoecologist Tom Van Devender discovered this down near the Camino del Diablo, in the Tinajas Altas Mountains of southwestern Arizona. Pulling out a chunk of crusty plant debris from an ancient packrat midden stuck back in the rocks, he encountered creosote fragments

11

embedded within. When radiocarbon-dated, these greasewood pieces confirmed that such plants had established themselves near the Lower Colorado River more than seventeen thousand years ago.

Larrea records nearly as ancient have been recognized for other areas in the western region of North American deserts. Van Devender now speculates that after migrating up from South America, creosote remained limited to a few lowland refugia throughout much of the Pleistocene. Then, as the Ice Age waned, greasewood began to spread. The Lower Colorado creosote probably extended up into the Mohave Desert. *Larrea* likely moved from another refugium along the coast of the Sea of Cortez to reach out across much of the Sonoran Desert. It spilled over into the northern Chihuahuan Desert around 4500 years ago, according to Van Devender's reckoning. Creosote has since dispersed further, so that it now covers a quarter of Mexico—some 30 million hectares—and another 18 million hectares of the United States.

Once greasewood gets settled, it sticks around. Take King Clone, near Old Woman Springs, California.

Flying two hundred and fifty kilometers northeast from the heart of Los Angeles's chaotic sprawl, pilots noticed odd elliptical patterns of growth on the ground below. Botanist Frank Vasek visited this area on foot and found an oval ring of creosote shoots averaging almost eight meters in radius. It was twenty-two meters in width at one cross section, with a bare spot of earth and dead wood stubble in its midst.

As Vasek studied the configuration, he surmised that it might consist of just one plant, instead of simply being a population of numerous individuals aligned in a curvilinear design. Vasek's colleague Lionel Sternberg confirmed through chemical studies that the population was in fact a clone of genetically identical *Larrea*.

It was not just *a* clone. It was the most extensive creosote clone known—King Clone. Yet how did the growth from a single seed end up covering a horizontal distance of twenty-two meters? And when did that pioneering seed germinate?

By observing younger creosote clumps, then delving deeper into the distribution of King Clone's shoots and roots, Vasek began to answer these questions. A new creosote sprout grows vertically until it reaches a few centimeters in height; then lateral branches develop. They shoot up diagonally, so that young creosote bushes are shaped like upside-down ice cream cones. As the plant matures, it begins to send up additional basal shoots from its root crown, but always at the periphery of the plant.

Sooner or later, the original stem dies and its dead wood slowly disintegrates, leaving a bare spot in the center of the clump. However, satellite shoots continue to branch out, gradually putting down their own roots in a ring around the original crown.

Concentric circles of new clonal shoots enable the original plant's genome to persist even as other inner stems die and leave a bigger hole in the "doughnut." Vasek decided to measure the rate of expansion of the creosote rings, to estimate how long it might have taken King Clone to attain its present size. His early estimates were on the order of eleven thousand years!

Vasek then measured the distance between concentric rings of dead wood stubble, and he radiocarbon-dated samples from several of these rings. Although the order of magnitude of his King Clone age estimate was still probable, these new data suggested that ring expansion rates may have varied through time. As the historic climate changed, both creosote growth rates and overall vegetation composition were affected. Vasek's more conservative age estimate for King Clone— 9400 years—suggests that this plant began to grow when junipers still dominated the valley. Today, near Old Woman Springs, King Clone's creosote progeny mix with a scattering of bursage to cover the valley floor, while junipers have retreated upslope several hundred meters. Whatever King Clone's exact age may be, it is older than the most ancient bristlecone pine known to humankind.

Like pine, greasewood is a resin reservoir. These resins are evident as an amber, tacky syrup exuded as droplets on its stems. More importantly, they make up ten to twenty percent of the dry weight of *Larrea* foliage, being found both internally and as a waxy sheen on the external surface of the leaves. These resins, a complex mix of flavinoids, lignins, volatile oils, saponins, and waxes, serve to protect the plant in several ways.

On the leaf surface, these resins decrease the amount of ultraviolet light and heat that can reach the leaf interior, where photosynthesis and other vital activities might be slowed or disrupted by more extreme doses. Resins also limit the loss of water from leaf surfaces, thereby reducing overall transpiration.

Furthermore, *Larrea* is protected chemically from overconsumption by browsing animals, ranging from cattle to tiny, nearly imperceptible insects. A number of compounds in creosote resin simply taste terrible and repel potential herbivores. Other compounds make creosote leaf proteins indigestible by forming new chemical complexes in an animal's gut which are resistant to digestive enzymes. Only one grasshopper is definitely known to have counteradaptations in its gut chemistry which can deactivate creosote's defense system. These *Astroma* grasshoppers, incidentally, are creosote cryptics. The females, which stay low in the bush during the day, resemble old stems. The males mimic young leaf sprays. In design, these insects are essentially extensions of their host plant.

To produce such pervasive defenses against their enemies and the elements, any single creosote bush generates an astonishing diversity of chemicals. Biochemist Tom Mabry has isolated more than 360 constituents from the oil components of leaves of various *Larrea* species. At least forty-nine kinds of volatile oils can be found in a single greasewood stand. These give the plant its characteristic odor. When warm summer rains wash creosote clean for the first time after months of drought, the desert smells like vinyl and methyl ketones, camphor, and limonene. No wonder Sonorans call it *hediondilla*—"little stinker."

It probably did not take desert cultures too long to realize that creosote's chemicals did more than stink—something that pungent might also be medicinally powerful. The Jesuit missionaries who pioneered in the Pimería Alta—present-day north-central Sonora and southern Arizona—documented the curative uses of creosote just as early as they did those of other major plant medicines. Ignaz Pfeffercorn complained that this *hedionda* "gives off an odor which is almost unendurable to a somewhat sensitive nose," but the old German did admit that "it is really a very powerful remedy...for worms in children as well as in adults." His contemporary Juan Nentvig believed that it was beneficial to those afflicted with syphilis, and that an ointment made from creosote branches fried in tallow was efficacious when massaged onto gnarled rheumatic limbs. He added, however, that "if the masseur washes his hands after applying the ointment, his hands will become gnarled."

Over the following two centuries, travelers, explorers, cowboys, botanists, and anthropologists documented an incredible diversity of medicinal applications of creosote stems, leaves, and gum. The richness of documented usages of creosote among a single tribe, the desert Cahuilla, is staggering. From David Barrows's seminal work as a visitor among the Cahuilla at the turn of the century to that of Katherine Saubel among her own people in recent decades, *Larrea* has been recorded as part of the treatment for at least fourteen afflictions and diseases: colds, chest infections or lung congestion, intestinal discomfort, stomach cramps associated with delayed menstruation, consumption, cancer, nausea, wounds, poisons, swollen limbs due to poor circulation, dandruff, body odor, distemper, and postnasal drip. Sprigs of twigs and leaves are boiled as a tea, and drunk; placed over a fire to create steam that is inhaled in a sweathouse; dried, pounded into a powder, and pressed into a poultice on wounds; and heated into an infusion that is applied to the scalp or to the pits. What's more, it cures horses as well as humans.

Perhaps women observers have been privy to more detailed information on *Larrea*'s cultural uses than have male anthropologists. Becky Moser learned from Seri Indian women that creosote lac has been used as a contraceptive by burning chunks of it over a small flame, catching the melted droplets in a container of water, and drinking this liquid with the goal of preventing conception. The crusty casings from the lac insect, *Tarcardiella larrea,* have also been used to mend everything from ceramic pottery to overheated, cracked engine blocks. Today, keeping a vehicle's motor running along the desert coast may be as important to the Seri as curing horses of distemper was to the historic Cahuilla!

When living with Papago families in the 1930s, Ruth Underhill realized that *shegai,* as they called greasewood, was their most universal remedy:

> It was used for stiff limbs, sores and poisonous bites. Men, after running all day barefoot, would make a fire, and when it had burned out, heap creosote branches on the ashes and hold their aching feet in the smoke. Women after childbirth or with menstrual cramps would lie on a bed of such heated branches. For rheumatism, the hot branches were wrapped in a cloth and laid on the joints. In the case of a snake, spider, or scorpion bite, creosote leaves were chewed and placed on the swelling. The leaves were also boiled and given to the patient as an emetic.

When all such uses were tallied, desert plant chemist Peter Duisberg realized that creosote "has been used by the Indians for the treatment of almost as many diseases as has penicillin." In fact, scientists have found it to have antimicrobial effectiveness against the fungus *Penicillium* and certain bacteria. Yet when biochemists and pharmacologists are asked if certain creosote compounds are truly effective in the treatment of these diseases and injuries listed above, they balk. Mexican scholar Carlos Zolla complains that when pushed, specialists typically concede that until further studies are done, the effectiveness of these folk remedies must be considered "more a product of the imagination or of necessity than of any concrete biochemical action."

Zolla, however, appears optimistic that scientists will soon confirm which chemical compounds in creosote are functionally responsible for dissolving kidney stones and are physiologically active as fungicides. Studies have indicated that the antioxidant NDGA, a phenolic acid extractable from creosote resins, has analgesic and vasodepressant properties, plus a remarkable ability to stabilize vitamin A. Vitamin A is not only essential to good vision, but may play a key role in normal growth, reproduction, and possibly in the control of cancer cells. Physiologists and pathologists are looking at how a variety of antioxidants themselves may be directly involved in the breakdown of developing cancerous growths. Chemist E. P. Oliveto has suggested that as a compound which makes up five to ten percent of dried creosote leaves, NDGA is a readily available, naturally occurring antioxidant with qualities that may be effective in the treatment of alcoholism and liver ailments.

At the same time, laboratory studies suggested that NDGA may have a detrimental effect on the kidneys. As a result of two studies done feeding pure NDGA to rats, the U.S. Food and Drug Administration decreed that NDGA was unsafe for human consumption. Ranchers in the Southwest who had hoped to turn their marginal grazing lands into lucrative NDGA extraction sites were left up the arroyo without a paddle.

Nevertheless, Papago Indians continue to harvest their own supplies of *shegai* for family use. They know where bushes are that produce particularly potent greasewood tea. Unlike other traditional cures that have been abandoned as the Desert People have become more modernized, creosote had kept its popularity among Papago families both on and off the reservation. Few of these O'odham have familiarity with FDA decrees. Few know that health food stores have been active marketing *Larrea* as a cure-all that they whimsically called "chaparral tea"— the plant never grows above the desert in true chaparral vegetation. Still fewer Papagos would ever believe that greasewood is hazardous to anyone's health.

Laura Kermen is a Papago woman who, at the least, is in her eighties. Since her family did not keep track of time on a Western calender when she was young, she is fond of saying that she was "born before the years had numbers." Whatever her age, winters wear hard on her. She therefore keeps a thermos of fresh-brewed creosote tea nearby to drink, and puts its branches in her bath water to ease the ache in her bones. The plant from which she gathers branches is the same one that her father used at the turn of the century. It is rich in waxiness on its leaves. Laura and her sister in an Indian nursing home near Phoenix still refer to this now-large bush as "Papa's tree." Laura periodically shares its branches with her sister, as she does with visitors who happen by her house when they happen to be in poor health. Laura knows that Papago, Mexican, Yaqui, and Anglo alike can be cured by creosote.

To prove her point, she tells a story about a snowbird friend of hers learning of greasewood's worth from an unidentified Indian lady:

"I had a friend, she comes from New York State. She spends winter here, up around Phoenix, and summer back home. One time she told me,

'I always like to go downtown and watch all the different kinds of tribes of Indians, in the colored clothes that they wear. Yes, I like to go and see how well their clothes match.

'One day I was downtown. I got tired. I saw a bench on the corner where the busses stop to pick up people. I sat down on that bench and I began watching people.

'After a while an Indian lady came up to me and said, "Can I sit here?"

' "Sure," I said. "I'm not waiting for the bus. I'm just sitting here resting."

'So she sat down next to me and we began to talk about things: their ways, the making of their clothes. After a while I had to cough—I always cough badly in the wintertime. Sometimes I get a coughing spell. So while talking to this lady I coughed; it made me think to ask her: "Say, do you have any native medicines? How do your people cure coughs when you have them?"

' "Oh, out here, the greasewoods are our drugstores."

'I asked, "Greasewood? What is a greasewood?"

' " It grows all over the state here I think."

' "Well, I have a cough that I can't get rid of," my friend said. "It's especially bad in the wintertime. Do you think the greasewood could help it?"

' "Yes," the Indian lady said. "You go and you get that greasewood. That will cure the cough. You go to the hills. That's where it grows." '

"Alright, my friend went home and waited for her son to get home from where he works in downtown Phoenix. He got home and went out to water the lawn. She followed him.

' "John," she said, "When you get finished sprinkling the lawn, take me out where the greasewood trees grow."

' "Greasewood?" he said. "Why do you want greasewood?"

'She said, "Never mind, you just take me when you're done."

'"Aagh!" he said, and continued with his watering.

'After a while, he came into the house and said, "Alright, mom, you get ready and we'll go for the greasewood."

"So she got in the car and they drove towards Camelback. After a while, he stopped the car and said, 'Alright, you go get your greasewood here.'

'"Where are they?"

'"Anywhere, right here!" he said.

"She remembered that the Indian lady says that it's kind of a brownish yellowish green tree and that you can smell it when you go near it. She walked around and broke a little piece off a bush. She smelled it and decided 'This is it.' She broke branches off the bush, filled up a paper bag with them, went back to the car, and they drove home.

"When they got home, she found a big can and put the branches in it and poured water over them. She boiled it on the stove and then came out with a big thermos. She filled up the big thermos and took it to bed with her that night.

"Early in the morning, I guess, her son and his wife were having breakfast not far from her doorway. It was the first time in a long time that they hadn't heard my friend cough during the night. They were sitting there and after a while they heard the doorknob turn.

"Her son turned to his wife and said, 'Well, I guess mother died during the night. For the first night in a long time, I never heard her cough!"

"My friend peeked out from behind the door and said, 'Yes, and it's the greasewood that did it!'"

Creosote often accompanies people as they leave this world. Creosote lac seals the pottery jars full of food and seed that several tribes bury with their dead, so that they may have well-preserved supplies of the resources needed for a good start in the next world. The aromatic sprigs of greasewood are sometimes placed atop corpses before their burial. Fragments of *Larrea* lac found during the excavations of prehistoric burials were first identified by ethnobotanist Volney Jones in the 1930s. From its elemental position in Papago creation stories, in traditional medicine associated with childbirth, and in burial practices, it appears that creosote has accompanied desert Indians from the beginning to the end of life.

Yet there is the strong possibility that it will even outlast us, enduring long after human cultures have vanished from the face of the deserts.

In 1962, at Yucca Flat, Nevada, the Atomic Energy Commission detonated a thermonuclear explosion nicknamed "Sedan." Creosote was one of the few perennials on the site prior to the blast, but it appeared to have been obliterated as the radioactive dust settled down on the land. Ten years later, ecologist Janice Beatley recorded that twenty of the original twenty-one creosote shrubs had resprouted. They were, in fact, scarcely distinguishable from those in the same population beyond the limits of dust deposition. Within the radioactive area, new creosote seedlings began to take root a few years after the explosion. They will likely be alive long after there is any Atomic Energy Commission. They have one quality that humankind still lacks, one which we still are struggling to obtain: persistence.

"I have never ceased to be amazed and delighted at the paradox of palms growing wild in the desert, for this tree must have abundant water at its shallow roots."

The Palms in Our Hands

AROUND Palm Springs, California, half of the sixty thousand residents are over sixty years old. In August, the asphalt running into the various retirement subdivisions drives the thermometer up over one hundred and seventy degrees. The pavement is so hot, you can fry a snowbird's egg on it if you can find one. Most of the old birds who stay year-round stay inside during the summer. They may take a couple of showers a day to stay fresh. Many of them pay Southern California Edison a thousand dollars a month or more to keep their air conditioners running straight through the summer.

Outside, there is little shade you can sit under. Carports or porches, if those can be considered "outside." A eucalyptus in the backyard, perhaps. A couple of lollipop-shaped citrus trees or an African sumac, though they are seldom manicured so that you can fit a warm body beneath their canopies. The Hollywood junipers in the front may throw a shadow on the wall, but they don't shade a soul.

Then there are the palms. All the planned adult communities have broad streets lined with widely spaced palms. They are lucrative commodities in the landscape-nursery industry of southern California, sold by the foot, hauled by truck, and propped up in yards as if a motion picture studio were making an instant oasis movie right there in the new neighborhood. Introduced date palms are placed in strategic locations, but they usually have a big puddle of irrigation water at their bases which keeps folks from sitting beneath them. And there are the lines of native palms: the shorter "California fan palms" with petticoats of dead fronds trimmed halfway down their stout trunks, interspersed every sixty feet with tall, slender "Mexican skydusters." Landscape architects love how these two variants of *Washingtonia filifera* "rise out of the bare earth" on the curbs of urban boulevards, either in monotonous rows "for cadence" or singly, "like an exclamation point." They are planted in these subdivisions to make each landowner feel that he is living within his very own "oasis paradise." Yet these palms are stuck out on the side of the street where hardly anyone walks. Separated from one another by irrigated lawns of empty space, each throws a tiny oval shadow down on the ground. Torn from their evolutionary history of being densely clustered with other palms of various ages, each is as lonesome as a fish out of school.

When the more speculative subdivisions dry up economically, the faucets close, and the flow of water from some subterranean aquifer slows. The billboard showing a life of leisure played out beneath a palm grove cracks in the wind, then blows over. On one abandoned boulevard near Palm Springs, a starved *Washingtonia* finally curls down, fronds gone, dead growth tip touching the dust. The whole plant makes a big, sad "U." It looks like a lean-legged ostrich hiding its head in the ground.

Nearby, a speculator leaves his office—a mobile trailer—and heads into town for a noonday drink. Parking his air-conditioned Oldsmobile, he locks the doors and walks, sweating, across the superheated paved lot. A palm silhouette shaped of menthol-green neon lights the window of the entrance to the Oasis Tap, promising paradise and lunch inside. His arms quiver and he makes a quiet grunt while pulling open the heavy door. Coldness rushes out. He enters. He can hardly see anything except for the flashing lights of the electric Coors ski-slope sign on the far wall. He takes off his sunglasses, and his eyes adjust to the dimly lit tavern. He is glad to have taken refuge in this little electrically simulated oasis, away from business, bright lights, and the blazing sun. He finds a stool. Perspiration cools quickly on his arms.

"Whatchou guys been up to, huh? Hey," he pants, "gimme a cold one. Hey, what they got on the tube today? Are the Padres gonna let the Goose pitch today? Is that game on? What time is it anyway?"

He reaches for the icy Coors in front of him and takes the first gulp. A chill hits his chest. He gasps. Staring at the TV, still sweating, he can't see a single Padre.

He never walks out of the Oasis Tap.

Three women ascend from a hole in a mound near their house as the shade begins to slide up the Sonoran barranca slope. It is after four on a June afternoon. They have been in the shelter of their *huki* since eleven or so. The two younger women joke while casually stripping palm fiber for the rectangular-shaped *petaca* baskets that they would begin the next day. The older woman, plaiting a new palm sombrero for her husband, is quiet, thoughtful. The last double-weave sombrero like this one lasted her husband for four years; his newer, store-bought plastic fiber hat hardly weathered seven months of his constant use. So she starts twilling its roundish crown, working down toward the pliant brim, and tomorrow will weave back to the top and tie it in. It will take several days of work for something that most people now buy at the store. But then again, having a durable hat is important. It is all that stands between her husband and the scorching sun on these June days when he has to work long hours to prepare his fields for the rainclouds that will soon cross central Sonora.

By noon on most days since early May, she has been retreating with the other women into the huki, a semi-subterranean shelter where a roof of logs, palm fronds, dirt, and brush covers a shallow excavation into a hillside. There, with her bare feet on the earthen floor, she hums quietly to herself while weaving, or giggles at the jokes the other two make about the men. There, in the musky dark, the frond fibers of the Sonoran palmetto, *Sabal uresana,* remain moist and workable. There, too, she has a break after helping her husband do the milking, after making breakfast and cheese, after sweeping the house and the ramada. Her thoughts are her own in the huki. Although she continues to work, the shadowy solitude somehow restores her freshness.

Hu-ki. Perhaps it means "basket-house," or possibly "menstrual hut." Whatever the derivation, it is an ancient word among the Uto-Aztecan languages, and *huki* is a term still shared by Mountain Pima, Cahitan, and a few Warihio in Sonora and adjacent Chihuahua. The structures remain in use in the foothills of the sierras of east-central Sonora, but most hukis have fallen into abandonment in the lowlands. South of 30 degrees latitude, and below 1000 meters in elevation in eastern Sonora, the Sonoran palmetto has been among the major weaving fibers for utility baskets, hats, sleeping mats, and other household articles for centuries. Two other palm species, beargrass, sotol, and agaves are also woven into baskets or cordage, but their association with the huki is not as strong.

Sonoran palmettos are used for myriad purposes. The fronds are employed for thatching the sides and roofs of Warihio and Pima homes, ramadas, and A-frame shelters. Sections of the trunks serve as uprights and crossbeams in houses. Whole lengths are stacked up to make corrals. The hearts of palm seedlings are infrequently roasted and eaten like agave hearts. Yet this practice apparently has not been too intensive or widespread in Sonora during recent times. The density and areal extent of certain palm stands in fairly accessible areas suggest that they have escaped overexploitation. *Sabal uresana* grows in extensive stands near Opodepe, Onavas, Soyopa, Mazocahui, and other ancient pueblos in central Sonora, well within reach of where thousands of people have lived for centuries. Perhaps only "surplus" palm hearts were used in years when there was an abundance of young plants resulting from the beneficial effects of burning the palmetto oases and savannas. Piman speakers are well aware that the whole palm dries up if the bud is used. Palm fronds are too important to let a whole plant be lost in just one meal.

Palms may have appeared as far north as central California more than seventy million years ago, based on reports of pollen similar to that of *Sabal* and *Washingtonia* found in Late Cretaceous sediments. Fossilized imprints of palm fronds have been found imbedded in Californian limestone strata twenty-five to thirty feet below the present surface of the ground. Some time less than five million years ago, other tropical plants such as wild figs began to drop out of sight of these northern palms, as summer rains decreased and winter temperatures lowered. For some reason, the *Washingtonia filifera* palms have persisted in more northerly, winter rainfall-dominated localities than those of *Sabal uresana* and *Erythrea* palms in Baja California or in Sonora. By themselves, the northern fan palms are considered relicts left over from earlier climates which were more favorable for your average palm.

They too may have been occasionally extirpated on a local basis from small canyons within their range by floods, freezes, borers, droughts, or disease. Later, they could have been dispersed to some of the same sites again as seeds in the feces of wandering coyotes. For periods prior to human habitation of the continent, *Washingtonia* palms had already earned the status of survivor, persisting in areas over long stretches of time, through varying climates, while other early-established plants were lost from the region's flora.

After people came upon palms in the western Sonoran Desert, it must have been difficult for them to conceive of a life in which these palms were absent.

Before A.D. 1500, there may have been a period of a couple of centuries when *Washingtonia* lined the shores of prehistoric Lake Cahuilla in the Salton Basin, if Richard Felger's hypothesis is correct. Prehistoric Indians harvested nearly forty species of plant and animal foods along the shores of Lake Cahuilla, and contemporary palm oases are situated close to this ancient shoreline. These shady oases would have been ideal sites for processing such foods, and many bedrock mortars used for grinding are found in the washes running through them. Virtually every palm oasis in southern California has prehistoric pottery or petroglyphs associated with it. Scratched and painted glyphs tell us of giants, big-horned animals, and solar visions dreamed by our antecedents. Under the tallest palm in North America, dreams grew large.

The Aguas Calientes group of Cahuilla Indians at Palm Springs tells a story about the creation of the first palm. As Francisco Patencio recalled, it began when one of the head men realized that his life as one of the People was about done, and that he should prepare to go:

> This man wanted to benefit his people, so he said, 'I am going to be a palm tree. There are no palm trees in the world. My name shall always be Palm. From the top of the earth to the end of the earth my name shall be Palm.' So he stood up very straight and very strong and very powerful, and soon the bark of the tree began to grow around him. And so he passed from the sight of his people.
>
> Now the people were settled all about the country in many places, but they all came to Indian Well to eat the fruit of the palm tree. The meat of the fruit was not very large, but it was sweet like honey, and was enjoyed by everybody—animals and birds too. The people carried the seed to their homes and palm trees grew from this seed in many places. The palm trees in every place came from the first palm tree, but, like the people who change in customs and language, the palms often were somewhat different…all, every one of them, came from this first palm tree, the man who wanted to benefit his people.

The benefits? Food from buds, flowers, and fruit. The fruit are produced on as many as thirty-one stalks per tree, with each fruit cluster weighing from five to twenty pounds. Fiber for sandals, skirts, trays and baskets. Petioles for spoons and bows. Fronds for thatched ramadas. Wood for innumerable needs. The pithy wood from the branches of the palm fruit clusters was used as tinder when fires were started by friction-spinning. Home, hearth, cloth, food, and fiber—the palm was to the Desert Cahuilla what the bison was to the historic Sioux.

The Cahuilla and other tribes probably dispersed palms to other canyons, both unintentionally like the coyotes, and intentionally like the Early People. Stands high in the San Jacinto Mountains have been traced back to Cahuilla plantings. The seeds are easy to germinate in moist soils, and young plants, carefully transported, could have been transplanted. *Washingtonia* palms, now found at the Papago oasis of Quitovac, Sonora, may have arrived on that scene in historic times via aboriginal trade routes. It could have easily been maintained there where western Papagos continue to transplant, burn, and irrigate various plants much the same way historic Cahuilla did.

Palm seed gets around, whether in guts of wildlife, in human guts, or in human hands.

In truth, the fate of various palms has been in our hands for centuries. Humans have long changed the age structure of "wild" palm stands by increasing the frequency of burning and by management practices such as irrigation and clearing of ground-covering plant litter. Go to nearly any palm stand in Baja California, Sonora, or Arizona, and you will see some blackened trunks that are the evidence of fires, often ones intentionally initiated by local residents. In 1909, botanist Parish saw that "it is almost impossible to find mature indigenous palms from which the leaves have not been repeatedly burned." Such torched oases have irked many a purist naturalist wishing to visit palms in their presumed natural state, with long skirts of fronds tapering down towards the ground. Instead they see charred, bared trunks that are ugly as plucked chickens.

However ugly they may have looked, only a small percentage of plants died in each oasis fire set by historic Indians. At the same time, brush, debris, and

competing plants were killed back. Water and nutrients were freed. Ecologist Richard Vogl estimates that Indian-managed oases were burned nearly every four years, and each fire stimulated a subsequent bumper crop of fruit to be produced. In one of his study sites, palms surviving a burn averaged twenty-one stalks of fruit after a fire, as opposed to twelve in the unburned control. Following a fire, fruit are so abundant that the surplus falling to the open ground may produce thousands of new seedlings. These bumper crops attract birds and larger mammals, some of whom were hunted. The fires also improve the nutritional value of oasis understory plants such as saltgrass and rushes.

If you live within a palm oasis for any period of time, you find reasons to burn, to clear away dead fronds and the creatures associated with them. Early Anglo-American naturalists claimed that the Cahuilla had spiritual reasons for burning oases—because dry fronds were the hiding place of spirits, or to offer fire to the dead and to send messages to departed friends. Cahuilla have also offered much more mundane reasons for setting fires in the palms near where they lived. Patencio remembered that "the bugs that hatched on top of the palm trees made the fruit sick, and no fruit came. After the trees were set afire and burned, the bugs were killed and the trees gave good fruit." Long after the Cahuilla began such a practice, the USDA undertook studies which confirmed that periodic burning is the most effective way to eliminate scale and spider mite pests, thereby increasing palm fruit harvests.

There are other motives for burning dried fronds. They get in the way of harvesters, and fallen ones provide shelter for rodents and other camp-robbers. Wasps and yellow-jackets often hang their nests among drooping fronds, and fires dispel them as well.

Such human modifications of palm populations probably began in prehistoric times, but the palms remained reproductive. All ages of one or two palm species could be seen clustered together in canyons where springs or seeps fed them, forming oasis microhabitats that sheltered cultures from the extremes of the open desert environment.

In early historic times, Spanish manipulations of indigenous human communities began to disrupt long-standing cultural relationships with palms. Jesuit Miguel del Barco, who lived among Cochimi-speaking people in Baja California for three decades, recorded the indirect consequences of the Spanish attempts to "mix" more acculturated people into resistant communities:

When the missions of the south were founded, there were many and frequent palm groves, because the Indians took absolutely no advantage of these palms [as lumber]. With the occasion of the uprising of the year 1734, people from the province of Sinaloa came to that part of California in order to participate in its pacification. These people began to cut the hearts of palms, which they called palmito, in order to eat them. The Indians learned to eat palmito from these or from others a short time before, because prior to that they did not know that it could be eaten. They liked it so much that in a short time they finished several beautiful palm groves.

Botanist Reid Moran has noted that palms historically extended west of the desert in Baja California Norte, though they no longer do as a truly wild plant. Valle de las Palmas, forty kilometers southeast of Tijuana, had its patron plant depleted, thanks to the wastefulness that botanical explorer C. R. Orcutt stumbled across in 1883:

We entered Valle de las Palmas, where we made our next camp among mesquite, screwbean, and other trees—but no palms! The next morning we proceeded through the valley till we noticed at our right, in a large canyon, two novel trees which proved to be palms (*Washingtonia filifera*). On further exploration we found 20 still standing but over 50 lying dead—cut down by an enterprising ex-governor that he might cover his house with leaves.

Rather than have his men climb the palms to cut a few fronds now and then, Moran guesses that they simply felled the rest of the palms in the same manner: "Apparently the ex-governor completed his work."

In April, 1782, the soldier-explorer Pedro Fages encountered two small oases of *Washingtonia filifera* around pools of water as his party traveled northwest out of the Imperial Valley. Numerous palm springs such as these had been used by the Kumeyaay ancestors since at least A.D. 1000. Yet one of the spots that Fages visited was singled out in the next century as *the* southern Palm Springs, owing to its accessibility to a foot trail that grew into the Butterfield Stage and Overland Mail Line.

Another, northern Palm Springs grew from campsite to stagestop to artists' colony to resort to unwieldy retirement community in less than a century. But it was the southern site that was more frequently visited earlier. In the 1840s, the Mormon Batallion recorded twenty to thirty native palms at this southerly oasis. These palms did not survive for more than a decade.

In 1853, Dr. W. P. Blake of the Pacific Railway Survey unknowingly stopped at the same site that the Franciscans and Mormons had camped on in earlier years. He commented upon the destruction left in the wake of careless Forty-niners:

> Three or four palm trees, each about thirty feet high, are standing on the bank from which the springs issue. They are much injured by fire and persevering attacks of emigrants, who have cut down many of the finest of the group, as if determined that the only trees that grace the sandy avenue of the Desert and afford a cool place for the Springs, should be destroyed.

Just five years later, J. M. Farwell rode the Butterfield Line to the southern Palm Springs:

> This place takes its name from a species of palm trees which formerly grew here, and which within a few years were standing, as I saw the trunks as they lay upon the ground, and the stumps from which they were cut.
>
> ...it was bright moonlight while we remained here, and the beauty and singularity of the scene will not soon fade from my memory...

Recalling these events a century later, historian E. I. Edwards lamented that the "picturesque oasis [had been] stripped of its crowning glory. The palm trees had been cut down. All of them." At the time of his visit to the site in 1959, "only one isolated stump remained as a visible reminder of the palms." Two other trunk fragments were uncovered within a mound of dirt. The springs had become seasonally dry.

In the meantime, the northern town of Palm Springs prospered. By the mid-1880s, Anglo-American settlers had begun to build irrigation ditches from other springs to support agricultural development. These ditches later fed not farms but urban landscaping. There are perhaps more cultivated palms today in *the* Palm Springs—the northern one—than in all the historic canyons of Alta California. Something different from mainstream agriculture developed—a myth of idyllic oasis life. Here, in the Perfect Land, you could live and breathe, and if you were so inclined, plant a backyard orchard. The *San Bernardino Weekly* ran this notice of a land auction in October, 1887:

> Invest at Palm Springs, where there is NO FROST! NO HEAVY WINDS! NO FOG! THE HOME OF THE BANANA, DATE AND ORANGE! Only spot in California where frost, fog and windstorms are absolutely unknown.....Best Opportunity for Men of Moderate Means....

Plans for the Perfect Land were, at that time, built on the presumption of Perfect Access to Water. Such perfect access remained in the bush, never quite coming securely into hand. Anglos and the Aguas Calientes branch of the Cahuilla Indians fought over water rights for three decades. During the 1894–1905 drought, agriculture in the valley almost turned belly-up under the hot, dry sky. But the government finally led the Indians into a complex settlement that returned to them certain water rights plus a checkerboard of land tracts in Palm Valley that they could then lease to non-Indians for 99-year periods.

Most of the Aguas Calientes families joined in the rush for the Perfect Deal and soon became prominent developers. Aguas Calientes descendants now have interest in condominiums, tract housing, hotels, and unrestricted bingo-game bonanzas. Once posing for tourist photos in Bedouin garb on the backs of camels, welcoming visitors to the "New Araby," some of the Aguas Calientes people have turned their dromedaries in for Mercedes.

This is not to say that agriculture failed to develop in the region. On the contrary, southeastern California is among the four richest agricultural zones in the United States. Yet the natural attributes which once attracted men of modest means to the area are now largely gone. The air is often dull gray in color, a stifling haze. Highway signs reading "Daylight Test Area" and "Keep headlights on for the next 50 miles" perplex unacquainted travelers. Surface water resources are overallocated. Groundwater overdraft per year has become so great that it would take decades without pumping to return the water table to its pre–1900 levels. The Coachella Valley's groundwater quality has also worsened. High levels of total dissolved salts, boron, fluoride, and sulfates severely constrain the future uses of this resource.

Is there negative feedback between southern California's Idyllic Oasis myth and natural oases left in the region? At first it appears as if the Coachella Valley's prosperity simply allows more people to appreciate the native oases—many are now protected, and they are elegantly interpreted at the Palm Springs Museum by enthusiastic, competent naturalists. It is believed that the number of palms in southern California canyons may be on the upswing. Most of these canyons are above the valley, in the zone of groundwater recharge, so that they are minimally affected by groundwater pumping on the plains below.

But it is the oasis as a unique microenvironment that has suffered, through fire suppression, exclusion of Native American gardening, and locally within the valley, changing water relations. Less than four hundred hectares of native palm oasis habitat persist in the wilds of the American Southwest.

Ecologist Richard Vogl has eloquently written of how "empty" southern Californian palm stands feel today:

> The original oases were largely open and foot-worn, free of accumulated plant debris. Springs were clear and impounded water holes were maintained for bathing and washing. In addition, hand-dug channels shunted water to small garden patches. Today's oases are usually cluttered and choked with plant accumulations, springs are silted in or taken over by emergent aquatic plants, and unimpeded streams tumble down to sink into the desert floors.
>
> Oases formerly smelled of charred wood, camp fires, burned grass, and moist soil, occasionally interrupted by cooking food. In some instances, oases could be smelled before they were seen. Today's oases take on the more subtle odors of the existing vegetation; they smell of willows, of mule fat, or of desert lavender, but seldom of smoke, char and fire.

Years of fire suppression allow the buildup of tinder to the extent that when a fire does occur, it damages many more palms. Similarly, there have always been flashfloods in southern California, but their frequencies and intensities have changed with urbanization. At Willow Hole near Palm Springs, twenty-one palms were evident in 1961. A 1969 flashflood, intensified by the amount of runoff rapidly dumped into washes from a paved housing development upstream, downcut the wash running through Willow Hole, dropping the water table there by six meters. By 1983, only nine palms were left, all scattered along the edge of surrounding dunes, where moisture bleeds out of their sandy shoulders.

Not too far away, the celebrated Thousand Palms oasis sits beside a series of sedimentary hills. Its three groves look fine from the summits of these hills. But when you meander under the palms you see that a number of them have been saved by supplemental water provided to them by a trickle irrigation system. It is like seeing someone fed intravenously, knowing that he might not survive without this lifeline. The smallest of the three groves, Powell Palms, has been particularly vulnerable to arroyo downcutting and water table droppage over the last decade. Groundwater use at nearby housing developments can only aggravate the situation.

It has become clear that no oasis is an island unaffected by surrounding land uses and abuses. Northeast of Palm Springs in the Mohave Desert, the National Park Service created Joshua Tree National Monument to preserve palm and yucca stands. Groundwater consumption in nearby fields and military bases has caused a five-meter drop in the groundwater over the last four decades. Spring-fed pools dried up in the Oasis of Marah (Twenty-nine Palms) over a decade ago. To avoid desiccation of the tourist attraction there, the wild *Washingtonia,* the National Park Service is running a pipeline up to the palms to keep them irrigated. With what? Pumped groundwater.

Somewhere within this rapidly changing scene, a man emerged who truly loved palm oases, as they have been and should be. Randall Henderson was born in the late 1880s in Ohio, but by the end of World War I, he was firmly planted in the deserts of southern California. From 1920 up until his death on the Fourth of July, 1970, Henderson visited eighty-eight native palm oases in Alta California and Arizona, and no less than eight oases in Baja California. Using a hand-held counter, he individually tallied the number of *Washingtonia* palms in natural habitats north of the border (11,000) as well as some 4500 of the estimated 18,000 palms of three species found within the first eighty kilometers south of the international boundary.

His quest for understanding the context of palms took him into remote areas with the likes of renowned botanist Liberty H. Bailey and the Pai-Pai Indians, seasoned oasis dwellers. The astonishing amount of information that he published on oases in his twenty-one years as editor of *Desert* magazine continues to dwarf that contributed by any trained scientist. His notes and photos form a baseline from which we can record change in these habitats. His compulsiveness for counting palms did not, however, diminish his wonder that any are able to grow in such an arid environment: "I have never ceased to be amazed and delighted at the paradox of palms growing wild in the desert, for this tree must have abundant water at its shallow roots."

What Henderson recognized is that much of the natural elegance of palms has to do with their specificity to certain kinds of places, their geological, hydrological, and microclimatic conditions. Most of the California palms oases are situated where springs and seeps well up at fault lines, such as the San Andreas, that are part of a tectonic-plate intersection. Hillside seeps caused by water outflow from exposed geological strata provide habitats for palms in Fishtail Canyon in the Kofa Mountains of Arizona and in Horseshoe Palms in the Indio Hills of California. Where water bubbles up on floodplains or in canyons due to impervious bedrock reaching the surface, oases such as Pushwalla Palms are formed. These islands of greenery float like mirages on the edge of sand seas surrounding the Salton Sea and Colorado River delta. Their beauty is in part due to contrast with their surrounding environment. Oases cannot occur just anywhere, for the natural habitats within which palms can persist for centuries are few and far between. Once established, the palms help create soil conditions and a buffered microclimate that encourage future generations of palms.

Henderson detailed the uniqueness of nearly every oasis he visited and pointed out differences and similarities with others nearby. Late in life, he became greatly disturbed that each oasis was rapidly becoming like every other in southern California, that suburbanization was making the landscape more homogeneous. The town of Palm Desert that he founded in 1948 currently houses more than 11,000 people. It now suffers from the same trappings that most post–World War II instant cities do.

One thing eventually saddened Henderson even more than the cancerous growth in his own backyard. It was the repercussions from a stripped-down jalopy that he adapted in the 1930s to drive down sandy washes during his oasis explorations. His modest homemade contraption became the prototype for the modern dune buggy.

When he realized what destruction off-road vehicles could cause, he retired from tourist-oriented *Desert* magazine in 1958 and poured his energies into the Desert Protective Council. He had hoped to put constraints on the all-terrain vehicles that were flooding the Mohave and Sonoran Deserts, but he was too late to turn the tide. By the time he died, there were an estimated 5 million off-road vehicles in the United States. Many of their Western owners had access to Henderson's earlier publications on how to get to remote places, including oases. For a conservationist loving tranquility, it was the equivalent of creating a Frankenstein. In his last days, he wondered when society would realize that it was "time to see what could be done about tooting auto horns, badly muffled exhausts, blatant radios…and the prattle of garrulous and ill-tempered humans."

Traveling over a wide washboard road on the edge of Laguna Salada, Paul Mirocha and I inadvertently ended up at one of Henderson's favorite oases, Guadalupe Canyon. We had missed the ill-defined intersections with two roads leading toward more northerly canyons in the Sierra Juárez of Baja California. Our road was considerably better than the winding course of a dry arroyo that Henderson had used as a path, but still it rattled our kidneys. When we reached sight of the first palms, we stopped in the middle of the road, emptied the truck cab and ourselves, and watched the sun go down behind the Sierras.

We were relieved to reach any oasis by sunset, let alone one where we turned out to be the only visitors. Not that we were the only people evident, for caretaker Arturo Loya Espinosa lives half a kilometer upstream from where we camped. We heard his dogs and chickens all night. He rents out primitive huts and camping spaces with fire pits, charges fees to enter the swimming pool and hot springs, and rakes up beer cans and plastic bags after visitors leave. He knows where the ancient fire pits are, and the bedrock mortars, the petroglyphs. He also knows the way to a cave containing clay ollas and palm sandals, but he won't take any-one there. He concedes that there is virtually no place near the oasis that you can go without finding evidence of human activities, camping debris, ancient or otherwise.

Yet palms, not public paraphernalia, dominated the habitat and consumed our attention. The last light glinted off of the Virgin of Guadalupe, a rock outcrop high above us. We sat down amidst a dense clump of *Washingtonia* and *Brahea* palms.

What music to wash the road-roar out of our ears! The flower stalks drooped down like streamers, rattling in the wind against the half-burned miniskirts of old fronds. From the background noise of the canyon bottom below, the rush and bubble of spring water wafted in. I looked up: a quarter moon, the Virgin, and the free flight of Western Yellow Bats leaving their roosts beneath the fronds.

As an inky darkness steeped into the canyon, my eyes worked harder. On a bench across the arroyo bottom, several hundred palms of all ages gathered around seeps. Arrowweed, carrizo reeds, screwbeans, and saltgrass grew in their shadows. Climbing down across the mineral-rich stream and up towards the bench, I found raccoon and skunk tracks in the mud. The best find, though, was as I approached the heart of the palm stand. There, in the ashes below a fire-tumbled giant, were palm seedlings. Scattered around in the darkness, there were
densely toothed new palm sprouts and seedlings of various sizes and ages,
manelike hairs emanating from their young, tender fronds. They were
growing in the protection of their elders, where the earth gave
freely of its waters. They would offer to future
generations the chance to see an oasis
as it should be, where it
should be.

To make bootleg mescal, Sonorans cut most of the soon-to-bloom paniculate agaves within their reach. This leaves nectar-feeding bats, the usual pollinators of these plants, little more than food for thought.

Mescal Bacanora:
Drinking Away the Centuries

"SOY un mochomo," Joaquin Martinez said as we headed toward his hidden mescal still in the hills of eastern Sonora. He compared himself to night-working ants, using an old Opata Indian word for them. Joaquin was reminding us that making mescal from wild agaves is a clandestine activity in Sonora. It is technically illegal since the mescaleros do not pay taxes on their alcoholic product. In the 1940s and '50s, a bootlegger caught in the act literally would be strung up in jail for three to four days without food. Today most authorities want only a kickback or a free sample from local still-keepers. As with the homemade sour-mash industry in Kentucky, even the local police chief will treat you to a glass on the proper occasion, bragging that his favorite uncle makes the finest in the country. Howard Scott Gentry observed that Sonora's mescal bacanora is to tequila what moonshine is to whiskey, and his statement holds for their legality, notoriety, and quality. Some of the wildest spirits the world has ever known have been conjured up out of the special agave that Sonoran hillbillies call *bacanora.* The term *bacanora* comes from the name of a town in the heart of Sonora's bootleg country. Yet others say it is derived from the Indian words for water and wild chiles, so that bacanora may be best translated as "pungent-hot water."

Like a worker ant, Joaquin spends plenty of time out on dusty trails searching for and picking up plants. Once found, they are transported back to his *horno* and *barranco,* the rock-lined pits where he will roast and ferment them. He can often tell when an agave is suitable for harvesting as it approaches sexual maturity, by the way the lower leaves are drying and drooping, and by the way the base of the plant is swelling with succulence. At other times, mescaleros use mature agaves which have begun to put up their flowerstalks from the center of a swirl of swordlike leaves. Before this poling flower stalk gets too large, expending the caloric supply the century plant has stored over its lifetime, it is carefully "castrated"—cut back to its base with a machete. Instead of being converted for growth into a huge branching bloom, the plant's carbohydrates simply well up into the leaf bases of the plant over the following two or three months, making the heart of the plant sweeter.

Joaquin later goes out and cuts all but one of the ends of the leaves off the agaves so that they look like pineapples with a carrying strap. Uprooting each trimmed head, Joaquin loads it onto his burro. When he has accumulated twenty or thirty plants, he returns home. After seven to ten loads of these heads, Joaquin goes out to cut three burro-loads of firewood, which are also brought back to the horno hidden in a little side canyon.

"Come, I have a batch that is running now." Joaquin gestured for us to duck under mesquite and hackberry branches in order to reach his rustic fermentation and distillation set-up. Here, he pit-roasts two hundred heads of agaves at a time in two cobble-lined hornos, shallow trenches in the ground that are coated with red-hot coals. After putting the heads in the pit, he places more coals on top of them and seals the pit with layers of brush and dirt thick enough to prevent any smoke from rising. He then tops it off with thorny branches to deter animals. At last, he lets them roast for one and a half to three days.

A sticky brown sugar with a somewhat smoky, earthy flavor clings to the leaf fibers of agave after roasting. If any of the heads are burned, they are tossed aside as the mescaleros unearth their pit roast. They take the well-roasted heads to a nearby wood trough called a *cuba,* where they are mashed with the butt-end of a tool. The macerated leaves are then tossed into the barranco where they ferment for four to seven days.

Barrancos are the pits into which the mochomos descend now and then to stomp on the roasted mash to turn it into the brewing juice called *saite.* Water and sometimes some fermented juice from the last good batch are added. A fire is made on the cap of this pit to keep the brew active. Joaquin tastes the bubbling saite and decides when it is ready for the still.

"Now it is time to load the train," Joaquin declares. His train of apparatus for the still is the oddest coupling of equipment that I've ever seen. The fermented saite is placed in a fifty-gallon drum capped with a sombrero or crude lid shaped out of wood of the tree called palo chino, *Pithecellobium mexicanum*. The edges of the sombrero are then sealed with a mud plaster. A woodfire built under and around the drum causes the liquid inside to boil and evaporate. It hits the underside of the sombrero, where it begins to condense and flow out of a rubber hose, into a five-foot-long copper distilling tube. This copper condenser sits in a long wooden *canoa* that is regularly refilled with cold water from a nearby well, in order to make more alcohol condense against the wall of the tube. Sometimes, at the end of or in place of the canoa, the tube runs through part of an old car radiator sunk in another fifty-gallon drum filled with water.

The first liquor to materialize out of the other end of the tube is called *mescal de cabeza* and is run through for a second distillation to produce *mescal bronco*, the uncut wild spirit of the Sierra Madre and adjacent desert foothills. To process the saite from all two hundred cabezas, the train is refilled at least seven times and the spent bagasse of the drained agave leaves is discarded. By this time, the mescal is being tested by all men present, blended with water, more mescal de cabeza, or with the tail end of the second distillation to balance the taste. Tired, and wired from too many sample swigs of full-proof mescal on empty stomachs, younger men usually end up passed out under nearby shade trees as the steady old hands finish up the work.

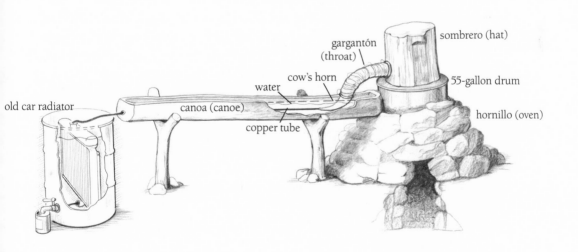

Joaquin pours a *trago* or "hit" of his newly blended mescal into a small glass and shakes it, staring at the sides of the glass where bubbles form—a good sign. He slowly sips the liquid century plant and lets it break like a gentle wave over his tongue. We wait for a judgment, but he says nothing for a while. The quality obtained with this final blending can make the difference between a gallon selling for 1600 pesos or for 2000.

Finally Joaquin volunteers some modest wisdom, and a trago for the rest of us to share now that he is apparently satisfied that the blend is as good as he can do for the time being. "No one really knows what conditions consistently make the finest mescal. Some say the taste of the spring or well water you use. Others guess that it has something to do with the soil that the plants were growing in. I prefer mixing the mescal bacanora [from the narrow-leafed agave, *Agave angustifolia*] with that of the lechuguilla [Palmer's agave, *Agave palmeri*]. Others insist that pure bacanora has the most distinctive taste. All I know is that the people here near the sierras know what is good quality and what is not; the commercial tequilas do not have the same taste."

A friend visiting Joaquin with us wanted to ask how long they aged the mescal there before they began to sell it. Joaquin's nephews laughed and pointed to the terminal of the copper coil running out of the radiator.

"...From the time it comes out of the copper to the time it hits the bottom of the glass! That's how long most of it gets cured! With so many drinkers around here, my uncle can hardly keep up with the demand!"

Joaquin laughed too, but then put on a sober look. "No matter how much the drunks want, I always put some aside and let it cùre back at my home. I know one elderly man who let his bacanora añejo cure for ten years, and that was as good as any I have ever tasted. It is true what they say about such things: the older it gets, the more musical...."

If music and taste come with age, they are naturally part of growing up for a century plant. An agave will inconspicuously sit as a gray cluster of leaves on a rocky hillside for decades, then suddenly will burst into a delicious song—hundreds of flowers, all buzzing with nectar-sucking animals, shoot up into the air on a 3–5 meter tall stalk launched in just a couple of months. Although no single rosette of leaves persists for a century, some plants do, in the sense that a mother rosette may sprout "pups" below her skirts that are genetically identical to her. These clonal pups, or "hijos," may outlive mama by ten or fifteen years. Yet if these successive generations produce pups in turn, they may leave a concentric ring of plants around the place where mama stood, visible for eighty to a hundred years after the old girl first sprouted.

It has been said that century plants kill themselves reproducing—not a bad way to go, when you think about it. The obvious drawback is that after a rather dull, prolonged adolescence, they have only the energy to do it once. When the time comes, the plants cannot take in solar energy and soil moisture rapidly enough to simply "add on" such a huge bloom. Instead, a leaf cluster sixty centimeters across loses about twenty-five kilograms of wet weight to satisfy the growth of a four-meter tall flower stalk—all in less than half a year's time. Although physiologists Bill Ehrler and Park Nobel have found agaves to be quick in their roots' responses to even the slightest of rains, and about twice as efficient in their water use as corn, the plants essentially die of thirst within two to five months after fruit set. Nobel has guessed that sixty percent of the water used for flowering is sapped from the leaves, which then wither for good.

Why such a swan song after years of merely humming along? Theoretical ecologists Bill and Val Schaffer feel that they know why certain panicle-bearing agaves, over evolutionary time, have traded away the option of repeated reproduction. "Big bang" plants, including both Palmer's and the narrow-leaved bacanora agaves, have likely become specialized for particular pollinators. These pollen-carriers can in turn insure that a high number of agave flowers will develop into full-seeded fruits during just one blooming spree per plant.

The mates which these paniculate agaves have saved themselves for are bats by the name of *Leptonycteris*. Certain agaves have evolved attractants to bring nectar feeders in by the flocks. First, their perfumed scent. Flowers which smell like rotten meat must make these long-nosed bats' mouths water. Second, if the Schaffers are correct, *Leptonycteris* bats favor flowers exposed on the largest erections that panicled agaves can muster. Third, nectar secretion (at least in Palmer's agaves) peaks between eight and ten at night, when the bats are most active.

Several agave species have coevolved with bats to serve these animals' nutritional needs. For instance, Palmer's agave flowers produce copious nectar with more than twice as much protein as that in the nectar from typical bee-pollinated agaves. It is likely that bat-size mammals would benefit from this enhanced protein supply more than hummingbirds or solitary bees would. Recently, ecologists from El Paso found that Palmer's and the narrow-leaved agaves have nectars that are rich in hexose sugars, and relatively poor in sucrose (eight to seventeen percent). Nectars of other known bat-pollinated flowers have roughly the same amounts of fructose and glucose that these agaves do. On the other hand, blossoms that bees prefer to work are usually richer in sucrose than the small amounts which these agave flowers have to offer. Hummingbirds generally favor sucrose-rich nectars too. Attracting bats by taste, touch, and smell, agaves definitely advertise what kind of creature they want to spend the night with.

The bats are certainly sucked in by all of this. Field biologist Donna Howell has documented how they end up doing for the agaves exactly what needs to be done to maintain the plant populations over the long run. Flocks of long-nosed bats are efficient at transferring pollen from one blooming panicle to others on nearby plants, insuring outcrossing within the island-like populations of agaves. This outcrossing is helpful in maintaining genetic variation within the agave population. It is also absolutely necessary to sexual reproductive success in Palmer's agaves. One of these plants will not develop fertile fruit if pollinated with its own pollen. Individuals are self-sterile.

To act as the pollen spreader most faithfully serving these agaves, long-nosed bats must show up at the right place at the right time. *Leptonycteris* flocks arrive in southern Arizona and northern Sonora at the time when the first Palmer's agave flowers begin to open in June. Earlier in the year, they visit the blossoms of narrow-leaved agaves and many other plants along their migration routes as they move up from Central America. Yet by midsummer, they have gone as far north as they ever go—the northward-running tributaries of the Gila River, which are also the range limits of Palmer's agave.

There, on summer nights, bats in small flocks take their turns swooping in to lap up nectar, primarily from agave flowers that have just begun to shed their pollen. Each bat takes a half-second turn drinking nectar as the others circle nearby. After several turns at flowers within close proximity of one another, the bats' head and shoulder fur is thick with golden pollen brushed off the anthers. The bats return as a flock to a roost on a cliff or in a cave nearby to digest the nectar and lick up some of the pollen that is stuck in their coats. They have, of course, left some pollen behind at other flowers as they moved from panicle branches on one plant to those on the next. Numerous bats, working several plants in close proximity to one another, insure that multiple cross-pollinations occur.

Repeated over numerous nights during a summer's time, the self-sterile agaves are outcrossed sufficiently enough for each of their 500 to 1000 fruit to fill with hundreds of dark-colored viable seeds. Of the hundreds of thousands of seeds produced by one adequately pollinated plant, perhaps only one of them will find a favorable site to sprout and avoid predators, diseases, and environmental stresses so that it will become a mature agave with a new genetic combination guiding it along.

With such a low probability of seed and seedling survival in the wild, one could wonder how agaves have persisted so long on this planet. Their other mode of reproduction, by vegetative means, helps maintain populations during periods when sexual reproduction is nil. And how much lower would their chances of persistence be if it weren't for bats and the occasional flow of genes which they enable?

Sadly—if you have any concern for long traditions—bats have not been able to work as much in their symbiotic role with agaves in recent years. By the mid-1970s, Donna Howell was noticing something peculiar about the capsule-like fruit of Palmer's agave whenever she cracked open a new one. Dark striations on the shiny inner wall of the capsules were few and far between. Those markings are stains made by pigments which only develop in fertile seeds and are in a sense signatures left by pollinators noting that they have done their work. When a capsule wall is a tawny color, with few dark stripes running across it, the message left is that the flowers were hardly fertilized, perhaps due to a shortage of pollinators. Howell became particularly disturbed by this message once she had gone back and checked the agave capsules on decades-old herbarium specimens that early botanists had made near her study area. The older capsules were richly marked with pigments, suggesting that a reduction in pollination has occurred in their population since the time of collection.

Two possible causes came to mind when Howell began to evaluate how this mutualistic relationship might have been recently disrupted after persisting for millennia. First, it has been documented that caves in southern Arizona which formerly harbored hundreds of thousands of bats now shelter a few thousand at best. Zoologists have linked this decline in bat populations with pesticide contamination. These chemicals accumulate in bat breast milk and the young die of nerve disorders when the pesticides exceed a certain level. Even after the ban on DDT in Arizona, *Leptonycteris* flocks continued to be exposed to this harmful chemical, since American manufacturers persisted in promoting its use in Latin American countries where these bats seasonally visit.

Another change affecting bats through their relationship to agaves has been occurring in recent years. Sonora's population has tripled since 1950. With such demographic growth, it is likely that there are a lot more drinkers in the northern Mexican state, not all of whom have constant access to ice-cold beer. According to their own testimonies, mescal makers have stepped up the harvest of agaves to quench this thirst, and overharvesting of wild agave stands has become increasingly evident in eastern Sonora. Has man's indulgence in spirits significantly diminished a major seasonal food resource for migrating bats?

Because the bootleg mescal industry legally does not exist in Sonora, there are no available statistics on how many agaves are harvested from the wild each year. Nor are there any definite ways to evaluate whether current harvesting rates are endangering the resource base of the industry itself. Yet mescal makers' complaints may be telling enough. In certain localities in north-central Sonora, near the northern limits of the bacanora plant's natural range, harvesters say that they must go farther and to more remote stands to secure enough cabezas for a *cuelga* (bunch). They note particular places where this species is now locally extinct, observing that bootleggers there have shifted to second- and third-rate species in order to produce their mescal. In other areas, nearly all of the harvestable plants on ejido or community lands have been utilized before reaching maturity, and mescaleros now pay nearby landowners or their cowboys for the right to take agaves from private property. Some now travel sixty kilometers to find agave stands thick enough to harvest.

The additional costs of harvest permits and increased time in travel and search have gradually been passed on to the consumer. Yet what mescal drinkers complain about most are not the real costs of today's production; they are outspoken about the few bootleggers who attempt to dilute their products with so much water and grain alcohol that the taste no longer resembles that of true bacanora.

It is difficult to ascertain how these diminished supplies in the face of steadily increasing demands have affected the number of mescal makers active in Sonora. As ethnologist Tom Sheridan found in Cucurpe, nearly every able male in the community claims that he has made his own mescal at one time or another. About twenty men in the Cucurpe vicinity make mescal in sufficient quantities to sell their *pisto* (liquor) locally, and a few bring in as much as $2400 to $3200 from the eight or so runs of mescal they do each year.

A diligent mescalero such as Joaquin needs to harvest about 1600 agaves during favorable seasons to distill the 320 to 400 gallons he sells each year. Most mescal makers in his area harvest considerably fewer plants, perhaps only averaging a single run each year. Yet there may be as many as a thousand to two thousand of these part-time bootleggers in rural Sonora. Considering the wild harvests of both the occasional and the more active mescaleros, on the order of half a million agaves may be harvested each year in Sonora. In wild stands near pueblos and ranches, harvesters probably cut most of the soon-to-bloom agaves they can reach. Beginning about 100 kilometers south of the border, most species of paniculate agaves are utilized for mescal clear on south to Sinaloa. Except in the most remote areas, this leaves nectar-feeding bats flying through Sonora little more than food for thought. Donna Howell may well be documenting a dying tradition if these agaves' rates of vegetative reproduction cannot keep up with the rate of harvesting. The remaining bats must search far and wide to find an agave giving off that familiar scent of rotten meat.

Aztec legends suggest that it was the animals who first showed humankind the edibility of agaves. In the Ocampo caves of northeastern Mexico, Professor E. O. Callen has documented human consumption of agave leaf tissue for food dating back to 6200 B.C. His evidence consists of plant fragments found in dried human excrement preserved in these caves. Euphemistically called coprolites, these dung samples were found in such good condition that Callen can reconstruct which foodstuffs prehistoric gatherers ate together as a single meal. At Ocampo, agaves were as major a food as prickly pears, meat, and mesquite. Agaves' importance continued even after hunting waned and agriculture became a more obvious caloric contributor. Oddly, the anonymous members of the *Infiernillo* culture who slipped into these caves to dump their loads unknowingly left us the artifacts for which their culture is now best known. Their dried feces, rather than any arrowhead or art object they created, have become famous specimens helpful in interpreting the early history of arid America.

Thus we have evidence of agaves' being a major food in northern Mexico for more than eight millennia. It is actually quite easy to overlook the use of agaves as food rather than as drink when observing the northern Mexican diet today. Only occasionally do the baked leaf bases of agaves show up in urban Sonoran markets today. These are typically trucked up from central Mexico to be sold as a sweet delicacy to recent immigrants to the desert. Otherwise, most contemporary Sonorans ingest agave calories only in liquid form.

It is ironic that a plant which most Americans think of only as "the cactus [*sic*] that produces tequila" has been a caloric mainstay, a fiber, medicine, and ceremonial element in desert cultures. There persists little more than mere fragments of agaves' many uses scattered out among the indigenous cultures of the greater Southwest—an Apache family harvesting *Agave parryi* for food, hauling them in a pickup truck in central Arizona; an old Papago man planting bulbils of *Agave murpheyi* at the Quitovac oasis; a Seri Indian using cooked *Agave cerrulata* leaves as an emergency source of potable liquids; a Warihio using *Agave vilmoriniana* for soap along the Río Mayo; a Tepehuan weaver shaping handbags out of fiber from species in the Sierra Madres. Introduced plants like bermuda grass, eucalyptus, and alfalfa play relatively more important roles in the lives of Sonoran Desert dwellers today.

Yet this was surely not the case in the past. Archaeologists Charles Miksicek and Paul and Susie Fish have recently uncovered evidence of intensive prehistoric reliance on agaves in south-central Arizona. Miksicek has identified numerous charred agave spines and leaf bases from the plant remains found in roasting pits located in the midst of rockpile fields north of Tucson. He and Vorsila Bohrer sometimes find agave as frequently as corn in the plant materials recovered from late Hohokam sites between Tucson and Phoenix. Such abundant agave remains in the Tucson area must have been derived from either long-distance transport or local cultivation, for no agaves exist as part of the present-day vegetation at the sites where they are found. The Fishes believe that local cultivation of agaves occurred on thousands of hectares of meter-wide piles of rocks, which could have served to capture runoff for these plants. Large rockpile fields were developed by the Classic Hohokam between A.D. 1150 and 1350, when the Tanque Verde phase of this culture achieved its highest population densities in the Tucson Basin. Thanks to innovative interdisciplinary detective work coordinated by the Fishes, it can no longer be denied that Precolumbian agave cultivation extended beyond Mesoamerica into the territory that is part of the present-day United States.

We know from Spanish documents that such cultivation persisted into early historic times in desert areas south of the border. Before 1620, Andres Pérez de Ribas observed that for the agave in Sinaloa and southern Sonora, "this plant only do they cultivate near their houses, and no other." Apparently mescal distillation had not yet been introduced to the Uto-Aztecan tribes of this area, because the only agave products which Pérez de Ribas mentions are fermented beverages, vinegar, syrup, and sisal-like fiber products. Agave cultivation also may be the only evidence of indigenous agriculture on the Baja California peninsula south of where the Yuman tribes farmed. In 1769, Junipero Serra, the famous wandering missionary of Baja California, encountered mescal plantations covering kilometers of desert between San Pacifico and San Telmo. His description of regular rows of agaves extending over the rolling hills, with only a few jojoba scattered in their midst, leaves no doubt that these succulents were intentionally managed.

Even where the Indians did not tend agaves, these plants were important nonetheless. When Edward Curtis visited the Apaches in 1906, he concluded that "nothing can give a better idea of the economic life of these people than a description of one of their annual mescal harvests." Their winter food then consisted largely of roasted mescal hearts baked in pits, some of which were "twenty feet in diameter and three feet deep; it may have been used a hundred years or a thousand, abandoned over a long period, then brought into use again."

Perhaps we are now too aloof, too impatient to wait for longer-term rewards, too cocksure that we are the controllers of the world to be able to participate in a mutualistic relationship with agaves. Yet botanist Howard Scott Gentry has tried to remind us that people from the Grand Canyon to Guatemala have in the past entered into true symbioses with agaves:

> During the several thousand years that man and agave lived together, agave has been a renewable resource for food, drink, and artifact. As man has settled into communities, agaves became fences marking territories, protecting crops, providing security, and ornamenting the home. As civilization and religion increased, the nurturing agave became a symbol, until with its stimulating juice man made it into a god. The religion and the god have gone, but agave still stands as a donor species of the first water. Among the world's crops, are there others that have played a more useful and bizarre role? If we are to ask more of the agave, we must give it attention and growing room.

We must also make a choice. At our levels of increasing population, it may be that the harvest of wild agaves for spirits or for any other intensive use is approaching parasitism. Several species of agaves deserve to be on endangered plant lists. We must choose between becoming parasites or symbionts.

Perhaps we can do the latter by giving agaves the "growing room" that Gentry suggested. By planting enough to make a self-perpetuating, frequently blooming population, we may also give the bats back their growing room. Long-sighted Sonorans have begun such an effort in the rolling hills east of the Río Yaqui, transplanting out thousands of bacanora pups on hectares of rainfed fields.

We need to resurrect agave cultivation on this side of the border as well. Susie Fish has initiated this process. She has organized a team to plant dozens of young agaves out on the bajada of the Tortolitas, amidst the rockpile fields and old roasting pits where agaves were grown and sacrificed prehistorically. It will be years before they reach fruition. Yet this experiment will be worth a visit in another thirty or forty years, if the progeny of Susie's plantings have persisted. Choose a moonlit night in the summer, and hike through the scattering of agaves in bloom. Hike past them, into the canyons of the Tortolitas where little caves lie hidden. Listen for the flutter of wings, watch for the bats, their shoulders cloaked in a coat of pollen, shining in the night like a poncho made of Precolumbian golden thread. Follow them back down to the scent of agave blossoms, where plants and animals again dance to an ancient American rhythm.

SPRING

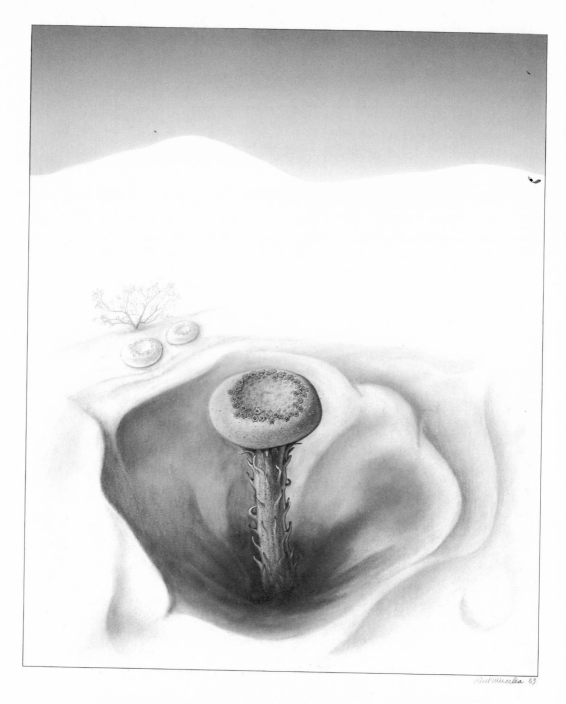

"I observed the Indian dismount from his horse and commence digging with his hands....He pulled out of the sand a vegetable-looking substance....He showed great eagerness to obtain more, and made a sign that it was good to eat."

Sandfood and Sand Papago: A Wild Kind of Mutualism

I T was May 17, 1854, in the sea of sand called the Gran Desierto, and temperatures were already reaching above one hundred degrees. Colonel Andrew Belcher Gray wondered why he had decided to stray from the line he had been surveying. He was hired to chart a route parallel to the new United States/Mexico border upon which the Texas Western Railroad could set tracks across the deserts to San Diego. Gray occasionally let his crew visit nearby pueblos or mining prospects, but this was as far as they had deviated from the straight and narrow. This day, there had been no mines nor towns, only sand sables, talc-like silt beds, and lava flows that looked as though they were still crazily creeping down from Pinacate Peak. His men were ill-humored and hungry; their horses, tired and dusty.

All this because of Gray's vain desire to become the first Anglo since Lt. R. W. H. Hardy in 1826 to describe the desert coast on the Sonoran side of the Gulf. As unproductive as this tangential jaunt had been, the desire seemed obsessive. Hardy at least had had some luck. He had charted new harbors and stumbled upon wild Seri Indians on Tiburón Island who believed him to be a great doctor. This had allowed Hardy to gain the intimate view of their primitive life that had later made his journals famous. Gray's own attempts to learn more of the "savage existence" of desert Indians had so far been futile. His old Papago guide, "Termite," who was "as thin a specimen of humanity as you would want to see," understood little English, said hardly a word all day as they had traveled, and rebuffed all inquiries. The worthlessness of the land was even more depressing to

Gray. He wrote that "towards the Gulf of California, the country presents more the appearance of a barren waste than any district I have ever seen."

Then, before dusk, Termite led them into the dunes overlooking Adair Bay and the open gulf with the sun setting over Baja California:

> Immediately upon entering these sand hills…I observed the Indian dismount from his horse and commence digging with his hands. At first I could not perceive his object, but shortly discovered that he had pulled out of the sand a vegetable-looking substance, which was shaped somewhat like a mushroom. He showed great eagerness to obtain more, and made a sign that it was good to eat.

The vegetable-like substance? It was what the O'odham have long known as *hia tadk*, 'dune root,' a vascular plant which botanists now know as *Pholisma sonorae* or simply "sandfood." Within an hour or so of discovering it for science, Gray had some in his belly:

> We encamped for the night in the sandhills, and the chief instead of supping with us as usual, made a fire, and roasted his roots or plants on the hot coals (which took about 20 minutes), and commenced eating them. None of the party seemed inclined to taste, but out of courtesy, I moved over to the chief's fire, and he handed me one. At first I ate but a little, and slowly, but in a few minutes, so luscious was it that I forgot my own mess and ate heartily of it; next morning each of the party followed suit and afterwards there was scarcely enough to satisfy us. The taste, though peculiar, was not unlike the sweet potato, but more delicate.

Gray sent specimens and a letter back to the famous botanist John Torrey, who hailed the discovery at meetings of a natural history society on the East coast. It was not then recognized that 170 years earlier, Juan Mateo Manje had encountered "poor people who lived by eating roots of wild sweet potatoes" on the same coast. Those natives, the *Hia C-ed O'odham* or 'Sand People,' had of course "discovered" the plant and its value long before that. When Termite took Gray's party to a Sand Papago fishing camp the next day, these wary Indians all ran away and would not meet the whites until the old Sonoita Papago chief gave them considerable assurances. Returning to where they had been processing their harvests of fish, shrimp, and wild grass seeds, the Sand Papago gave Gray the glimpse of aboriginal life in the desert that he had been craving:

> In this naked spot, I found a band of Indians (Papagos) almost in a state of nudity living on fish and crabs caught in the salt creeks and lagoons on the Gulf; and a

sort of root, which was ate after roasting upon hot coals; or dried in the sun, and ground on a metate (curved stone) with mezquite beans, forming "Pinole."...

Not withstanding it appears to be the most desolate and forlorn-looking spot for eighty miles around the head of the Gulf...Nature seems even here, where no rain had fallen for eight months, to have provided for the sustenance of man one of the most nutritious and palatable vegetables.

Yet there was a problem with this vegetable that Gray failed to advertise. Forty years later, his sidekick Pete Brady recalled the Sand Papago encounter with mixed emotion. Brady was somewhat aroused by the beauty of the thinly clad maidens present. Then they smiled at him:

Most astonishing of all, their teeth were all decayed and were level to the gums. Even the young Indians of twelve or fourteen years of age were in the same fix....[Present in the sand root was] a great deal of a certain kind of acid...that destroyed the enamel on their teeth and it was this that caused the Indians to present such a frightful appearance.

We are not sure if the Sand People were toothless because of some undescribed acid in this plant or because of all the crunching and gnashing of sand and shell that came along with many of their foods. Fear of tooth decay has not kept others from dreaming of eating this luscious foodstuff, no matter how far it may be tucked away in the hottest, driest areas of Arizona, California, and Sonora. Its renown has grown through the decades since Gray and Brady brought it out for the rest of the world to see. In the 1930s, USDA and BIA bureaucrats even funded a feasibility study to see if sandfood could be cultivated, culled, and canned in order to buffer Papago Indian reservation residents from the food scarcity that comes with the droughts that hit their homeland.

The trouble is, sandfood defies domestication. Over the years, USDA technicians and university scientists have all failed miserably in their attempts to germinate its seeds. You see, the root of the dunes is not a root at all. It is a parasite on the roots of desert shrubs. The edible portion of this plant is actually a subterranean flower stalk which reaches up from its attachment on the shrub roots, in order to let its flowers open on the surface of the sands. Scientists speculate, but have not proven, that sandfood seeds will germinate only if they are on or near the roots of certain host plants. How then do the seeds which mature on the burning surface of summertime dunes ever get dispersed through a sea of sand to the proper harbor? And why is the vegetable which Gray found to be "very abundant in the hills" now considered a good candidate for endangered species lists? It is doubtful that it was eaten into oblivion, for soon after Gray's visit, the Gran Desierto was largely deserted by its human gatherers. More troublesome yet, where did those Sand Papago go?

If you were a Sand Papago who knew your gathering grounds well, you could go to certain sand swales two moons after winter solstice and dig. Not just anywhere. Dig at the edge of selected sand-loving shrubs. Dunes buckwheat. White bursage, maybe. Or look for the two kinds of mat-forming bushes with quiltlike leaves. There is no common name by which they are known today, although botanists call them *Tiquilia*. Find a circular marking in the sand around these plants, sculpted by branches dipping and sweeping with the wind. Dig down, down until you hit the cooler moist sand, then dig another meter.

There, on shrub roots no thicker than a baby's little finger, look. Looking hard, you might sight a pale mass of undifferentiated cells, wartlike, waiting. Wait yourself.

Come back a moon later, when the sand is warmer. As the days lengthen, so lengthens this mass of cells, shaped like a spear, pushing up through tons of sand toward light. Not much longer, and a wooly gray cushion the size of a small fried egg will burst the surface of the now-hot sand.

Yet it still hides from the untrained eye, for drifting sand lingers in the gray fuzz, camouflaging it. This coating of silica grains reflects light back to the sky, reducing the plant's heat load. It is hidden amidst the dazzle of wildflowers that pop up with the winter rains. Devil's lantern primrose. Gran Desierto sunflower. White-stem blazing star. Desert lily. Sacred datura. Sandfood's subtle lavender flowers, only millimeters wide, are seldom seen beneath the leggier dune flora.

Only when the wildflower show fades in the spring, and water becomes scarce or scummy in mountain *tinajas* or pisstanks nearby, does sandfood loom larger in the gatherer's eye. Now dig at dawn, because by noon in May, the sand surface reaches above one hundred forty degrees. Dig where the last flowers wane on the puckered seedhead, while some seeds mature, hidden in the wooly mat. Widen a hole around the two to ten mushroomlike tops that converge down into the loose sand, but try not to break the yard-long, wrist-thick succulent stalks. At this stage, sandfood may weigh more than thirty times its host plant's weight. It is ready to eat.

Breaking the stalk off close to the shrub roots in the excavation you've made, you jar the seedhead with enough force to cause several hundred seeds to fall into the hole. A few find themselves pressed up against the shrub's roots. You have inadvertently dispersed them to places from which they can germinate. They have landed in a harbor, rather than being lost in a sea of sand. While gathering food, you have participated in a wild kind of mutualism.

Outsiders often try to freeze desert Indians. Freeze them in time and space, restrict them in our minds so that we feel secure that we know who they are. Freeze one moment of how they lived and looked. Hang on to this snapshot, and forget that the movie rolls on.

One time at the Hopi mesas, a pigeonhole in which I had unconsciously placed a friend collapsed before my eyes. I was talking to his wife about native foods. She had been telling me when to gather the wild potatoes from the sand dunes below the mesas. "Those *tumna* are good, good with venison." I inquired, "Do you eat much venison?" imagining Hopis hunting deer in canyons nearby. Her husband, who was carving a katsina at a workbench nearby, replied, "I had some yesterday and it sure was good. That's why I feel tired today. I just flew in from the Explorer's Club luncheon on the East coast, where we had venison, caribou, kangaroo, and even shark meat. It was a real feast."

With the Sand Papago, visitors have always called them "poor." Poor people in a barren land. From Manje's first visit to them in 1694, outsiders have tried to pin them down. Manje pinned them naked to a place "full of rocks and all kinds of brush and cacti—an arid sterile land with no water for pasture....We gave them a supply of food since they were poor and hungry, living on roots, locust and fish." Early observers viewed them as desperate enough to eat even snakes, lizards, and toads.

Poor. No gold to give to the conquistadors. No agriculture that an outsider could recognize as such. No permanent housing or fixed residences. No cuisine except that prepared from herpetological oddities and plant parasites.

To lock them up further, Anglo folklore claims that there are no Sand Papago left. They were wiped out by an epidemic around the time that Gray visited the Pinacate. They were rounded up by a Mexican posse and all were shot for having robbed Camino del Diablo travelers. They left the sand, never to return. Or only one hermit lived into this century, and Lumholtz was the last to see his traces. Or they all took to living on the Papago Indian reservation, and studying at BIA boarding schools, where they have become part of the American Indian melting pot. They gave up sandfood for Coca-Cola, which not only rotted their teeth, but killed them as well.

The last few years, however, Sand Papago families have been gathering together with one another. They have known all along that they were not extinct. Nor do they have exactly the same traditions as the 12,000-plus Desert Papago (Tohono O'odham) native to the villages where the present-day Papago Indian reservations are located. However, some Sand Papago have married Desert Papago and now live in these villages. More often than not, they still live beyond the margins of both these reservations and their former Gran Desierto gathering grounds, scattered through such towns as Ajo, Caborca, Gila Bend, Sonoita, Stanfield, and Roll. Some wish to have a reservation of their own, to be located near Ajo, while others prefer not to have to deal so much with the BIA.

Wherever these families now reside, there remain a few old folks, some still quite lively, who roamed the dunes and lava fields when they were young. Oral histories have been collected in the O'odham language by their kin, in-laws, and descendants. These scattered records document a manner of living that has been rich in ways that modern society can hardly fathom or measure. Clearly, the Sand Papago do not see their ancestors as having been poor in things that matter.

These people remember a dynamic life, a life too varied to be caught like some overexposed snapshot out in the dunes. Seldom did they have a year or even a season exactly like the preceding ones. The Sand Papago might have resided parts of the year in sites one hundred fifty kilometers away from one another, and now travel similar distances in pickups to stay with relatives for a few days at a time. They could be at the ocean when the tides brought in fish, then move up to the Tinajas Altas to hunt. After digging in the dunes for sandfood, they might trek to Yuma or Gila Bend or Caborca to help harvest wheat. The wheat harvest was followed by a reunion of relatives at Vak (Quitovac, Sonora), where organpipe and saguaro fruit were gathered for the *Vi'igita* celebration. If rains came in July and August, they would plant fields hidden between the lava flows of the Pinacate, fueled by the runoff from infrequent storms. After harvests, some would take their produce up to Quitobaquito, Sonoita, or Ajo, to trade for dry goods. On a visit to the Gila River, they would catch freshwater fish, perhaps humpbacked suckers; they would exchange "fish stories," medicines, and other products with relatives.

Mobility kept them healthy in an area where today Park Service, Border Patrol, and military men go stir-crazy, resulting in a high turnover on various government jobs. Now in her eighties, Candelario Orozco recalled her rambling days: "A long time ago, moving around did not cost very much. People could walk anywhere to change their residence." They generally traveled lightly, but devout Catholics had more of a burden in that they carried around all of their santos, as one woman explained to Ofelia Zepeda; they took holy pictures and small statues with them wherever they went.

Miguel Velasco remembered roaming across areas where today's boundary fences and border guards inhibit human movement: "It was the custom of the Sand Indians to travel all over....They went to Mexico, because there was no fence then." They drifted, Miguel told his relative, Fillman Bell, because they were like the sand they had come from:

> We are all Sand Indians. We are not known as on top of the sand. We are from the sand, and known as Sand Indians, to find our way of life on the sand of the earth. That is why we go all over to seek our food to live well. We cover a large portion of land in different harvest seasons to gather our food to store in the time of the winter season....Yes, we are one of the same the Mexican Papagos call *Hia Tadk Ku:mdam*, 'Sand Root Crushers.' We have been given many names. We don't stay in one place. We are the Sand Indians originated out of the sand to roam on top of it.

To live well, Molly Jim Orozco said that they drew upon a diversity of foods, sandfood being primary:

> They also call us Sand Root Crushers. It must be true. We do dig the sweet potato-like plants with long roots. It is very good and sweet. We eat many different plants. The mesquite beans we pound and make a drink out of it. The desert asparagus [broomrape] that grows in the soft banks of the arroyo...We eat fish from the ocean...Sometimes we come [to the Pinacates] to gather cactus fruit and deer.

Scientists have occasionally tried to reconstruct the diet of the Sand Papago, guessing from what adjacent people are known to have eaten and from what potential food resources exist even in this arid core. Such lists of foods contrast oddly with that which can be compiled from the oral histories of Sand Papagos themselves. As foods that they truly relished, they casually mention twenty-one wild plant species, nine cultivated plant species, and at least twenty-three animal species. Altogether, these represent thirty-two families of flora and fauna. Sand Papago elders such as Miguel Velasco lament the demise of this dietary diversity:

> Long time ago, this was our way of life. We did not buy food. We worked hard to gather our food. We never even knew what coffee was until the white people came. We drank the desert fruit juices in harvest time. The desert food is meant for the Indians to eat. The reason so many Indians die young is because they don't eat their desert food. I worry about what will happen to this new generation of Indians who have become accustomed to present food they buy at the markets.

They will not know how to survive if the Anglos stopped selling food. The old Indians lived well with their old way of life.

Fillman Bell was told by Alonso Puffer at Hickiwan that since Papago gathering had diminished, sandfood itself may be changing for the worse:

> There was plenty of rain in those days and the desert yielded lots of food....The Sand Indians dug a sweet potato-like plant with long roots that grows in the sand, and [they] ate it raw. Now these same plants are very bitter. They don't taste the same.

What does sandfood taste like growing in superheated asphalt on a late May day? Just off the edge of old U.S. 80 in California's Algodones Dunes, it comes up through fifteen centimeters of soft tar next to a metal fencepost. This is one of the few spots in the surrounding thousand hectares where sandfood can grow without being run over. Dune buggies dodge the fencepost, tearing off the old road that is now half inundated with sand drifts, on their way to tackle the monstrous dunes a hundred meters high nearby. Host plants such as *Tiquilia* regularly get creamed as off-road vehicles (ORVs) cross and crisscross the Algodones.

Here, another nomadic group currently inhabits a portion of sandfood's natural range, at least on weekends. I have not the anthropological expertise to know if this group can properly be considered to be a tribe of its own. At first glance, their material culture sets them off from other humans: balloon tires, Honda ATC-110 three-wheelers with Enduro front suspensions, Escapade trailer homes, and beer carried only by the caseload. They crack off pop tops from their beer cans, hop on their seats, tip their sunglasses down over their eyes, and scream away. I take flight from their trajectories, landing in the shadow of a telephone pole, where I notice one last sandfood poking up out of the sand. No host plant in sight. Perhaps it is parasitic on the telephone pole.

Few of the dune-buggy jockeys ever notice sandfood. They are in a place where one looks for fun, not for food. Instead, they gather food at a U-Totem fifty kilometers away. This storehouse regularly provides foods derived from forty-two species of plants and six species of animals, which cumulatively represent twenty-four families of flora and fauna. On holiday weekends, ten to fifteen thousand of these southern California nomads bring in two to five thousand bikes and buggies for their tribal rituals in the dunes. The Algodones Dunes bear the brunt of more ORV use than any other dune area in southern California. Hilary Kaye and Harold Koopowitz tell of one weekend when 151 competitive ORV events were held in this sandfood habitat, drawing 67,000 participants and 189,000 spectators. The dust raised by this fossil-fuel-powered powwow was so thick that it showed up in satellite photos as a huge cloud over the Algodones Dunes.

But do ORVs actually have any effect on sandfood? Since the plant is so cryptic, we can only answer this question indirectly. Roger Luckenbach and Bruce Bury have compared Algodones Dune areas where buggies and bikes abound with those which are off-limits to ORVs. They found marked declines in herbaceous annuals and woody perennials, in arthropods, lizards, and mammals on the tire-compacted dunes. Even low levels of drag racing significantly decrease the volume of vegetation on the dunes. They further observed that "all sand-adapted species, including several plants considered rare or threatened species, were greatly reduced in habitats where ORVs operate."

Sandfood may be grouped with this latter bunch. It is particularly vulnerable, since it is dependent upon shrubby host plants easily mauled by oversized tires. Accordingly, it has been placed on California and Arizona special-plants lists and has been nominated for listing as an endangered species in the United States. Yet because much of its natural range lies in northern Mexico, some have claimed that it is not really endangered over a significant portion of its range. That claim was stronger in the years before dune buggies spent much time playing in the Gran Desierto of Sonora. Today, the ORVs crisscross the Gran Desierto, from Puerto Peñasco and El Golfo on the coast to the jeep trails of the Pinacate to the east. Whenever I see a dune buggy down there, I pray for a way to teach both sandfood and its host plant to duck.

Still, there remain places within sandfood's 6250-kilometer-square range that dune buggies seldom reach. During a full moon, go south of the border, between the Colorado River delta and the Pinacate lava fields. Stop your vehicle, take your shoes off, and walk. Walk toward the soft shape on the horizon, dunes like hips of women sleeping on their sides. Wander through the tracks of side-winders, lizards, windswept bushes, and beetles. Look down at your toes. There it is, like another moon coming up through the sand: sandfood, reflecting back at you.

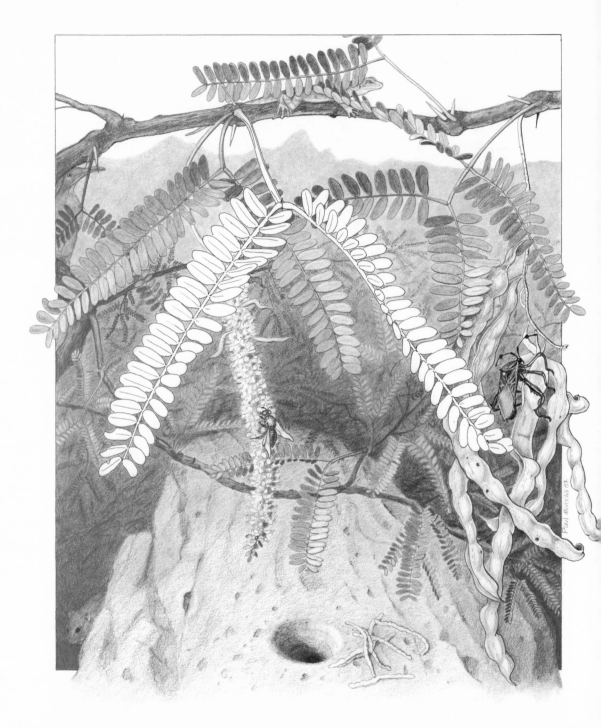

In the ocean of extreme heat and drought which we call the Sonoran Desert, Prosopis
is a protective harbor, an island of shade, nutrients, and moisture.

Mesquite as a Mirror,
Mesquite as a Harbor

I N forty seconds, mesquite can carry you from darkness into the heavens. Twenty-six mesquite stairs rise in a spiral from the musky floor of the windowless mission, Nuestro Padre San Ignacio de Caborica. On adzed, cantilevered planks the size of huge human thighs, you climb to the vaulted roof where white-winged doves take flight into the wide desert sky. Up on the roof, you look out over the fields, orchards of Spanish-introduced fruit, and native floodplain flora of Sonora's Río Magdalena.

Entering the cylindrical stone stairwell, with light sprinkling down on the mesquite from the doorway above, you feel like pressing the palm of your hand against the old wood. Subdued in color, this mesquite is smooth, even shiny in places, from two centuries of contact with human hands and feet.

The age of the stairs and the antiquity of the wood itself are uncertain. A church was first begun in Caborica by Jesuits in the late 1680s. It was short-lived, as were many other Sonoran missions during two centuries of frequent Apache raids and occasional uprisings of the Pima, the tribe to which the local Imuris-area people belonged. After the Pima Revolt of 1751, the seasoned padre Gaspar Steiger slowly rebuilt a church on the present site, completing it in 1756. Either then or when Zuñiga renovated the mission in 1775, the stairway was likely constructed from more than a dozen enormous trunks selected out of a nearby mesquite *bosque*, a virtual forest at the river's edge.

The stairway endured while the Steiger-Zuñiga edifice fell down around it. Around 1830, the church was redesigned and took the shape of what you see in

San Ignacio today. All the wear and tear of centuries has hardly harmed the wood in the stairs. Though each of the planks has its own minor stains, scars, and markings, they are still all within a few centimeters of thickness in length, breadth and depth of one another. Yet what stuns you is the way in which every stair shows gentle impressions of the human soles on the rise. The ancient mesquite holds the images of feet—some four centimeters deep—ascending to the sky.

As you wind up the spiral, hands reaching for the next stair above, you carry a feeling of moving through history. Mesquite's own heritage comes to mind. It is a mirror of that of humankind. Or at least, it reflects the ways men have made their living from the land.

Take a step up the mesquite stairway, and let the old wood talk to you. It is mute on the centuries before the arrival of the Spanish, but was alive as a tree in a *bosque*—a closed-canopy floodplain forest—when Precolumbian giant mesquites still stood. The stairs will remember that mesquite pods were ground into flour on bedrock mortars to provide the food given to Alvar Nuñez Cabeza de Vaca's group in the early 1530s. Southwestern Indians offered mesquite foods when they first discovered these Europeans, a disoriented, hungry, and odd-looking bunch. From Texas onward, Cabeza de Vaca saw clusters of mesquite trees trailing down the washes wherever he went in the dry lands north of the Valley of Mexico.

Within the growth rings of that same step, Hernando de Alarcón was given mesquite bread, corn, yucca, rabbits, and macaw or parrot feathers as gifts from the tribes residing near the Colorado River delta. These members of the Yuman family were adorned with body paint, shells, bundles of feathers around their waists, and small bags on their wrists full of seeds that could be mixed with water to prepare a beverage. Whatever the other details of their diet were, it supported a heavy human population on the delta in 1540. These delta dwellers were tall, well-built people.

Take another step up, and you'll hear the feet of Andrés Pérez de Ribas traveling up from the Río Sinaloa to meet with the peoples of southern Sonora at the start of the seventeenth century. There, he observed that "a principal form of sustenance in its season is the pod of a tree which is called mesquite. These pods, when ground, they drink with water. This drink, being somewhat sweet, is to the people what carob is to the Spaniards."

Step one higher, and you can hear Father Francisco de Escobar describe his 1604 visit to Río Colorado communities where "these Indians obtain much food from the mesquite, with which the entire river bottom is covered; and from the seeds of a grass which they gather in great quantity; which does not argue for a great abundance of maize."

The fourth step—after discovering mesquite and realizing its primacy over cultivated grains—was a change in the man-mesquite balance. This change came on the hoof. Breeding herds of cattle and horses became established in New Mexico in 1598. Padre Eusebio Kino began breeding Spanish criollo cattle in Sonora in the 1680s, setting up stock ranches at many settlements on the edge of the frontier. He distributed some of this stock to Baja California in the 1690s, where they became progenitors of the *chinampos,* perhaps the hardiest cattle in the world. These formed the bases of permanent herds in the Sonoran Desert which began intensive grazing and trampling of plants in certain localities.

Unlike your average pale-faced Herefords, criollos are browsers that eat the leaves and pods of a diversity of shrub species, including mesquite. Paleoecologist Paul Martin has argued that such browsing bovines and equids filled ecological niches left vacant in mesquite country when wild camels, horses, mastodons, and other megafauna bit the dust near the end of the Pleistocene. Mesquite had evolved under the influence of such browsers, and the introduction of additional large herbivores in the Southwest meant that mesquite seeds had increased means of dissemination. Papago elder Angelita Enríquez tells of her people's recollection that the Avra Valley uplands were grasslands until horses brought mesquite and wheat up in their hooves from the watercourses below.

Angelita's oral history has a curious correlation with fact: when horses and cows are fed mesquite pods, the seeds within have a much higher germination rate than shelled seeds which have not passed through any animal digestive tract. Pods found on the ground have only half the germinable seeds of those found in cowpies, and only a third of those found in horse manure. As many as 1600 germinable mesquite seeds have been found in a single cow chip. Spanish stock were driven across the desert uplands, and they increased the density of mesquite by leaving in discrete fertilizer packages seeds which had a high probability of germination and establishment. As ecologist Dennis Cornejo joked to Bil Gilbert, mesquite trees "…were just lurking in washes waiting to pounce. They were biding their time until something came along and disturbed the land to let them get up in the flats. Cattle did that, disturbed the land and let them out." Yet Angelita mentioned the arrival of both wheat and mesquite in the same mouthful. Perhaps the next shift in the mesquite dynamic came when Piman-speaking Indians accepted wheat as their first wintertime planting. When put into bread or puddings, the addition of wheat to mesquite dramatically increases the protein quality of such foods. The catch is that wheat became a crop to be harvested in late May to mid June, just when the first pulse of mesquite pods was ripening. Archaeologist William Doelle has surmised that the harvesting and threshing of winter wheat disrupted the customary Piman scheduling of mesquite gathering. When farmers realized that they could obtain their summer maize and beans plus winter wheat off the same piece of floodplain land, they may have been encouraged to open up more fields in mesquite bosques. Until the introduction of barbwire, these oval fields remained bordered by curvilinear hedgerows of mesquite, which protected the fields from winds and their evaporative pull, as well as from grazers. Except in drought years, mesquite pod harvests on field margins could hardly compete with the combined yields of the double cropped fields. For desert floodplain farmers, mesquite's primacy as a food began to wane.

Gradual adoption of Spanish culinary preferences may have been the next step in mesquite's demise as a Sonoran foodstuff. Padre Pedro Font expressed revulsion at the aroma of the Gila River Pima diet, based on velvet mesquite (*Prosopis velutina*) and its corkscrew-podded cousin, the tornillo (*Prosopis pubescens*). He complained that because the River Pima "eat much *pechita,* which is the mesquite pod ground and made into *atole,* the tornillo, grass seeds, and other coarse things, when they are assembled together, one perceives in them a very evil odor."

Coarse, uncultivated foods. Mesquite breads and beverages could be made without cooking and therefore without the expenditure of fuelwood. Such energy-saving foods were probably considered crude or primitive by the standards of European sophisticates. As the Indians became missionized through the church's *reducción* program, at least some of them accepted the negative connotations associated with "wildness" and "rawness" that European colonists carried into the yonlands. While mesquite seeds were being dispersed throughout Southwestern watersheds, seeds of dislike for the plant as a food were also being sown.

In areas more remote from colonial influence, mesquite somehow remained the staff of life until a century or so ago. Then changes so dramatic occurred that remaining steps rose and fell in rapid succession. With the Gadsden Purchase, Civil War, and rounding up of most of the raiding Apaches, the westward movement of Anglo-Americans seeking riches reached into new areas of the Sonoran Desert. The human population of the Territory of Arizona doubled in the 1880s, largely because of the mining boom. Fifty different mines started up during the Tombstone Bonanza in southeastern Arizona, and with an ore find in the heart of Papago country, Quijotoa grew into a boom town of over ten thousand people. The resource which these mines consumed on the largest scale was wood—mostly mesquite.

Silver stamp mills consume more than a tenth of a cord (.4 cubic meters) of fuelwood to process a ton of ore. By going back through Tombstone area newspapers and mine records, geographers Conrad Bahre and Charles Hutchinson realized the tremendous quantity of wood cut to keep the Bonanza alive for less than a decade. Nearly 50,000 cords (170,000 cubic meters) of mesquite, juniper, and oak were cut locally between 1879 and 1886 for use in the stamp mills, and perhaps an additional amount of the same magnitude was cut to fuel steam hoists and water pumps. Bahre guesses that at least another 30,000 cords of oak and mesquite were cut for Tombstone domestic use during the Bonanza's boom years. This short spurt of woodcutting depleted local floodplain bosques and reshaped the nature of upland vegetation for as much as forty kilometers away.

In 1887, Indian Agent Elmer Howard complained that Anglo woodcutting had upset Papago subsistence: "The mesquit [sic] wood is rapidly being exhausted, being cut to supply mining camps and towns, thus depriving them of the mesquito beans, which have always been one of their principle articles of food." Boomtowns at Gunsight, Comobabi, and Quijotoa rapidly extracted the small veins of silver, copper, and lead found nearby, probably devouring all large mesquite within their reach. The towns were soon deserted, leaving a degraded desert in their wake.

At the same time that miners invaded southern Arizona, so did another wave of ranchers and their cattle. Durhams, Alderneys, Shorthorns, and Devons were brought in alongside the already numerous Sonoran *corrientes* and Texas Longhorns, but few of these breeds were hardy enough to persist. Nevertheless, cattle numbers in the Arizona Territory swelled from 35,000 in 1880 to well over 720,000 by 1891. Then, beginning with the failure of summer rains that year, an unprecedented calf crop had to face three consecutive years of drought on desert range already denuded of much of its palatable vegetative cover. As a rancher named Land later reminisced, the results were that "you could actually throw a rock from one carcass to another" nearly all the way across southern Arizona. The unacclimated stock died off quickly while ranchers desperately tried to place their remaining emaciated animals on ranges in other states. By July 15, 1893, when a substantial rain finally fell again, southern Arizona ranchers had lost fifty to seventy-five percent of their ranching investment. Gaillard, a soldier-surveyor visiting the Papago at this time, found their situation to be critical: "a drought of nearly three years had destroyed their crops, exhausted their waterholes, cut off their supply of fruits and seeds, and killed many of their cattle."

When the rains finally came in the following years, floods were "flashier" in that there was less ground cover to slow their flows. The downcutting of arroyos that followed has been intensively studied over the last century. While scholars are not in agreement regarding cause-and-effect relationships, most have been stunned by the magnitude of the effects. It is unlikely that the Sonoran Desert has ever regained the carrying capacity destroyed at that time. Grasses never came back at their former densities. With reduced competition, and with fewer fires carried by the clumps of grasses that remained, mesquite began to dominate the semidesert ranges as they had not done for centuries.

Along watercourses, however, scientists observed that some mesquites were left high and dry by the deepening of arroyos and depletion of springs. In the 1920s, geologists O. E. Meinzer and Kirk Bryan suggested that the presence or absence of deep-rooted mesquites could be used as an indicator of changes in groundwater levels in arid zones. Little did they realize the extent to which dead mesquites would indicate a major shift in the Sonoran Desert economy over the following half century.

Although mesquite wood was used to fuel steam-driven water pumps in Arizona in the 1880s, such pumps were considered relatively costly then and were generally used to pump groundwater that was less than eight meters below the ground. By 1904, electric pumps had been introduced to Arizona and became increasingly available to farmers over the following two decades. At Casa Grande National Monument—the site of the huge Hohokam edifice—the first well was dug in 1902, and water was only five meters below the desert mesquite woodland. By 1918, the well was dry, for the water level had dropped to fourteen meters—still high enough to sustain mesquite. A new well drilled in 1931 more rapidly extracted the groundwater there, and the mesquite began to die as the water table dropped below sixty meters in 1952. As Ira Judd has documented, the famous prehistoric ruins now sit in the midst of a dead desert woodland.

When pumping occurred near rivers, deep rooted mesquites at first replaced emergent marsh plants such as sedges and rushes, as well as cottonwoods and willows. Yet mesquite roots could follow the water down only so far.

At the San Xavier Road crossing on the Santa Cruz River south of Tucson, mesquites were twenty meters tall at the turn of the century, and the bosque stretched for miles. In 1940, Arnold found 111 avian species and twenty-five species of mammals in bosque remnants that had been badly damaged by wood-cutters. Despite the already considerable degradation, Allan Phillips recalled that it was still "a paradise for birds." By the end of World War II, continuous surface flow on the Spring Branch of the Santa Cruz had ceased, and pumpage in the area was already one and a half times the estimated safe yield.

Paradise had begun to dry up. Subsequently, as Tucson derived a quarter of its water from a well field nearby, water levels plummeted below fifty meters, then to eighty meters. Only the most exceptional mesquite has roots which reach deeper than fifty meters. Now, on hundreds of hectares, dead mesquites stand like fossils on the dry ground that was once a lush, marshy ciénega.

Even before Paradise had evaporated away, mesquite had come onto tougher times. Perhaps World War II itself escalated the mesquite conflict. As two mesquite species came to dominate 34 million hectares of desert and semidesert in the American Southwest, range managers more frequently came to refer to them as "increasers" and (erroneously) as "invaders." These plants were native to the United States, so they weren't invading American soil as much as they were invading an American dream—that economic prosperity comes with beeves and grass. Shrubs "infesting" potential grasslands were spoken of as enemies or pests, diminishing American productivity. It was a fight for control of American soil.

Following the war, the baby boom put increasing pressure on ranchers to produce more food from the land. Ranchers who had inherited overgrazed land sought ways to improve range quality without reducing the number of livestock they were running. Range scientists showed them that the conversion of mesquite-covered uplands to grassland temporarily increased the forage available to their favorite grazers. Yet their own economic studies indicated that a rancher needed a twenty-percent increase in forage production for seven years to make mesquite control financially worthwhile. If cattle prices were low, if mesquite resprouted in significant numbers, or if drought or overgrazing reduced grass yields, the costs were hardly worthwhile. Not all range managers paid attention to each of these variables. Instead, some of them concentrated nearly all of their efforts on finding a technological fix that could completely eliminate mesquite resprouting. They sought a complete kill of mesquite, despite the fact that many ranchers consider mesquite browse to be valuable cattle feed during drought months when grasses are not as available.

After experimenting with fire, chaining, and diesel oil dumped around the stumps of cut mesquites, they still did not kill all the shrubs as fast as they had hoped they could. Some shrubs that looked dead immediately after treatment would resprout from their bases. If the land was overgrazed or poorly seeded with grasses, the rancher would never realize the long-term return in forage and beef that had been promised to him. As ranchers became dissatisfied with the results of costly vegetation manipulations, scientists became more outlandish in their attempts at what they called "arid land ecosystem improvement."

In short, the "improvement" was the use of herbicides to disrupt mesquite's growth. No single herbicide—2, 4-D; 2, 4, 5-T; tebuthiuron; dicamba; or picloram—is known to produce a hundred-percent kill of mesquite. Range managers therefore began to test combinations of chemicals on mesquite-covered range. While increasing the percent mortality of mesquite, these tests also affected other life forms. Environmentalists grew uneasy, for they had heard of adverse affects on humans and wildlife when some of the same chemicals had been used as defoliants in Vietnam.

These environmentalists claimed that all-out chemical warfare had been initiated against mesquite, but that it could potentially damage other life forms within proximity of this targeted plant. They argued that although 2, 4, 5-T contains miniscule amounts of dioxin in it, this "impurity" is a confirmed causal agent of cancer, miscarriages and birth defects. The closely related phenoxy herbicide, 2, 4-D, is less persistent in soil and plant tissue, but is also a known mutagen, carcinogen, and embryotoxin. Workers exposed to this chemical while applying it have reported dizziness, double vision, stomach pains, nausea, and a burning sensation in the mouth. Picloram may also be carcinogenic. Still, scientists and government agencies could not agree on whether field workers applying these herbicides are sufficiently exposed to the dangers of these chemicals during their routine work to warrant permanent bans on their use.

It was then realized that those involved with spraying these herbicides were not the only ones potentially exposed to them. What of Papago woodcutters and mesquite pod-harvesters who did not understand that tribal herd lands near their villages had been sprayed in a mesquite-control program in the late 1970s? As a result of concerns for public safety, in the summer of 1980 the Papago Tribal Council voted to suspend such sprayings and pellet applications, overruling the opinions of their government range managers.

Ironically, while most range scientists considered mesquite's beneficial values to be small compared to the economic losses it caused by reducing forage production, others had begun to reevaluate and appraise its true economic value. It was found that on floodplain acreage in southern Arizona, the economic value of mesquite-flavored honey and mesquite wood for fuel or furniture-making on a sustained yield basis outpriced the returns from the same land if converted to pasture for livestock grazing. On poorer lands, mesquite firewood-cutting could be an important additional renewable resource for land that was economically marginal when livestock grazing was the only use considered.

Yet not all business-minded people cared whether mesquite was managed as a renewable resource. A new industry simply treated mesquite harvesting as a one-shot deal. In northern Sonora, *ejiditarios* had begun to clear-cut mesquite for the production of charcoal to be imported to northern California and New York. Whereas woodcutters typically leave trees with trunks smaller than fifteen centimeters in diameter, charcoal makers take everything. Mesquite, which produces more BTUs of heat than the same volume of pine or juniper, probably loses half its energy when made into charcoal. Yet, when its volume is reduced down to four-tenths of the original wood mass, charcoal is considered "convenient" to export to other regions. Desert watersheds where scrubby mesquite has historically increased in density are now being shorn of every leguminous scrub that can be cut by axe or chainsaw. The rate of cutting is staggering—hundreds of hectares are denuded in a season's time, left to cast their dirt to the winds.

A mesquite forest can now be clear-cut, smouldered down into a truckload of charcoal, bagged, and hauled to a big-city steak house with little trouble. The steak itself may be Sonoran beef which got its start on overgrazed land where stocking rates are 283 percent higher than the biological community can sustain. These cattle then may have been sent to Arizona feedlots to be fattened into the marbled slabs of meat that Americans love. The Wild West is now shipped off to East Coast restaurants that advertise mesquite-broiled, smoky-flavored Marlboro Country meat. Even though charcoal gives off little of the mesquite wood scent, the whole pitch is lucrative as hell. The demand for mesquite for charcoal is so strong now that decades-old corrals and fences are being dismantled at night and hauled off before their owners can figure out what has even happened. Churchgoers in San Ignacio de Caborica beware—you may go to the mission one Sunday morning to find that your stairs have disappeared into thin air!

Somehow, mesquite, like the coyote, has persisted despite all such chingering-around with it and its habitat. As Bil Gilbert has eloquently written,

> Like the coyote, ranchers and their public servants see the mesquite as a ferocious enemy....both mesquites and coyotes are remarkably tenacious and successful. They have enormous ecological impact on everything around them....The coyote, of course, sometimes preys on livestock. The mesquite's crime is that it "preys" on grasslands that feed livestock. And neither the coyote nor the mesquite can be rubbed out.

Like a resurrection plant, mesquite crops up again and again regardless of increasing numbers of woodcutters and "ecosystem improvers." Trees demolished by chainsaws resprout at their bases, growing back into multitrunked shrubs. Chemicals fail to achieve the complete kill of all *Prosopis* pests for which they are targeted. Pods lodged in adobe bricks for forty-four years, when unearthed, germinate and grow into vigorous seedlings. Mesquite is too tenacious, too resilient, too variable to be simply subsumed by man's manipulations. Its abundance reflects our failure to control the desert environment more than any harmony with it. Mesquite is like a funhouse mirror, exaggerating our actions so that we may see them for the follies they really are.

Mesquite may be a mirror held up to human failings, but it remains much more than that. In the ocean of extreme heat and drought which we call the Sonoran Desert, *Prosopis* is a protective harbor, an island of shade, nutrients, and moisture. Mesquite's sheltering attributes have been intensively studied by an International Biome Program team coordinated by botanist Beryl Simpson. The team uncovered details of mesquite's magnetic hold on many of the members of the biotic communities inhabiting Sonoran bajadas and bottomlands.

You can hear all the life hovering around a single mesquite, often before you see it. Approach a small watercourse in desertscrub, and listen to the hum, buzz, and banter of hundreds of animals congregating on each of mesquite's many inflorescences. Over a season's time, a mature velvet mesquite produces well over a million flowers. Rich in nectar and pollen, these attract more kinds of animals than do the blooms of any other plant in Sonoran Desert scrublands. Sixty-four kinds of solitary bees have been found visiting a stand of mesquite on the Silverbell bajada north of Tucson. Toss in tarantula hawks, mantids, thrips, crab spiders, beetles, assassin bugs, hummingbirds, and flycatchers, and you get enough flower feeders and predators to make for a sizeable menagerie.

As pollinated flowers develop into pods, leaf-footed bugs, bruchid beetles, and weevils jump into action. The leaf-footers suck some ripening pods dry of their goodies, thereby causing them to abort or shrivel. Several kinds of bruchids lay their eggs in green pods, and their larvae bore into the seeds, leaving them empty and lifeless. Mesquite presumably produces such a large mast of pods to swamp the number of bruchids damaging them. Even so, three quarters of a season's seeds may be destroyed by these boring beetles.

Those seeds which survive are often the ones which have passed through a vertebrate gut, since gut juices kill the beetles before they have completely cored out the seeds. Pod-feeding vertebrates range from pocket mice and kangaroo rats to pronghorn. More impressive, perhaps, is the diversity of backboned animals using mesquite bosques for various combinations of food and shelter. Tom Gavin encountered fifteen mammal and ninety-five bird species—including twenty-eight kinds nesting—in a single bosque on the Río San Pedro.

Animals are not the only organisms which take shelter under mesquite's boughs. Roughly twice the number of herbaceous plants grow under mesquites than in exposed areas between them. On the Silverbell bajada, Beryl Simpson and John Neff collected thirteen species of summer grasses and wildflowers beneath mesquites that could not be found in nearby openings. Highly nutritious browse plants such as panicgrass, six-weeks grama, and fringed amaranth often nestle in the skirts of scrubby mesquite.

I once guessed that herbs were clustered under mesquites because blowing seeds came to rest up against trunks and broken branches which blocked their tumbling. Once trapped, the shade there offered a buffered environment where moisture would be temporarily held once it had rained. New sprouts would begin in microhabitats where heat and evaporative pull were reduced compared to those of bared areas.

On the other hand, each herb growing in the shade may have fewer evaporative demands but more overall competition for water, both with other herbs and with mesquite itself. Typically, 1500 kilograms of water are used to produce a kilogram of mesquite, so that considerable soil moisture is gobbled up by the tree shading the herbs. And yet, despite this competition, herbs are often huge, with large seed sets under mesquite.

The discovered existence of another kind of harboring effect can help explain the herbal abundance below mesquite. Nitrogen becomes concentrated in mesquite islands, even though the usual deficiency of this nutrient is nearly as limiting to desert productivity as is lack of water. Mesquite trees have long been known to be nitrogen pumpers. That is, their extensive root systems pull in whatever available nitrogen exists in the soil and rock strata below, and it is pumped into the canopy. Leaves and pods falling are essentially dumping nitrogen as litter below the canopy, enriching the topsoil. Recently, however, scientists finally confirmed that symbiotic bacteria also associate themselves with mesquite rootlets as they do with other legumes, forming nodules which fix nitrogen as an additional source for the tree. In an otherwise nitrogen-poor desert, mesquite and its entourage of herbs sit in a pocket of riches.

All in all, *Prosopis* has the ability to accumulate more of this scarce macronutrient than can nearly any other desert plant. With the help of rhizobial symbionts, mesquite islands are essentially self-fertilizing. Peter Felker once calculated that on a hectare of mesquite-dominated vegetation, the equivalent of 300 kilograms of ammonium nitrate is added to the soil by a year's litter accumulation. Relative to its fellow bajada-dweller, the foothills paloverde, mesquite contains about fifty percent more nitrogen in its canopy, trunk, litter, and soil system. Barth and Klemmendson have confirmed that soil below mesquite grows richer as the tree grows, while this is not necessarily true for paloverde and other desert trees.

Visiting a Papago Indian wheat field with me once, farmer Wendell Berry noticed a side effect of mesquite's nitrogen harboring. There, in the midst of the floodwater-fed wheat, he observed a round patch of plants that were much taller and darker green than any others. We asked the farmer if he had fertilized that patch or done anything else special there. No, he replied, except for having cut down an old mesquite there a year before. The patch of vigorous plants covered about the same area as the tree's shadow once did. For such reasons, I later learned, Papago farmers would often let large mesquites persist amid their fields, and formerly gathered up the litter from field-edge hedgerows to dig into the soil around their crops.

The nitrogenous riches of *Prosopis* become a currency in the Sonoran Desert. When summer thunderstorms break loose, rain hits the ground with such force as to carry away considerable mesquite litter in sheetfloods. Litter-laden runoff drains into watercourses and washes as flash floods down to alluvial fans, where the flows spread out, dumping their suspended loads. The detritus left on these alluvial soils is about one percent nitrogen, thanks to all the mesquite leaves, pods, and rodent feces found within it. It greatly contributes to the fertility and tilth of such fans. Whether it be the dense blooms of wildflowers found on natural alluvium, or the best farmlands found in Sonoran Desert river valleys, plant productivity in these spots is nurtured by mesquite growing upstream.

The most peculiar places that mesquite currency is invested are the shabby hovels of desert packrats. These nocturnal rodents gather thorny mesquite branches and cholla cactus joints to construct a protective armature over their messy mounds. When mesquite pods begin to drop to the ground, packrats gather them up and bank them in underground chambers below the mounds. Mesquite pods are carefully sorted and piled separate from those of paloverde, acacia, or other desert plants. However, seeds of some of these pods may fall under the mound-wall debris, perhaps eventually germinating just as those in adobe walls do.

Once, humans knew of and drew upon this mesquite-packrat connection. Elderly Yuma and Seri Indians have recalled how their families had uncovered mesquite pods in packrat middens long after their own harvests had been used up.

Upon finding a packrat mound, teenagers would use a stick or foot to remove the branches on top. Then, digging around in the mound, they would expose the carefully sorted caches and remove considerable quantities of pods, handful by handful. Occasionally, youngsters would disturb a hidden packrat, but did not always catch it to throw into the larder. In a way, taking just the packrat's cache was like short-circuiting the energy flowing through the food chain. It was gathering nutrition from the packrat without losing ninety percent of the food energy that would have become unavailable if the packrat had eaten the pods and then the people had eaten him. By knowing that packrats were as fond of mesquite pods as they themselves were, Sonoran Desert dwellers extended the availability of this food for several more months.

It's November, near Thanksgiving time, ten years since I first had mesquite pudding at a Pima Indian family's holiday feast. I am out on the bajada of the Santa Ritas, where mesquite-lined arroyos run down toward the Santa Cruz River. Below on the Santa Cruz floodplain, heavily irrigated pecan orchards now shade the earth the way mesquite bosques did in the past. Above on the bajada, amidst scrubby mesquites surviving on a much more modest water budget, a number of packrat mounds are built into the larger arroyo banks.

Popping off the top of one of these middens, I expose a small pile of pods, still fine for the eating. An idea pops into my head—packrat ranching. Rounding up packrats who round up pods. Ranching not for meat, but for mesquite. What would have happened if we had pursued this connection with legume and rodent, rather than gambling all our chips away on cows? Would ranchers hire "ratboys" to wrangle rodents? Would we learn to "make mesquite while the sun shined" instead of "making hay?" When we looked in the mesquite mirror once again, would we see that it could also be our harbor? Is that too remote a dream?

I gently placed the mesquite boughs and bark fragments back in place atop the midden. "Sleep tight, little packrat," I murmured. "And guard your cache of mesquite pods. We may need them someday. Someday we may need the both of you."

*It is as if the blooming organpipe, branches reaching skyward, serves as
the Sonoran equivalent of the lightning rod.*

Organpipe Cactus:
Bringing in the Rainfeast

A SOFT stream of sound reaches the cactus-covered Quitovac hills on a full moon night in late July. Songs rise from the small Papago-settled Vak oasis below. They rise from the *Vi'igita,* an O'odham ceremony variously interpreted as a cactus fruit harvest feast, a rainmaking rite, a blessing of newly sown crops, or a community identity renewal. The masked Naviju dancer has already gone around to sanctify the houses that still stand, as well as those fallen down, rubble piles of stone, mesquite posts, mud and cactus bones. Most Papago have returned to the bare earth of the dancing floor, across the wash from the houses, to celebrate some more. During the next few nights, they will watch the pantomime of remnant tribal lore, sing the barely remembered songs, and splash down hundreds of liters of saguaro and organpipe wine. Whether Arizonan or Sonoran by citizenship, these Papago are glad to be together again with old friends, distant relatives, and seldom-seen spirits.

Up on the rocky slopes where the sung notes drift, the columnar cacti stand, lively in the moonlight. Organpipe, saguaro, and senita reach above the squat, spinescent shrubs of the desert scrub. There, another feast is in the works, one which even fewer people witness, but one which is ever more ancient and persistent.

This feast takes place near the tops of organpipe, or *pitahaya dulce,* as it is called in Mexico. Pale, funnelform flowers flare out laterally from the sides of the tapering branches. By eight at night, they are fully open, laden with cream-colored pollen. At the base of the floral tube, nectar is welling up. These pastel-tinged flowers stand out in the drab landscape, and give off a skunklike scent.

Nectar-feeding bats hover around the flowering, towering cacti. Perhaps they will linger within reach of this dense stand for several weeks before moving to where agaves bloom to the north. As one bat approaches an open organpipe blossom, a drop of crimson stains the perianth. The bat turns its head slightly and its snout glints in the moonlight, shining blood-red. As its tongue dives into a flower to lap up nectar, it treads in mid-air, then darts away. Other droplets blotch the organpipe blossom, remaining after the bat has gone.

Not blood but pitahaya juice taints this pollinator and flower. For in addition to administering the cross-pollination necessary for organpipe fruit set, bats are among the seed dispersers of this succulent, *Stenocereus thurberi*. Since flowering and fruiting periods overlap on any single plant, a long-nosed bat may feed on both nectar and fruit during the same evening.

Donna Howell discovered that another kind of bat gathers rewards from pitahayas too. Visiting a mine shaft full of desert pallid bats near the Arizona-Sonora border, she noticed that many of them were red in the face, much the same as the long-nosed bats. At first she wondered if they had been in a massive fight, for they are quintessential insectivores, not fruit eaters. Then she observed that the fresh feces on the mine shaft floor consisted of one part cactus pulp and seed and three parts moth fragments.

Moths and cactus fruit together? As the fruits ripen, their frontal ends become soft, and their thin skins are easily punctured by the frugivorous long-nosed bats that slurp up pitahaya pulp and juice. Noctuid moths then enter the openings left by the bats, drinking juice in a frenzy. Desert pallid bats, primordially strict insectivores, block the opening through the fruit's skin and glean any moths attempting to escape. They primarily consume the trapped moths, but they must gain some nutrients from the organpipe adventitiously. They feed on this protein- and calorie-rich combination, then return to their mine shaft roosts as the sky begins to lighten.

In the desert heat following dawn, fermentation occurs within the remaining juices of the punctured fruit and in the nectar of still-open blossoms. Fruitflies and bees go to drink in these ephemeral pools. They become drunk, fall in, and drown. Doves and hummingbirds get in on the dregs. A multitude of insects swarms in as the day proceeds, working to finish off the mild wine before mid-morning, for the flowers close by then. They soon forsake the wine and escape for shade, about the same time that the Papago do below, down on the burning desert flats.

Drinking wine. Dealing with the desert heat. These are old, old rituals.

Have these old organpipe rituals been commonplace? We don't know. The only sites where organpipe cacti have been studied in any detail are near where they reach their northernmost limits, and no one is sure how representative this information is. They peter out in the Papago country of southern Arizona near Ajo, Ventana Cave, Hecla, and the Pichacho Mountains. Such locales are closer to desert research labs and universities than they are to the heart of organpipe's range. In terms of their ecological relations with other species, Arizona organpipes may be out on a tangent.

This holds true too for the borderline pitahayas featured at Organ Pipe Cactus National Monument, situated within the hundred kilometers between the Sonoran oasis of Vak and the floundering mining town of Ajo, Arizona. Because the monument sits at the northwestern limits of the genus *Stenocereus,* the spotlighted plants are chubby, stubby, scarred from frost damage, and few and far between. In the monument, organpipes are restricted to rocky slopes above where cold-air drainages settle. They cling to slopes facing the south and southwest, where extra solar exposure keeps the air and soil temperatures up a few more degrees. In this habitat they may be kept from being killed by most freezes, but they still show the wounds of close calls.

It seems that organpipes have been studied where it is most convenient for U.S. citizens to visit them, but in populations that are atypical for the species as a whole. The sparsely distributed dwarf organpipes of the north may tell a different story than those which dominate the landscape for hundreds of kilometers to the south. In their heartland, we are not sure that nectar-feeding bats still slurp up pitahaya fruit juice as they do in the north, nor do we know whether other species become more important in pollination and seed dispersal.

As for native cultural interactions with pitahayas in the north, they have been limited by low densities of the plants within reach. Certain Arizona Papago families formerly walked or rode wagons a hundred kilometers to the south to harvest the fruit they call *chuchuwis.* However, most Papago in Arizona would simply stay closer to home, gathering the abundant saguaro or *bahidaj* within a half day's walk. Whereas saguaros figure prominently in Papago folklore and religion, organpipes are on the margins.

It was supposed to be a gathering of experts on organpipe, its environment, and its management. Yet by nine o'clock, the few desert biologists that were in the room had begun to glance at the door off and on—wasn't someone else going to arrive who knew something about the topic at hand? There were a few state-level land managers from Phoenix and landscape architects from Tucson whom they had seen away from their offices once or twice before. Then there were government agency administrators from Denver, Albuquerque, San Francisco, and Salt Lake—Westerners, but with little experience in the Sonoran Desert. Two other men had come to southern Arizona for the first time, directly from Washington—business suits on a May day in the desert gave them away. A game warden and a theoretical ecologist had been invited from Mexico, but neither could attend. No Mexican scientists, no students, and no enlightened amateurs who had lived in organpipe stands were in attendance.

The talk went on, but it was hard to tell what it was about. There were phrases thrown out like "maximizing visitor use days in targeted environments while protecting the periphery" and "developing integrated methodologies to monitor rodent and cactus thief impacts on the demography of roadside populations."

Suddenly a grizzly bear rose up in the audience and started to roar.

Well, not exactly a grizzly bear. Instead, a grizzled old desert biologist. But the effects were the same. The bureaucrats looked frightened, queasy, and concerned. Some beast had barged in and spoiled the picnic. And he was still roaring:

"Cactus! Rocks! Birds! Nests! Bats! Bugs! Snakes! That's what we should be talking about, that's what we should be learning about! If you guys want to set aside land for 'visitor use days' and 'roadsides,' count me out."

The gray-haired, hulking figure in wrinkled khakis and dusty workboots pawed at his neck to open the collar of his shirt more, as if something was suffocating him. He sat down, looked around the room, and sneered:

"And by the way, how many of you have ever seen an organpipe cactus? I don't mean through the viewfinder on your Kodak...I mean out in the boonies where you can't just snap a photo then trot back to your air-conditioned car! How many of you have ever taken the time to look at them away from scenic-loop drives or nature trails? Do you guys go to Mexico, other than to visit the beach or to hear mariachis play in the border towns? How in the heck do you think you're gonna figure out what to tell the public about organpipes if you just sit around in rooms like this?"

He glanced around the room again. Distraught bureaucrats were frantically writing notes to themselves, in case they were called upon to cover their peripheries. Then the bear lumbered out of his seat and over to the door. He turned around and looked at them one last time.

"I shouldn't have been so impolite. Some of you are here in the Sonoran Desert for the first time, so I shouldn't expect you to know anything about organpipe. And I myself know a lot less than I should. So let's get a fresh start. I'm going out to my Carry-All there in the parking lot, I'm gonna straighten it up, and make a little more room. I'll be leaving for Sonora in a couple hours, and you are welcome to go with me to see some great organpipe stands about a half day to the south. I'll loan you all the camping equipment you'll need. In fact, I'll be happy to pay the way of anyone who wants to go down and learn a little about organpipe. As for the rest of you, I wish you a pleasant visitor use day...."

He held his paw up to them for a moment, gesturing farewell, then stormed out the door.

Go south. Drive south of the border as far as you can in one day. Find a dirt road and drop off the pavement. Follow it down to where there is no more road sound of mufflers on semi-trucks, no more plastic diapers and beer cans. Park your vehicle. Grab a flashlight, a groundcloth, and a light sleeping bag. Walk, by moonlight, to a dry sandy wash at the base of a rocky knoll loaded with organpipes. Sleep. Sleep.

When you awake, you realize that you are not far from Topolobampo, Sinaloa. You are not far from where the Spanish first saw *Stenocereus thurberi*, and first learned of its usefulness from the Indians. Its southernmost limits are not too far to the south, in denser drought-deciduous forests, but here they begin to dominate certain landscapes. You are still far from understanding just what this plant really is, what it can mean to humankind.

Walking, walking, you zigzag under the dense canopy of this tiered Short Tree Forest. In a sense, the forest is not all that short except in comparison to the pine forests in the Sierra Madres up the barrancas to the east. The upper boughs of the tallest trees seem to float more than four meters above the continuous canopy. These giants include the *pochote,* with its fruit full of feather-like kapok; the huge-trunked *palo barril;* the *palo joso,* with its hundreds of tiny leaflets; and the *torote* or elephant tree. The more continuous middle canopy is made up of brasilwood, tree morning glories, the wide-crowned *guasima,* and the spiny-fruited *papache.* Occasionally, the mass of the arborescent *cardon echo* cactus breaks through this canopy, or makes an opening for itself. Below, wild jicama, sennas, *chocolas,* and birds-of-paradise seek light through small openings. Particularly near the bases of hills, this forest is too competitive, too wet for organpipes to thrive. To find them, you often have to move upslope, to the cliff faces of barrancas or steep sides of volcanic hills with too little moisture-holding capacity for more tropical plants. Sometimes, however, you find them on rocky, soil-poor bajadas, stretching for miles, such as the ones Andrés Pérez de Ribas visited north of the Río Sinoloa some time after 1604. He was the first to describe thoroughly the pitahaya fruit and plant, and their use by Indians, in memoirs written around 1644:

> The fruit which they enjoy for the longest period is of the pitahaya, a tree unknown in Europe. Its branches are several centimeters in diameter and of the nature of thorny green striated wax tapers extending as much as ten meters in height.
> The fruit grows from these thorny ribbed branches and is, of itself, covered with thorns. It is similar in appearance to a chestnut or prickly pear. Its interior consistency is much like that of a fig, although softer and more delicate. Its color is at times white, at others red, or yellow. It is very savory, particularly when harvested before the rains come in the summer. The abundance of these pitahayas is such that one may travel among them for a distance of fifteen to thirty kilometers.

At least as far south as the Sinaloan organpipe which Pérez de Ribas relished are those described by Spanish padres in Baja California Sur a century later. There, organpipe enters the subtropical Cape Region, where it is found with several other columnar cacti, including the endemic known scientifically as *Stenocereus littoralis.* It remains more abundant in true desert areas north of La Paz, where its fruits are still sold in markets for the equivalent of a dollar per kilogram. Other columnar cacti fruit, by comparison, are seldom eaten near La Paz, due to the superiority in taste of pitahaya dulce. There, the vegetation receives between 150 and 200 millimeters of rain and supports more arid species, such as an ocotillo locally known as *palo adan,* the peninsular palo verde, the *chilito* cactus, *palo jito,* the *datilillo* yucca, and organpipe's tart counterpart, *pitahaya agría.*

Miguel del Barco, who knew the natural history of the Loreto and San Xavier areas better than any other priest in Baja California, was particularly curious about the organpipe:

> The fruit is born stuck to the branches, near their tips. There, it is produced from beautiful white blossoms tinged with red. When these dry and the fruit begins to swell, it is so covered with thorns that you can't see the fruit itself. As the fruits increase in size and are about to mature, the thorns become more widely spaced, and you can see through to the skin of the fruits, be they green, yellow or red as

when completely ripe. Those that have red skins are always red inside as well. Others are yellow, white or buff.

All of them are excellent fruit, worthy of being on the table of the greatest of kings. Their flesh is juicy, mild, delicate and very delicious. They have no pit to cause problems in eating, and the seeds which are no bigger than those of mustard are imbedded into the pulp of the fruit, each separate from the others. For this reason the seeds go down easily, as part of the pulp, without you even knowing that they are swallowed.

...Some years there are so few organpipe fruit that it is fair to say there wasn't any. In the winter of 1739–1740, it rained so many times that even though these rains were gentle, the arroyos were swollen and ran swiftly. This event I witnessed only that winter in the thirty years that I was there in Baja California. All the country was cured of the drought, and the following months brought a dressing of herbs and wildflowers. In contrast, the organpipe of that year did not bear fruit, complaining perhaps of too much moisture.

While Miguel del Barco recorded patterns of pitahaya variation that scientists have yet to study, his colleagues in lower California looked at the columnar cacti in only one way. They served as the medium of the most lowly tradition that the Baja California peoples practiced—a food-recycling technique known euphemistically as "the second harvest." In 1740, Father Consag provided a brief description of this tradition, later highlighted by geographer Homer Aschmann:

> When the pitahaya dulce was ripe, food was so abundant that the Indians could remain in one spot for some weeks. They made a practice of defecating in a selected spot. When the feces were dry, they were collected in flat baskets, ground up by hand, and the undigested pitahaya seeds winnowed out. These seeds were toasted, ground on metates and eaten.

During months of drought, the columnar cactus seeds provided a needed source of protein, oil, and calories that the people of Baja California, coastal Sonora, and Tiburón Island could not afford to waste. The large-seeded *cardon,* or *Pachycereus pringlei,* may have been used more frequently in this way than even the organpipe. Whichever species was utilized, the seeds were meticulously cleaned and washed, ground, and then thoroughly cooked before being eaten. Regardless of how much preparation went into making this food acceptable to the desert peoples, it was hardly palatable to Europeans.

It was with unclerical delight that Consag spread a story of what had happened to the finicky father, Francisco Mario Piccolo. Visiting a ranchería of Pericu

Indians near Mulegé for the first time in a long while, Piccolo had been treated to a specially prepared feast. After the meal, Piccolo asked out of curiosity what it was that they had eaten. To his discomfort, they began to explain that it was from a flour made of ground pitahaya seeds.

Not just any pitahaya seeds, they continued. Ones that they had painstakingly gathered from feces found on a favorite rock nearby....They didn't need to go into any more detail for Piccolo, who all of a sudden was feeling ill.

Go east as far from Baja California as you can reach, without letting organpipe drop out of sight for good. Rise up from sea level as high as you can without freezing them out. You might take a train, the Ferrocarril Pacifico, with tracks that traverse the edge of the Barranca del Cobre. If you are roadworthy enough, you might endure a truck or jeep bouncing up and down the switchbacks, from Sierra Madrean summits of 3000 meters to canyon bottoms of 500 meters, dodging landslides and potholes. This will put you into other *barrancas,* the word Mexicans use when "canyon" just doesn't encompass enough.

At 1400 meters, not far below Chihuahuan oaks, organpipes edge themselves out on slopes of volcanic tuff. Here, the dominants at Los Mochis persist, more widely spaced, at the limits of their distribution too. But the barranca microclimate serves to mix a wider range of plants together: the *amole* agave, which I nickname the "turn-of-the-century plant," growing upside down on cliffs; *guamuchil;* coral bean; *sotol* or desert spoon; boat-spined acacia; sycamore or *aliso;* mesquite; and *chichiquelite,* an edible nightshade. In addition, the wild relatives of many cultivated plants cluster below organpipe and echo cactus, particularly in more open areas: figs, chiles, teparies, manioc, and a tequila-like agave. With such a diversity of flora, the predominantly pine-zone dwelling Tarahumara Indians often descend into the barrancas to gather plants not found closer to home.

It was with the Tarahumara that Carl Lumholtz first encountered the pitahaya, which he claimed produces "the finest fruit in Mexico's Northwest." He observed that this harvest allows the Tarahumara a chance to feast during the otherwise food-poor dry season. It may be for this reason that organpipe came to play a role in Raramuri mythology and calendrical cycle:

> With the Indians, the pitahaya enters, of course, into religion, and the beautiful macaw [guacamaya] which revels in the fruit is associated with it in their beliefs. The bird arrives from its migration to southern latitudes when the pitahaya is in

bloom, and the Indians think that it comes to see whether there will be much fruit; then it flies off again to the coast, to return in June when the fruit is ripe.

The following gives the trend of one of the guacamaya songs: "The pitahaya is ripe, let us go and get it. Cut off the reeds! The guacamaya comes from the Tierra Caliente to eat the first fruits. From far away, from the hot country, I come when the men are cutting the reeds, and I eat the first fruits. Why do you wish to take the first fruits from me? I eat the fruit, I throw away the skin. I get filled with the fruit and I go home singing. Remain behind, little tree, waving as I alight from you! I am going to fly in the wind, and some day I will return to eat your pitahayas, little tree!"

Once harvested with a pronged rod, the fruit is split and dried in the sun. On ripened fruit, the thorns so easily fall off that there is no trouble handling them during processing. The Tarahumara then scrape the hardened pulp out of the brittle rind and store it as small cakes. Sometimes the fruit is boiled down and the seeds are skimmed off the top. The thickened fruit juice and pulp are poured into a mold, where they congeal into a *queso* or sweet of cheeselike consistency. The skimmed-off seeds are ground and added to pinole.

As masters in the making of fermented beverages, the Tarahumara also make a mild cactus beer or *tesguino*. The juice from mashed pitahaya pulp is collected, mixed with water and boiled in a huge clay pot for several hours on top of coals. They throw in a piece of bark, most often from the shrubby papache, to serve as a catalyst as the juice begins to ferment. The Tarahumara tesguino pots are used over and over again, building up within their pores a special culture of beer yeast. The tesguino reinforces the culture of the Tarahumara themselves. Adults spend around a hundred days a year participating in ritualized *tesguinadas* where the beer serves as a social lubricant, whether it be made of sprouted maize, mescal, manzanitas, or pitahayas. Like the flying guacamaya, the Tarahumara partake of the fruit, and go home singing.

Some 250 kilometers northwest of the Tarahumara, pitahaya is too important as food to be made into wine. In 1737, Padre Felipe Segesser commented that the pitahaya, with its exceptional flavor, was used intensively by the Pima at Tecoripa whenever they had a summer shortfall of grain. Two hundred and fifty years later, old Pedro Estrella, one of the last Pima speakers at Onavas, affirmed that the fruit "was purely to eat, not for wine."

As Don Pedro said this, he sat beneath his ramada made of organpipe bones cut lengthwise to form what looked like a corrugated roof. Much of the paraphernalia near his ramada was made of this bone-like xylem tissue which remains after organpipes die and their watery flesh rots away. Pima gatelatches, corrals, and fences, plus chicken coops, bird traps, and boxes are regularly made of cactus bones.

On the banks of the Río Yaqui, Onavas lies just outside the true Sonoran Desert, in subtropical thornscrub. Here, organpipe may outnumber the echo, the other common columnar cacti. Both serve as roosts for vultures, so that their branches are often streaked by the whitewash of these scavengers. The vegetation is rich in legumes such as feathertree, boat-spine acacia, ironwood, mesquite, Sonoran palo verde and kidneywood. Birds are thick within the patches of fruiting wolfberry, hackberry, and graythorn. At least one bird stays so close to the organpipe during fruiting time that in Onavas, it has become the organpipe dove: *paloma pitayera*. You can hear the white-winged doves calling "o'koko'i" early in the morning from the tops of the pitahaya, the Pima say.

When fruit is scarce, the Seri Indians suggest that you listen for the call of these white-winged doves. Follow the sound. Where the doves are, there are ripened pitahaya.

I followed them along the Sea of Cortez coast one week eight years ago, in the heat of early July. I was with the late great chaotic desert rat Paul Schneider, working for ethnobotanist Richard Felger, trying to estimate the yields of desert foods used by the Seri. We would awake with the first calling of the doves and dive into a desert heat that not even the night diminishes. By the time the sun came up, we would already be sweating, running down the desert coast, counting the fruit of organpipe.

It was like working for the Census Bureau, except the citizenry we had to interview were all columnar cacti.

"Good morning, Mr. Organpipe. Your address? The Desemboque dump? Yes, I guess there's only one prominent dump in this area. Age? You don't know? What do you mean you don't know? You're older than that little one over there, aren't you? Well, yes, that's right, taller and more arms. Maybe that will do, yes? Paul, could you count the arms, while I estimate height? Mmmmm, let's see there—3.5 meters. Paul? You're having trouble? Yessir, keep them up in the air for just another moment until Paul is done counting....How many? Twenty-seven arms. Not bad. There's another one over here that's your height that has only six. Okay, Paul, I'll count the fruit and flowers on this side, and meet you at that dead branch....Your subtotals? Fifteen and twelve? Let's see, with my counts, that makes a total of thirty-one fruit and twenty-three flowers. Thank you for your patience, sir. Yes, you can let your arms down now. Yes, thanks again. Next?"

We would get several dozen cacti interviewed by ten-thirty or so in the morning. By then, the temperature had climbed over a hundred and ten degrees, and Paul had climbed into his old, battered pickup. I pushed so that Paul could jump-start it, and we would then joyride through the gorgeous forests of cardon, wood, desert lavender, brittlebush, and foothill palo verde. Swerving down the sandy road into Desemboque, we'd bounce with every bump. His truck was free of air-conditioning, so whenever we stopped, we had to peel ourselves from the wet seatbacks—I never knew that pickup cabs could sweat that much. We would then kick the doors open and swagger around the humble town of Desemboque looking to see if an ice-cold Coke could be had.

The same schedule followed in Punta Chueca and Bahía Kino as in Desemboque—do our cactus counts, collect a few fruit for nutritional analysis, jump-start the truck, dig the truck out of sand pits, then head into the nearest Seri village. Within the previous five years, the southerly Seri had moved from the low brush and wood huts to fancy fiberboard frame houses. They still used old truck bodies for walls of storage sheds, and they eyed Paul's soon-to-die pickup with envy. We would drink our sodas, Paul would juggle, I would finger-wrestle with the kids, then we would show them the cactus fruit we had collected earlier.

"*Imam imam,*" a youngster would say of the ripe fruit.

"*Ool,*" said another, acknowledging that it was from organpipe.

A man with shoulder-length hair under his cowboy hat would then lift his sunglasses to take a good look. He said in Spanish that it was a good harvest for so early in the season.

Our last night in Bahía Kino, we carefully packed all the fruit to be taken back for nutritional analysis. We wrapped each in paper and placed it on a cardboard liner inside a wooden fruit box. We covered the entire box with paper and wrapped string around it. Several boxes were fit snugly together in the back of the pickup.

We went to sleep in our hammocks at eight in the evening, hoping to get an early start to escape the heat. The truck sat not ten meters away from us, waiting with its load. We got the jump on dawn, and were back at the border by midday.

That's when we discovered that all the boxes of cactus fruit were gone.

In the long run, perhaps the loss of our additional data didn't matter that much. We had our census statistics, just no seed per fruit and nutritional composition information for another year. Besides, Richard Felger and his collaborator Mary Beck Moser had already accumulated what may be the most extensive set of data on Indian use of columnar cacti that will ever be assembled. Following up on W. J. McGee's suggestion that cactus fruit was the most important wild fruit harvest of the Seri, Moser and Felger spent over two decades documenting the nuances of the relationship between columnar cacti and the last hunter-gatherer culture in arid America.

Their treatise not only covers the Seri use of organpipe as food and drink, but also the plant's use as medicine, shelter, toys, in games, as paraphernalia in hunting and in smoking out bees, and as an image in folklore.

The Seri still gather pitahaya fruit every year, despite the fact that in the last few decades, their economy has shifted more towards the sales of wood carvings, baskets, and sea-turtle meat. The ripe fruit, *imam imam*—which Padre Gilg wrote as *himamas* in 1692—remains a special treat. Traditionally, the first ripe fruit brought into camp was opened, and bits of its pulp dabbed on the cheeks and nose to bring good luck.

According to Moser and Felger, the Seri were aware of geographic variation in organpipe traits at a level of detail beyond that which botanists have ever investigated. The Seri know a place near Pozo Coyote where certain plants flower and fruit twice a year. At Pozo Peña, the fruit produce a particularly strong but pleasant odor. At other sites, they found fruit that came on fairly late, in the autumn. The care for detail by persons who noticed such things was prominent in Seri culture. Would such fine observations count as much in a symposium of so-called cactus experts?

For me, the most remarkable Seri use of organpipe was for keeping boats afloat—a strange duty for a land-loving plant accustomed to less than 100 millimeters of rain per year. The caulk called *hoco ine,* 'wood's mucus,' by the Seri was first described by Edward Davis in 1924:

> I witnessed the operation of making a certain kind of pitch or tar which the Seri use to make the seams in their canoes or boats tight. The women pound up the dried pulp next to the outside skin of the dead *pitahalla* cactus (organ cactus). This is very dry and brown in color and the pieces are pounded up to a dry powder with a wash or shore rock in a dried deer hide. This is placed in a *batello,*

or flat basket, and manipulated so that the coarse pieces come to the top and are scraped off and thrown away. The fine powder is then put in a five gallon can and some porpoise [*sic*] or sea-lion oil or horse oil is poured on it and stirred into a thick gummy mass. When thoroughly mixed it is put over the fire, in an olla, to boil continuously for an hour or two until it is the consistency and has the appearance of coal tar. While being worked it is kept heated and applied to seams inside and outside the boat. It hardens just like tar and answers the same purpose.

Well, almost. Early in this century, the plank boats coated with this caulking leaked so badly that they needed constant bailing. A Seri boy with a bucketlike pot had to be sent along with the men to keep them from going under. No matter how detailed a culture's botanical knowledge is, no remedy, no technology is foolproof. Let us praise such failures as the Seri in a sinking ship, for that is what sends us back to the drawing board.

Keeping afloat in a tide of water. Throughout most of Sonora, countrymen will say that the fruiting of organpipe begins around San Juan's Day in late June, with the initiation of the summer rains. It is as if they ready their fruit to ride the coming floods.

To ensure greatest establishment and survival of seedlings, columnar cacti such as organpipe gear their seed-ripening period to coincide with the summer rains. Those seeds which have not already been passed to the ground by birds or bats are then knocked loose by the thunderstorms. There, they wash downslope and are often left in sight or scent of a number of predators ranging from coyotes to harvester ants. The few which become established are often those which have been washed or defecated down beneath spiny desert shrubs. With this protection, they are allowed to emerge and grow until they eclipse the size of the nurse plant below. To pass on a favor, it seems, they themselves often serve as a protective platform for *Mamillaria* cactus, and as a support structure for vining herbs. To extend the favor, the nexus of their branches regularly provides a base for nests of cactus wrens and other birds. Organpipe fruit are of course eaten by these birds, as well as by dozens of other kinds of animals.

Rain delivers organpipe seeds to new homes, but do organpipes themselves bring the rain? It is as if the blooming organpipe, branches reaching skyward,

serves as the Sonoran equivalent of the lightning rod. When the fruit on the
columnar cacti are ripe, the Papago say, we make wine from them, drink, and sing
to throw up the clouds. The clouds build and bulge, dark and heavy
over the desert hills. Suddenly, one weighty cloud sags,
touching the top of the thorny cactus
below. With the touch of just one
thorn, it bursts into a
thunderstorm.

SUMMER

"One man's weed is another man's vegetable," a Papago might say.
And he might be both men at the same time.

Amaranth Greens:
The Meat of the Poor People

"SOMETIMES they have the amusement of setting themselves to graze like beasts."

Miguel del Barco wrote with amazement of seeing the Pericu, natives of Baja California, down on all fours, "nipping off the top of the amaranth, and eating it, saving the work of taking it by the hand to their mouth." He had been struck by the unabashed manner with which these desert dwellers responded to the first flush of wild leafy vegetables, or *quelites,* that suddenly appeared after months of drought.

To del Barco's readers—Jesuit intellectuals of eighteenth-century Europe—it was difficult to imagine a behavior, a diet, a foodstuff as lowly as these. His note must have reinforced their notion that desert hunter-gatherers were always at the brink of starvation. A little religion, and perhaps some irrigated agriculture, mining, or forestry might leave these people with more in life than an existence so bare that they pounced upon whatever sprang up from the earth. Perhaps they could learn to toil for a stable supply of bona-fide vegetables, rather than lazily waiting for unpredictable, uncultivated desert plants to appear. A local, renewable resource such as desert amaranths hardly merited mention, let alone future consideration in Jesuit schemes. The Jesuits of the time were educated sophisticates in an organization rapidly reaching out to all parts of the globe, "with a lack of interest in or a capacity to fathom the viewpoints of the Indians," as ethnohistorian Edward Spicer concluded. They would pray for the day when Baja California colonies would bring in enough lumber and minerals to encourage European gardeners to settle there, replacing wild greens and cactus fruit with good Mediterranean grapes, lettuce, and olives.

Still, wild-amaranth gathering persists to this day in local pockets of Baja California, Sonora, and Arizona, as in other parts of the *tierra caliente*. Those who gather *Amaranthus palmeri* sprouts in the Sonoran Desert region today do not look like wild Indians down on all fours. Indian and non-Indian alike, farmer and urbanite, are among this bunch. To be sure, there are still holdouts. There are those who consider amaranth greens and other *quelites* to be "the meat of the poor people," as one old Sonoran told anthropologist Tom Sheridan. They served well in earlier, leaner times, but only the most impoverished families ask wealthy land-owners for access to harvest them on private land. The trick today for quelite eaters is how to avoid being seen gathering them, thereby admitting that you're so poor that you can't buy greens from the store.

Less than a century and a half after del Barco, another European visitor to arid America took issue with this point of view. Explorer Carl Lumholtz sensed that amaranths were an impressive item and that those who looked down upon their use had missed the boat. Lumholtz felt that the culinary quality of amaranths was fine enough to make their gathering a fitting harvest even for farmers:

> In and near the fields of some of the ranches, where the soil is rich, the quelite, in Spanish *bledo* (*Amaranthus palmeri*), grew in great profusion, sometimes present-ing the appearance of a large, dark, dull-green mass of vegetation. This plant, when young and tender, furnishes an excellent vegetable much relished by the Indians, but as only an insignificant part of the luxuriant growth is utilized, in his fields it becomes the most formidable weed he has to contend with. When freshly gathered and immediately cooked, this vegetable is superior in taste to spinach, resembling more in flavor fresh asparagus. In the neighborhood of Tucson it is appreciated by Indians and Mexicans alike during its short season, though the Anglo-Saxon, in his assumed superior knowledge, has so far ignored it. Quelite, inexpensive and easy to cultivate, should be accepted by civilized households. It grows prodigiously fast and several crops may be raised each year.

Prodigiously fast. I wince when I think of that, for it has been less than a month this season from the first amaranth sprouts I was able to eat, until their present, enormous condition as they come into flower. Already, this quickly, most have grown too tough, too bristly, to swallow. This year, the summer rains came to the Sonoran Desert the day that folklore says they should—June 26. The rains are said to follow the Feast of San Juan, when Sonoran Folk Catholics congregate at dawn to wash themselves in what little water may be left running in irrigation ditches.

They do this to baptize the season known as *las aguas*, an understated way to speak of the time when the monsoons storm in and all hell breaks loose. Because amaranths typically germinate with the first good cloudbuster of that brief rainy season, they are regionally known as *quelites de las aguas*.

I wince, too, because by the time amaranth plants grow beyond edibility, they are also letting loose hundreds of thousands of pollen grains per plant. I wince, wink, blink, blur, itch, and sniffle, for within a month's time, my amaranth friends turn into foes of my eyes and nose.

I'm allergic to them.

Allergic is not strong enough a word. There is something masochistic about this relationship with my favorite vegetable's pollen grains, those microscopic whiffle balls that smart when they hit me. The more I have studied these plants, the more sensitive I have become. Allergists decree that my immune system has gone wrong, for my skin perks up into welts if the wind guides even a few grains to land on my forearm. My voice drops to a baritone, then leaves altogether. My nose flows like a monsoon-season arroyo, and my eyes puff up like those of a spadefoot toad's. By late summer, amaranths have changed me as dramatically as they have changed the desert floor.

Wincing, I think back with nostalgia to those days in late June when it looked as though the arroyo banks had been stained green by the first rains. Wherever floods had deposited their bedloads, churning up alluvium and scarifying the seeds hidden in its midst, a steady sheen of greens quickly covered the earth. In the Sonoran Desert, amaranth seeds are often thrown down into open habitats, where light and heat are highly available, but soil moisture is temporal. There, where other disturbance-adapted plants also germinate in great densities, they can waste no time in using what water their little roots can reach. The seedlings of *Amaranthus palmeri* shoot their large leaves up quickly, shading out others, perhaps depriving them of the resources they need. Scientists suspect that amaranths inhibit the germination of seeds and growth of seedlings of certain other plants, through the allelopathic chemicals their leaves contain. It is as though amaranths jump up above the other plants, taking advantage of as much light, heat and moisture as they can during their brief life cycle.

Early in the season when soil moisture is not yet limited, *Amaranthus palmeri* is actively converting solar energy into plant matter in a rather special way. Amaranths are of the C-4 pathway, a kind of metabolism which allows them to use efficiently any carbon dioxide they let into their stomatal pores. Rather than always having to open their pores to provide more carbon dioxide to their photosynthetic machinery, thereby losing water through these pores at the same time, they pump it into compartments where water loss is least. They then recycle it. C-4 plants can convert twice as much light into plant growth for the same amount of water as conventional plants do. This water conservation, so essential in desert environments, has a cost attached to it. C-4 plants require extra energy to do all this fancy pumping of carbon dioxide into specialized compartments. But as prime performers under high light and heat, amaranths usually have access to the additional energy needed to accomplish this conservation. Physiologist Jim Ehleringer has found that *Amaranthus palmeri*'s photosynthetic effort peaks under high temperatures (107 degrees) and light fluxes too extreme for most plants to comfortably work.

Wild desert amaranths are quintessential sun-lovers. They grow at the hottest time of the year, in the habitats with the least shade, and all the while their leaves follow the sun through its daily movements across the sky. Each leaf pivots on a *pulvinus* or hinge cell, as its turgor changes during the day, tracking the sun so that the leaf surface has maximum exposure to direct sunlight. Ehleringer and his student Ivan Forseth estimate that these solar-tracking leaves are over 150 percent more effective in intercepting the sun's light than are stationary, vertical leaves of other kinds of plants. Solar-trackers are thirty-eight percent better at capturing sunlight than leaves stationed in a permanent horizontal position. By allowing amaranths to take in more sun around dawn and dusk when water loss due to evaporation is not so severe, solar-tracking results in thirty to forty percent more carbon gain for plant growth. Desert amaranths had evolved into amazingly dynamic solar collectors long before the pages of *Sunset* and *Better Homes and Gardens* argued the merits of energy-efficient architectural designs.

Their efficiency in solar interception goes beyond what any single leaf does, for overall plant shape is involved as well. Desert amaranths invest much of their energy in above-ground growth, many of them assuming the shape of an elongated pyramid or cone as time goes by. As sunlight cascades through this conical canopy, whatever rays fail to hit the smaller, upper leaves may ultimately be intercepted by those larger ones in lower strata. This early, rapid trapping of solar energy allows them to escape late-season water stress by completing their life's reproductive cycle before damaging drought sets in.

Such a splendid manner that amaranths have for combining water and energy use efficiency...yet the net effect is that the plants grow so rapidly that they begin to flower and flow with pollen much too early for my own liking. I must hurriedly schedule my personal "Amaranth Appreciation Week" as soon as I see the plants surging up from the earth, or else my palate will not have a chance to respond before my nose goes on strike.

In 1984, on July 16—less than twenty days after amaranth seedlings emerged from the drenched earth—there was a festive feeling in the air. Something was telling me, "Take a Quelite to Lunch."

I carefully harvested all of the sprouts from each of several areas less than a foot square (or nine hundred square centimeters). The number of amaranth sprouts per plot varied from seventy-five to one hundred-sixty. They averaged twenty centimeters in height—roughly a hand's breadth tall—the rule of thumb that Papago friends use to decide when to harvest the greens. Anything much taller than that is also much tougher, so that only individual leaves rather than the young stalks and leaves combined make a suitable harvest.

I discovered that each of my little plots in Avra Valley held over one hundred grams of fresh weight of usable greens. I then pulled out some food composition tables I had to see what each little plot might provide in terms of nutrients, since 100 grams of raw amaranths makes a modest serving of about a cup and a half of raw salad, or half a cup of cooked greens. I compared the nutritional return of my couple of minutes of fresh greens gathering to that of walking down to the neighborhood Circle K to buy a nice, dead head of iceberg lettuce, an effort that takes at least as much time where I live.

The raw *Amaranthus palmeri* greens contain nearly three times as many calories (36), eighteen times the amount of vitamin A (6100 international units), thirteen times the amount of vitamin C (80 milligrams), twenty times the amount of calcium (411 mg.), and almost seven times the amount of iron (3.4 mg.) as one hundred grams of lettuce. Even when compared to other well-endowed wild greens such as lambsquarter (*chual*) and purslane (*verdolaga*), they are exceptionally rich in iron, calcium, and niacin content, and nearly the same as the others in riboflavin and vitamins A and C. From the pioneering wild-foods studies of Ruth Greenhouse, Edith Lantz, and other Southwestern food scientists, it is clear that wild greens are worth their weight in nutrition.

If wild leafy amaranths were no more than a parsleylike garnish which desert dwellers touched only on rare occasions, their chemical profile would be academically interesting, but of no real import. There are millions of plants that look great on paper which people hardly ever use due to harvesting and cleaning difficulties or to inferior taste. However, *Amaranthus palmeri* cannot be so easily dismissed.

In the central Sonoran Desert, the amaranth season was short, but these and other kinds of green plants filled critical gaps in the diet of the historic Papago.

After gathering saguaro cactus near the mountains, on rocky bajadas, the Desert People customarily headed down to floodplain fields to plant with the rains their cactus-wine singing had brought. There, the crops would take another two months before they ripened, and only a few of their cultivated plants such as squash could be used before the fall, while still immature. Stored saguaro seeds, remains of last year's grains, mesquite, and cultivated beans provided protein, oils, and calories, but these foodstuffs are low in vitamins, and by themselves would be monotonous. Before the crops matured, volunteering amaranths, lambsquarters, purslane, and annual saltbush greens were the major products harvested from Papago fields. Some families would fix amaranths frequently when they were around, as salad, or as boiled or fried greens, as a filling with beans in fat little corn tortillas, or in a mixture with meat or eggs. Versatile while available, amaranths were also essential to rounding out the Papago diet before the plantings began to supply other kinds of fresh vegetables for consumption.

Considering that these quelites have been so widely eaten in the Americas for centuries, it is hilarious that some scientists have suggested that these plants are poisonous threats to humankind. There are textbooks which give the impression that amaranths and lambsquarters are so toxic that it is lucky anyone has ever survived after eating these potherbs. Contemporary Sonoran Desert Indians should be amazed that their amaranth-eating ancestors lived long enough to produce progeny! This notion of poison begins with fact—that these plants accumulate nitrates and oxalates, known antinutritional compounds—but somehow this modest fact gets swallowed up by unwarranted fear that gruesome suffering lies in store for any wild-greens consumer. Knowledge of what nitrates and oxalates may do, if ingested in considerable quantities, needs to be put in the context of how much of these chemicals is actually present in desert greens, and how much of these greens was eaten relative to other foods in the diet.

When most kinds of green leafy vegetables are eaten, a portion of the nitrates in them are converted to nitrites in an acidic digestive tract and absorbed by the blood stream, where they are available to combine with hemoglobin. If produced in high enough levels, the resulting compound, metheglobin, can cause headaches, flushing of the skin, vomiting, and dizziness. In particular diets, a certain amount of nitrites can be beneficial, since they may detoxify cyanogenetic glycosides such as those in lima beans. However, in extreme cases where nitrate intake from other food sources has been exceptionally high, the result has been respiratory paralysis, collapse, coma, and eventual death.

These symptoms, to my knowledge, have never been reported in humans eating desert amaranths. Pigs in the Midwest have been poisoned from eating the temperate-adapted careless weed, *Amaranthus retroflexus,* under drought stress. Nitrate poisoning is possible in livestock that eat fresh desert amaranth plants in quantities above two percent of their body weight, but other forage plants are abundant at the time amaranths are available, so this seldom occurs. In contrast, a daily serving of amaranth greens as sizable as my hundred-gram portions provides a dietary intake of nitrates well within what the human body can assimilate. To reach the two-percent body weight level of consumption—equivalent to what is toxic for livestock—an adult would have to eat a hundred of my servings of amaranths, an unlikely achievement.

Surprisingly, the fifteen samples of *Amaranthus palmeri* greens that I have had analyzed from the Sonoran Desert are generally lower in nitrates than most other amaranths and many kinds of commonly used leafy vegetables. This is intriguing, since in Midwestern careless weed, nitrates are supposed to accumulate with increasing drought stress. Although Sonoran Desert droughts impose much more severe water stress on *Amaranthus palmeri* than temperate zone *Amaranthus retro-flexus* ever experiences, these desert plants apparently have a physiological means of keeping nitrates from reaching such high concentrations in their foliage. Even in late season samples taken from nitrogen-rich soils, desert-amaranth nitrate levels were not particularly outstanding. In fact, Jim Ehleringer has found that nitrogen content of desert amaranth leaves decreases with prolonged drought, since late in the season, this nitrogen is being transported out of the foliage and into developing seeds.

Similarly, oxalate levels in desert amaranths are quite low when compared to other leafy vegetables. Since oxalate binds calcium and makes it nutritionally unavailable to humans, high levels of consumption of oxalate-rich plants such as rhubarb and wood sorrel have been of concern to nutritionists. Again, eating desert amaranths should not normally be a cause of concern as far as oxalate levels are involved. Only forty percent of amaranths' oxalates are available for binding up calcium. Vulnerability to oxalates is serious only in diets that are extremely low in calcium to begin with. Papago, Yaqui, and Pima populations in the Sonoran Desert had access to many calcium-rich foods, including beans, cholla buds, prickly pear fruit, and mescal.

It is curious that Papago farmers have come upon their own way of reducing the amount of amaranth consumption by livestock at any one time, thereby making nitrate poisoning of livestock even more remote. I didn't realize this until I went out to a Papago floodwater field on the twenty-first of July one year to count densities and cut amaranth greens in meter-square plots. When I arrived at a friend's field, she and her mother were already out in the amaranths themselves. They were pulling up all the young plants—some nearly a meter tall already, though three-quarters of them were less than thirty centimeters tall—and were bundling them into oval stacks for a wheelbarrow ride back to their adobe shed.

"Sure a lot of *chuhukkia*," I said, looking out over their field, thick with amaranth. My plots averaged 230 grams of fresh greens per square meter. There were well over a million amaranths per hectare volunteering near the mouth of this alluvial fan.

"A whole lot," Elizabeth replied, standing up to stretch her back. "Help yourself. We can't cut it quick enough and it's beginning to cover our squash and corn seedlings."

"What are you going to do with all that *chuhukkia* ꞌ*iiwaki*?" I asked, sensing that if it was too much to cut, it was too much to eat as well. Were they giving the greens to neighboring families to eat?

"Hay."

"What?"

"Hay, I guess they'd call it, though it's not from grass or alfalfa. We put it in the open side of that shed over there to dry down, then we feed it in the winter to the horses. If we fenced them into this field now, they'd just have to eat it now so they'd get sick on it. Besides, they'd trample whatever crops are coming up. But when we dry it in bundles like that, and give them some off and on over the dry season, they do fine."

The cutting went on for hours. The feeding, for months afterwards. That winter, there remained an ample supply of amaranth hay with which to supplement their horses' foraging. And enough plants escaped the sickle blades, enough seeds washed back into the planted area, for another mess of amaranths to fill the field the following year.

It was late August the following year. I was in Big Fields village, off Sells Wash, where Delores Lewis was leading me across the floodplain toward his field. I followed a few feet behind him, as he trudged his way through the rank growth there, and sneezed every time he bumped into an amaranth plant, launching a few million more pollen grains into the air. He trampled down the plants in an especially thick stand at his field edge—leafhoppers, robber flies, cucumber beetles, and mesquite bugs bounded out of the foliage. Some, I later learned, were insects beneficial to crops, but others consume certain cultivated plants as surely as they would eat amaranths. For the moment, I only wondered how many invisible pollen grains flew up out of the greenery for every bug I noticed doing the same.

I knew that Delores regularly ate amaranths and other field greens, or, as the Papago call them, *'oidag 'iiwaki*. Yet I also realized that he had spent years working for Anglo- and Mexican-American farmers in the irrigated fields near Continental, Arizona, cultivating or cutting these plants out of cash crops where they were considered worthless weeds. What did he think about those who simply rogued out amaranths, to bury or burn without any use of them whatsoever?

"Those farmers don't like the *'iiwaki* in their cottonfields."

"But I've seen them in your fields. I've seen some left growing in other fields of the Tohono O'odham. Do those Papago think those plants are okay there?"

"Well, the O'odham, they just leave in the field whatever they need, especially that *chuhukkia 'iiwaki* (amaranths) and *'opon 'iiwaki* (winter spinach), because they get them to eat. They leave those plants there in their fields, except when there's too much chuhukkia covering up their plantings. Grass and chuhukkia bring lots of worms…worms and crickets come from there. *So:'o*, the grasshopper, comes from weeds…they will spoil the plantings and eat the leaves. If the farmers don't cut them, the chuhukkia will cover up the crop, so they cut them and throw the rest into a hole or feed it to the cows or mules."

Delores could see amaranths two different ways, simultaneously, as if they were like the double image of a flicker toy. They were a traditional food, savored or left to remain in their place in certain modest numbers. When they became too dense, too rank, their value changed. The plant itself was neither bad nor good. It was how you looked at it, what context it had, how many you had to deal with, how large they had become. Amaranth greens could become too much of a good thing, and Papago farmers know what that can mean. Work.

"One man's weed is another man's vegetable," a Papago might say. And he might be both men at the same time.

Amaranth pollen grains, like the weedy plants themselves, mean various things to various people. More properly, I should say *cheno-am* pollen, for weedy amaranth's male grains are virtually indistinguishable from those of cultivated amaranths, wild lambsquarters, wild saltbushes, and a number of other plants in the Amaranthaceae and Chenopodiaceae. When archaeologists look at the pollen record of a particular site, they are often intrigued by dramatic increases in the frequency of cheno-am pollen types at specific points in time. When one of these "blips" comes near the end of the occupation of a prehistoric village, they sense that this cheno-am increase must indicate a rather substantial change in the local or regional environment, and in a culture's subsistence. Yet few archaeological palynologists have interpreted these blips in the same way.

In the absence of seeds, it is impossible to tell whether the cheno-am pollen is derived from wild plants, or from domesticated grain and dye amaranths which diffused into the American Southwest from Mesoamerica around the time of Christ. Yet some archaeologists have guessed that a cheno-am increase means the addition of amaranth cultivation to a particular environment. Others argue that a cheno-am abundance means that people had to rely more heavily on wild resources (including bledos, lambsquarters, and saltbush) because the most important crops (beans, corns, and squashes) failed.

Yet how might cheno-am pollen abundance relate to the factors causing crop failure? If failure was due to drought, a few of these species, such as saltbushes, narrow-leaved *Amaranthus fimbriatus,* and some *Amaranthus palmeri* might survive when other food sources did not, and therefore contribute more to the diet. If failure was due to floods or fires, weedy amaranths might subsequently thrive, since they are responsive to the nutrients released by these events. Following a flood or fire, farmers might not weed their fields as carefully as in years of good crops, thereby allowing more of these volunteer plants to flower and fruit. If social factors caused the demise of agriculture, some of these weedy plants would make up much of the vegetative cover on abandoned fields for the first few years.

Beginning with one of these assumptions on how amaranths or their relatives respond to a particular factor, archaeologists have used prehistoric cheno-am pollen to tell various stories of the rise and fall of Southwestern civilizations. Yet do amaranths and chenopods cumulatively respond more strongly to one of these factors than to others? Do they really respond to natural phenomena and human activities in all the ways that archaeologists have hypothesized? Does *Amaranthus palmeri* contribute more pollen in one particular environment—uncultivated floodplains, recently plowed farmlands, or abandoned fields—than do other cheno-am types? Or is it some sort of changeling, seeming to alter its ecological niche to fit the dream of whomever it meets on the street?

I wondered if I could sketch *Amaranthus palmeri's* ecological amplitude as it exists today around Native American villages and desert fields. Maybe, I thought, the desert amaranth has a more specific niche than what the archaeologists have outlined in their doodlings. Possibly it occurs only in certain habitats, particular kinds of fields, or even in specific plant associations within fields. Perhaps I could catch a glimpse of the underlying nature of this changeling, if I could keep my eyes open long enough between sneezes.

That's when the real trouble began. As soon as I set out to pin amaranths down, they came up everywhere I looked. I found them around spring-fed oases, along concrete irrigation ditches running from perennial rivers, in faucet-watered kitchen gardens, and in floodwater fields in the remote Pinacate lava flows. They made up less than five percent of the plant cover in some Papago fields, and over sixty percent in others nearby. Although they are commonly considered field weeds responsive to plowing, they appear just as abundantly in unplowed areas adjacent to Papago fields. In my survey of seventeen Papago fields and adjacent uncultivated floodplain environments, desert amaranths were documented in six floodwater-churned "natural" environments, but only in five fields. Apparently the seeds don't care whether floods, digging sticks, draft horses, or John Deeres do the plowing.

I realized that desert amaranths aren't just agrestals, or weeds primarily restricted to areas of agricultural disturbance. Nor are they simply ruderals, or plants responsive to roadside disturbances, though roadsides are an easy place for folks to gather their greens. They also crop up on little footpaths made by Papago schoolchildren running from buildings to baseball fields. They rim the highwater mark on *charco* reservoirs where livestock drinks storm runoff.

I walked around Pima and Papago villages, noting other places where amaranths occur. There they were, in dump heaps where uprooted garden weeds, last night's tamale corn husks, and last year's Coors bottles all found an ultimate home. There they were, rimming the melted adobes that crumbled down around an abandoned home.

And they don't even restrict themselves to the ground. There they were, growing on top of a dirt-covered roof of saguaro ribs, ocotillo branches, and mesquite vigas, holding together a sandwich-style shed where an old man kept his farming tools.

I felt my vision blur. My nose ran. I was seeing amaranths before my eyes, everywhere I looked. It was time to escape their spell.

After a month of allergies in early fall, I was given an excuse to leave the desert, and, I hoped, "to dry out" away from the influence of summer, rainfed amaranths. I headed to Los Angeles, where I hoped that the lack of summer storms would mean a pollen-free break while I attended the U.S./Mexico Borderlands Environment conference. I was to give a brief lecture on wild relatives of food crops that grew in the borderlands, but amaranths would only fill a couple of sentences of that presentation. With luck, they would be off my mind and out of my sinuses for most of my visit.

Then, as I was being rocketed along the L.A. Freeway by a maniacal taxicab driver, I noticed something out of the corner of my eye. There, on the highwayside, some people, bent at the waists, gathering something green. I turned around to see if I could be sure what it was they were picking, but it was too late—the freeway divided, we went up into the air on a concrete curve and came down, going another direction.

My mind flashed back to an odd little article written in 1969 by Dick Marsh of California State College at Long Beach. There, in the midst of the urban cesspool of greater Los Angeles, Marsh had met a Papago family that continued to use wild amaranths, although displaced five hundred kilometers from their homeland. Marsh scribbled down a recipe from a Papago woman, who boiled the lead-laden L.A. greens in saltwater, drained them, then fried them in vegetable oil with tomatoes and onions for another ten minutes. He took a sample of the plants that the woman said her brother brought home from the Long Beach nursery where he worked. It was weedy *Amaranthus blitoides,* a species which doesn't even reach into traditional Papago country. But it was amaranth enough to be recognized by a Papago, and green enough to eat. No matter that it was California. No matter that it wasn't the same species of amaranth their grandmother had picked in the Sonoran Desert. There was the simple connection: "This looks familiar. It has a taste we know. Because of that, we are nourished."

"The Milky Way is said to be the white bean. He lives clear across the sky. Beans grow in abundance and we see them scattered across the sky."

Tepary Beans and Human Beings
at Agriculture's Arid Limits

W E were flying over that crazy sprawl of Pinacate lava which darkens two thousand square kilometers of the Gran Desierto in northwestern Sonora. Beyond the black lava lay a sea of cream-colored sand, and beyond that, the flashing waves of the Sea of Cortez. What a wild panorama, I thought. But at the same moment, I gained perspective on what we were doing. I couldn't help laughing at my own impracticality: spending a hundred dollars an hour to buzz over this barren area in pursuit of a strange tangent in the agricultural history of beans. The flight was arranged under the pretense of learning where Native American agriculture historically reached its most arid limits. How far had Indian farmers pushed their hardy beans and grains within the grasp of dangerous drought and hopeless heat?

Looking out about this land of lava and sand, I thought that searching for an answer here seemed absurd. It's tough enough for tenacious wild organisms to endure the extremes here, let alone domesticated plants weakened by centuries of man's dickering with them. We scanned the sparsely covered scene again. Impressive vista, I conceded; bad research plan.

Suddenly the plane dipped and turned. Julian Hayden, the archaeologist sitting in the next seat and guiding the pilot, nudged me out of my high-elevation daydream. Tan and sinewy as an old Sonoran *corriente* bull, Julian leaned toward the window and muttered, "Now there's the place you've been wanting to see...Suvuk!"

Described in 1912 by Carl Lumholtz as the "single agricultural site that may be attributed to the Sand People," Suvuk sits between the lips of two lava flows below the southeastern slopes of Pinacate and Carnegie Peaks. Lumholtz noted that a few years before his own visit, Papagos had planted tepary beans, maize, and squash there, using digging sticks.

Recently, various scientists scoffed at the idea of Sand Papago agriculture in an area as arid as the Pinacate. One desert ecologist dismissed the notion by arguing that "agriculture was impossible in their environment." An anthropologist summarizing presumed Sand Papago subsistence patterns asserted that "farming in their territory was possible only at its fringes, near rivers and springs." I looked down on the Suvuk valley—no springs or rivers for miles—hoping for hints that would set the record straight.

The answer was there, written as a pattern of recent plowmarks.

"Why, son-of-a-gun," Julian mumbled through his white moustache, "it looks as though the Romero boys have tried their hands at farming again! They haven't done that in years."

Julian squinted into the sun, then let loose of a few of his forty-some years of observations on Pinacate life. "They're probably farming the same spot that Lumholtz spoke of, just like their father did when he left Trincheras to come here in '46. His family had done *temporal* farming over there, so he knew how before he had even set eyes on the overgrown field here. Suvuk, the place name, should truly be reserved for those hills over there, close to where the Romeros had their house for a while." He pointed eastward, to a granite ridge half a kilometer away. Suvuk, pronounced *s-wegi* by most Papagos today, means "reddish."

Below the hill and not far from this century's house and litter, three ancient sleeping circles were outlined on a brindled lava bench.

"There've been people camping here for a good long time, but no evidence of *prehistoric* agriculture here that I know of. That's not to say that *Areneños* on this side of the Pinacate didn't plant here historically. Areneño Papagos, Sand People, that is. Old man Romero thought that someone had farmed here before him, even though it was all grown up in mesquite when he arrived. He and some friends found a big clay olla full of crop seeds, including those of Spanish melons, in a cache that they pulled off a shelf in that lava flow not too long ago."

The plane circled, and so did history for me. Here it was, a Mexican family renovating an historic Papago field in an area nearly as hot and as dry as Death Valley, years after Papagos had left the place. An ancient farming tradition had not completely died—it had simply changed hands.

"You should go talk with those Romero boys," Julian suggested. "They live down at the Cholla Bay beach over by Rocky Point. If you see La Viuda de Romero, tell her hello for me. Give that lovely widow my warmest regards."

If I had felt awkward searching for agricultural history in a plane hovering above the Pinacates, I felt downright out of place pursuing it in Rocky Point. Or properly, Puerto Peñasco, a Mexican beach town which gringos think they own. In effect, they do. I had always avoided the Point, not wanting to catch tanner's skin cancer or a worse disease—tourism. If I had my druthers, I'd always see Mexico while working like a reverse wetback rather than lounging around with the Beautiful People. Now, as a last resort, "work" had brought me to this ungodly beach town, around which no agriculture exists for miles, to seek out some semi-retired desert farmers.

The irony was too much to endure at eleven in the morning on a burning June day. I popped open a Tecate can, slugged down some beer, and tried not to ask myself, "why here?"

Heading into Cholla Bay, we noticed some locals who had also begun to nurse themselves with beers that Saturday. We drove up to where they stood around a grease pit, a tin ramada hanging above them.

When I remembered my mission, I looked at these four amigos in cutoffs, stained teeshirts, and thongs. They were bitching about the *pinche* clutch of the car parked over the grease pit. Could one of these guys be a farmer incognito?

Not a single one of them looked like Mr. Green Jeans.

As they stared back at us, I could hardly bring myself to ask the preposterous question:

"Excuse me, do any of you cultivate a small field stuck between two lava flows way the hell in the middle of nowhere?"

Eric, my Sonoran sidekick from Caborca, saw that I was tongue-tied, and intervened. He asked if they knew who Ricardo Romero was. Two of them gestured to the one standing in front of the ailing vehicle. He held up his monkeywrench.

"We're friends of Don Julian Hayden, and wish to give his greetings to the widow."

"Ah, sí, Don Julian, el viejo," Ricardo murmured, remembering visits from a wiry American whose old four-by-four was the first he had ever seen in the Pinacate. Ricardo set down his monkeywrench, gesturing for us to follow.

We crossed the sand and entered a small house where the widow lived. There, I gave the Romeros aerial photos of their field, which stimulated all their memories and expectations of Suvuk. Yes, they hadn't cropped there for six years for lack of rains, but they had begun to prepare the field again in case a storm came their way.

"Who knows?" Ricardo shrugged. "Perhaps we will get a good rain this summer. All it takes is one good flood to give us enough water to mature our beans."

"Beans on one rain?" I asked in disbelief.

"Just one rain strong enough to make the wash flow across the field. We have a well there that is usually dry, but even when it has some water, it's for us, not the crops. No, we rely on the runoff from the mountainside that drains into our field."

The widow had tears in her eyes from all this talk about the old homestead. "When it did rain, we could grow crops so easily. People would travel out of their way just to come and buy our produce. And we would invite them back on the holy days, for San Isidro's feast and Santa Cruz, to help us bless the plants or petition for rain. Those were beautiful times. When we finally moved into town, it broke my husband's spirit. He missed the tranquility we had, so much that he died within a year of leaving there."

"Is it okay for us to visit there, to study it this summer?" I asked.

"Sure," Ricardo replied. "Nothing is planted. But who knows how the summer goes. It may bring rain, and the rain, beans."

Two hours later, Eric and I arrived at Suvuk, each of us heavier for all the desert talc we were wearing. The Pinacate lava flows were bone-dry, and the surrounding silt flats were pure powder. The heat was overwhelming. We made haste.

First, on a hill above the field, we set out a cross of white butcher paper twenty meters long to serve as a scale for future aerial photos. Not exactly a cross suitable for the Fiesta de Santa Cruz, but it would serve our purposes. Then we set up a rain gauge and a maximum-minimum thermometer in the middle of the field. Finally, I half-heartedly planted some white tepary beans in the powdery dirt at the edge of the Romero's most recent plowmarks, in case it happened to rain soon. If the Romeros hadn't planted the site for six years, why would they consider trying this summer? If by chance it did rain, at least I could come back and watch those Papago teparies grow.

If by chance. I knew that the odds were bad. I knew that nearby, in the Gran Desierto, one place had gone a full thirty-four months without any measurable precipitation. I had calculated that the coefficient of variation in rainfall—a measurement of unpredictability critical to understanding how arid a place really is—

was greater here than in the Negev Desert of Israel, considered by some the most arid area where rainfed agriculture had been practiced. I would probably return to find little more than dry, roasted beans sitting unsprouted in the soil.

When I returned, it was by air again, the first day of August. I had decided to rephotograph the field vicinity, using the paper cross for scale, to help estimate the amount of arable land near Suvuk. As we approached the Pinacate around eight in the morning, it looked weird from the plane. It was gleaming.

Nearby, the Sonoyta River was running toward the coast. Along drainages on the east slope of Carnegie Peak, we could see stretches that sparkled, reflecting the early morning sun. It had rained enough for the Pinacate to shed some runoff!

Reaching the Romero field, we were in for a greater surprise. Below us, as we circled the water-stained valley, we could see new lines being made as the moistened earth was turned over. The Romeros had driven up from Puerto Peñasco. They had attached a plow to the bumper of their pickup. One of them was driving across the field, pulling the plow, while another walked along, guiding it and tossing seeds into the opened furrow.

Sonorans have come a long way since the digging stick.

We took our photos, waved, and hollered "Buena suerte!" out the windows as we left.

When I returned on land the next time around, the Romero's seedlings had emerged. My seeds had been washed away. Roughly five centimeters of rain had fallen, all in one storm. We later learned that the washes had flowed for several hours, flooding the entire valley a half meter deep. The air temperature had peaked at one hundred-and-eighteen degrees sometime within the previous weeks.

I was joined this time by Charlie Hutchinson, an arid lands geographer, and Chuck Bowden, an incurable masochist for desert heat. They helped me pack into Mexico some sophisticated scientific equipment for measuring plant-water stress, equipment that we were afraid we'd have trouble explaining to border officials. So we placed flippers and a diving mask atop one instrument's compressed air tanks and gauges, to make it look like scuba gear we were taking for a wild weekend at Rocky Point.

Instead, we dove into a full day of measuring the sizes of bean plants, the water potential of their leaves, and taking soil samples for estimating moisture content. We quickly realized that none of the plants were yet water-stressed, despite a month without rain. Digging into the soil a little, it became obvious that its moisture-holding capacity was great.

The Sand Papagos, then the Romeros, had chosen a place remarkably suited to farming. Less than ten hectares in the surrounding 100,000 were as well-endowed. I later learned from oral histories that the Sand Papagos in the vicinity of the Pinacates had at least four such field areas beyond where scientists had believed rainfed farming could reasonably exist. By drawing upon runoff from large watersheds, situating their fields on soil that absorbed rain like a sponge, and cultivating heat-hardy, deep-rooted crops, indigenous farmers could produce plenty of food per area of planting.

Heat-hardy crops. When they realized it had rained in the Pinacates, the Romeros had grabbed all the seeds they had in the house and had raced to take advantage of this rare event. As a result of their haste, they sowed both unadapted crops like zucchini squash and pintos, and desert-adapted ones like cushaw squash and a few tepary beans. This latter group of crop ecotypes can be considered Sonoran Desert "land races." They have not been improved by the breeding techniques of modern science, but instead have been grown in a particular land so long that they are generally well-adapted to the conditions there. Would these plants' different tolerances to stress make a difference in the long run?

At first we didn't notice the tepary bean seedlings scattered in amid the pintos. Then noon rolled around, and the pintos tried to close up shop. They tilted their leaflets parallel to the sun's rays, for they had already received too much heat load for their own good. It was then that we spotted a few bean plants that had kept their leaflets open, tracking the sun, continuing to work through the noon hour. They had thinner, narrower leaflets, and vines that were already fifty percent longer than those of pintos.

They were the tepary beans.

Their name, derived from the Opata Indian word *tepar,* has long been used in Sonora and Arizona for the little white, brown, rust, and beige seeds of cultivated *Phaseolus acutifolius.* As far as legumes go, tepary means "desert-adapted." Virtually no other cultivated beans can bear the intense heat of the Sonoran Desert and produce viable pollen and pods full of seeds in temperatures above one hundred-five degrees. Their roots are known to reach twice as far down as those of common beans in the same amount of time, allowing them to tap deep reservoirs of soil moisture when upper layers have already dried. Whereas common beans continue to produce more seed with more water given to them, tepary-seed yields peak out with a modest amount of soil moisture and decrease with overirrigation. They need a certain degree of stress to trigger all-out seed production, or else they will simply continue to put on more foliage.

Although we now use an Opata Indian word to describe this bean, it is with Papago Indians, or Desert People, that teparies are most closely linked. Both old Papago and two-century-old historic documents suggest that the term Papago is a condensation of *Papavi Kuadam,* or "Tepary Eaters," a name they gained from growing and eating so much of this desert bean. Their own folklore contains this tidbit:

> ...so that is why the white tepary bean is the child of the Desert People. It was born here and endures dryness. When it doesn't rain enough, the white bean still comes up. The Desert People will always eat it and live here.
> The Milky Way is said to be the white bean. He lives clear across the sky. Beans grow in abundance and we see them scattered across the sky.

Chuck, Charlie, and I spent a night under that crystal-clear Milky Way, then a full day taking notes on the field's plants, animals, and soil characteristics. There were many variables to consider when assessing whether a crop could be produced this year in such an extreme setting. Yet for me the whole story of Suvuk was boiling down to a bunch of beans.

In late September, we began to see that Suvuk was home to many members of the bean family, but all of these legumes were not equally comfortable there. I came with Tony Burgess, the essence of a field botanist, who quickly noticed two wild legumes that must have germinated in the field just after the Romeros had planted. One of them was *Psoralea rhombifolia,* kin to the prairie turnip, a major food resource of the Plains Indians. The Romero field became the first known locality of this plant in the Sonoran Desert. The other legume which Tony and I found was *Phaseolus filiformis,* a wild desert bean. It is quite closely related to teparies and pintos, though not able to outcross and produce fertile hybrid seeds with them under natural conditions.

With the appearance of this wild desert bean, we began to make a three-way comparison to contrast its adaptations with those of pintos and teparies. Our other companion, a tepary bean physiology expert named Rich Pratt, kept us hopping around the clock, following the course of these beans' leaf temperatures and transpiration rates for intervals over twenty-four hours. At that date, the plants had gone two months with less than two centimeters of rainfall.

As the measurements in our notebooks began to fill page after page, certain patterns became clearer. The teparies behaved much the same way as the wild desert beans, with leaflet temperatures and transpiration rates remaining rather high during midday hours when pintos were partially shutting down. We guessed the tepary and wild bean plants were keeping their stomatal pores open wider, allowing more rapid production as a tradeoff for water loss. By this time, their roots were probably much deeper, so that they were tapping into a greater amount of soil moisture to accommodate these losses. They were way ahead of pintos in their flowering and fruiting. All this meant that they had used water rather liberally, particularly early in the season when it was in abundance.

Phaseolus filiformis, a wild desert bean

Native desert plants wolfing down more water than non-adapted, introduced ones? It sounded whacky at first, since we tend to think of desert dwellers as those which conserve the most water by using as little per day as possible. Instead, tepary and wild mitten-leaved beans save water in the long run by using it for a shorter period of time overall.

How does this work? Through rapid growth and early fruiting, they are able to complete their reproductive cycle weeks before other plants are able to mature. Under irrigation, teparies can be done producing a crop in two months' time, whereas other cultivated plants may need as many as two more irrigations over an additional five to seven weeks to complete their seed yield. Knowing when to time planting, irrigating, and harvesting, Pima Indian farmer Albert Cooley continues to produce teparies on only two irrigations, less than half that used by nearby Anglo farmers.

Domesticated teparies stay true to the way of life pioneered by their wild desert relatives: get up fast as soon as the summer rains come, reproduce while the moisture is handy, and die before a late season drought comes and kills you. Like most desert wildflowers, they are ephemerals. Each is only on the face of this earth for a brief moment, though their legacy has lasted for hundreds of centuries.

By late October, the value of being ephemeral was manifest. No rain had fallen in the last month, and only sixty-eight millimeters over the entire rainy season, if you could call it that. The scorching winds of far western Sonora had pulled much of the moisture from earlier runoff out of the root zone. With soil moisture depleted, nearly all of the plants were rapidly approaching permanent wilt. All this stress didn't much matter to the tepary and wild bean plants at this point, for they had already matured hundreds of their seeds. Unlike the pintos, their reproduction was essentially over.

It was almost like the story of the three little pigs. In this case, however, only the pinto had not worked hard enough to insure safety from the blowing winds of the big bad wolf. Only three percent of the pinto pods were mature, and the still-green seeds inside had begun to shrivel. They had not made it through the work of producing fruit when the water was there. For them, the drought came too quickly. Soil-moisture depletion was too profound.

Because the Romeros had hastily and randomly grabbed seeds when they had gone out to plant, parts of their field turned out to be disaster areas, while others were richly green. While pintos and zucchinis were on the verge of total crop failure, the Sonoran land-race squashes and teparies returned an abundance of seed. Had the Romeros planted a hectare's worth of teparies instead of the unadapted lot of seeds that they did, they would have ended up with a three-ton crop of dry beans on that hectare. The few teparies that were planted were burgeoning with seed. They carried four times as many pods and a hundred times the dried seed per plant as the pintos.

At first glance, the Romero field appeared so dominated by failing pintos that most of it hardly seemed worth harvesting. However, we noticed one of the younger Romeros out in the bean patch gathering something we couldn't see from the field edge. When we approached him, I could see that he was stooped over a wiry wild plant, salvaging its seed.

"Do you know what this is?" he asked, holding out a handful of tiny beans, dark and angular like the lava backdrop behind him. "We call it *frijolillo.* Its taste is almost like lentils. We sometimes eat the *ejotes* too. Those green pods are small, but fine in flavor, and there's always plenty to pick."

He had shelled a few dozen seed of *Phaseolus filiformis.* Not only were Romeros recycling an indigenous farming tradition, they were also the last Sonoran Desert dwellers known to harvest wild beans. And that tradition, many times older, was even less understood.

I had clumsily questioned many Sonorans, many Indians, regarding the harvest of wild beans, hoping to hear the kind of comments which the young Romero had just volunteered. Most everyone I had probed about wild beans responded in one of four ways.

A blank stare.

An unqualified "No."

A "¿Quien sabe?"

Or with another question: "Why would anyone ever have wanted to do that?"

I had just about resigned myself to the fact that wild bean harvesting in the Sonoran Desert had slipped out of sight.

Still, we have clues to the former importance of this subsistence activity. In a cave not far from Globe, Arizona, archaeologist Neil Ackerly has found bean debris associated with cultural remains from pre-pottery times. The spent pods are those of the same wild bean as that in the Romero field, *Phaseolus filiformis,* and each is tightly twisted around itself since the seeds have been shed.

At Fortified Hill Site near Gila Bend, students of the late, great prehistoric Hohokam encountered the pea-size seeds of *Phaseolus metcalfei*. These were likely traded in from mountain habitats more than one hundred kilometers away, since this wild species is not known to reach as low as the lower Gila River valley.

More recent research by Vorsila Bohrer has demonstrated that the prehistoric Hohokam consumed a number of wild herbaceous legumes in addition to the many leguminous tree species they utilized. The historic record suggests that the herbaceous bean eaten most in the Sonoran Desert was the wild progenitor/ relative of domesticated teparies. It is a delicate vine that twines high in mesquite canopies, crawls over cliffs, sprawls into fencerows, and slips into field plantings. With a few hunter-gatherer friends, I was able to round up over half a kilogram of wild teparies in the Santa Rita Mountains in a couple of hours. At the densities and productivity of these desert legumes, a hectare's harvest could meet the average American's bean-consumption needs for three-fifths of the year. The little that we later cooked up had a nutty but delicate texture, with a dozen or so midget frijoles perched on every spoonful.

I thought the taste was delicious, but my opinion is so biased that it isn't worth…well, never mind.

The first time I met ethnobotanist Richard Felger was when he had just returned from the fourth aborted *haap* bean expedition. He was tired, but at the same time excited, frantically trying to type up notes from a week's trip in Seri Indian country.

"The Seri once used this bean, and we don't know what it is scientifically. They know what it is. It's an *haap*. It grows with the summer rains around Sierra Kunkaak on Tiburón Island. This was my fourth time crossing out to Tiburón to find it, walking for miles and miles without luck. One year, we arrived at the wrong place, and ran out of time. The second time, we got to *haap caaizi quih yaii*, the *haap* user's place, but there were no *haap* seedlings that year. The fall that followed, we showed up too late. And this year," he moaned, "there had been a drought and no summer ephemerals were to be seen at all."

By the following year, I was working on Richard's ethnobotany projects when he left to journey out to Tiburón once more. This time, he was accompanied by Rosa Flores, who had not visited the *haap* user's camp for thirty-four years. She led Richard Felger and his friends Ike Russell and Cathy Moser up a barren slope of black volcanic scree. There, below a mulch of boulders, two tepary plants remained rooted, maturing seed, far beyond their known distribution. The *haap* and the wild broad-leaved tepary, *Phaseolus acutifolius,* were one and the same.

Rosa told how Seri women would gather pods early in the morning, before they would dry to the point of popping and projecting their seeds meters into the air. The women would gather the pods in their skirts to carry them back to camp. To shell the unpopped pods, the Seri would roll them between their hands over deerskins or blankets.

Old Sara Villalobos told Becky Moser how they were cooked, either alone or with deer meat: "They are boiled just like regular [pinto] beans. You do not grind them at all. They cook right away—regular beans take a long time to cook because their skin is thick. You don't use a lot of water. You don't salt them because their water is sweet."

The Seri at times shared their wild tepary resources with other Indians. Around 1900, when the Yaquis had to flee southern Sonora to escape extermination or slavery in the henequen plantations of Yucatán, some took refuge within Seri territory, on Tiburón Island. There, hiding in the interior of the island, they survived on a number of wild foods, including *tepari del monte.*

Other Yaquis fled to Arizona to live with the Papago west of the Baboquivari Mountains, where wild teparies grew along the same washes that had domesticated teparies planted on alluvial fans. Yet by the time the Yaquis arrived, the gathering of certain wild foods had already begun to take a tailspin among these floodwater farmers. Only the oldest Papago alive today have any notion that wild teparies were named, let alone used by their people.

Laura Kermen is one who let such little facts settle deep down in her memory, to well up more than seventy years later. Perhaps she recalls relatives' using wild beans early this century because she soon thereafter worked for Dr. Robert Forbes, the first scientist to organize a team to collect and evaluate tepary beans as a desert genetic resource. In any case, she remembers the time when her people still had to depend now and then on this wild bean called *chepurina bawi.*

A woman and her children had decided to walk all the way to Hickiwan, on the other side of the Santa Rosa Wash, to visit relatives there. En route, near a *wo'o,* or floodwater-filled pond, she noticed some wild teparies growing in the shrub understory. *Chepurina bawi.* They gathered them, and being otherwise low on food at the time, the little beans helped to tide them over.

George Freeman, the leader of Forbes' tepary team, visited the Santa Rosa Wash a few years later, stalking the wild tepary. With the help of a few Papago hands, he gathered up six kilograms of *chepurina bawi* in November 1914, which when broadcast at Yuma produced 400 kilos of dry hay the quality of alfalfa. There, in the wash, though, he was even more stunned by the lushness of this desert annual, for it was "...found in abundance growing in thickets and climbing in great profusion upon the surrounding brush. Many of the vines ascended to a height of 10 to 12 feet and bore a bountiful crop of pods as high as 6 to 8 feet from the ground."

Amidst that bounty, the last recorded Papago harvest of wild teparies took place.

As an *ingeniero frijolero,* a college-trained beaner, I may have been born fifty years too late. By World War I, the harvesting of wild beans had waned. Among those who call themselves O'odham, from the River Pima near Phoenix to the Nevome of central Sonora, the ancient name of this bean was slowly forgotten. When seen, it would be provisionally described as *tepari del monte* or wildland tepary, as Coyote's tepary, or simply, black tepary. To others, it became just another vine stuck out of sight, out of mind, in the desert scrub.

By the 1930s, the sowing and consumption of domesticated teparies also began to wane among the Papago. Irrigated crop production based on big dams and groundwater pumping pulled them off reservation to work for wages. When Clem Maristo, a Papago from Big Fields village, left there in 1931 to work in California, "the fields stretched for miles, from the Cowlic road to over by the Church, and again farther south on the other fork of the wash." Other young men left their families' fields behind at the same time, and when they returned a few years later, the place could have reasonably changed its name to Little Fields.

"I couldn't believe what a change it was," Clem recalled of his first visit three years later. "So much land was out of cultivation," and with the abandonment of farming, certain crop seeds became scarce. He said that many of the people had gone to work near Eloy, Sahuarita, or Coolidge, and would be away from their fields from August to January. The summer crop work had been disrupted. During this time, the forty-six color variants of teparies that Forbes and Freeman had found in southern Arizona earlier in the century dwindled down to six. Today, only two are regularly found among the Papago and Pima.

In the decades following World War II, government "welfare" programs began to provide low-income Papago families with staples such as pinto beans that were readily available in the national food market. These replaced teparies as the legume most frequently eaten by the Papago. Worse, it served as a disincentive for planting any beans at all. One Papago woman spoke candidly of this cause-effect sequence: "When the commodities program first reached here, most families could get all the pinto beans they needed that way....Pretty soon, the only kind of bean most of our people ate was pintos, and hardly anyone grew the old kinds anymore...."

Does it actually make a difference whether the Papago or anyone else eats wild beans, teparies, pintos or for that matter, no beans at all? Nutritionally speaking, is it fair to say that a bean is a bean is a bean?

My gut reactions are that yes, it does matter, no, all beans are not equal in chemical composition nor in health benefits. Although there are indications that the pintos which have replaced native beans in Southwestern Indian diets are slightly lower in protein quantity and quality, and in mineral content, these differences are probably negligible when integrated into a well-balanced diet. Yet we know that as Southwestern Indians in this century have become more acculturated, their diet has worsened and they have become more vulnerable to nutrition-related diseases. That teparies do have higher iron, calcium, and protein content and fewer antinutritional factors than your "average" grain legume may make a difference in the diet of a pregnant or lactating Papago woman, who may be at risk for these nutrients. The diversity of legumes which Native Americans once ate in the Southwestern deserts insured that a range of sources of minerals, B vitamins, and essential amino acids were available, each one with peculiar deficiencies being balanced out by the others. As their diet shifted to fewer leguminous sources, then to fewer beans altogether as fast foods replaced home-cooked meals, the magnesium and iron intake of the Pima measurably decreased.

In the long run, the fiber contribution of beans may be considered even more important to Native American diets than their nutrient composition. Most beans provide between six and eight grams of fiber per serving, more than almost any other food except bran flakes. Wild beans and teparies are on the high end of the fiber chart, although we still don't know how much of this is functional dietary fiber. Whatever the actual portion of viscous dietary fiber that can be gained from eating a bowlful of beans, we know that it is crucial in reducing the health problems that Papago and Pima adults accrue from diabetes.

These tribes have among the highest incidences of diabetes recorded among any population in the United States, roughly fifteen times the national average. One in eight people on the Papago reservation today knows that he or she is diabetic. This percentage has increased over the last few decades, as have the side-effects: arteriosclerosis, gangrene, acquired blindness, and kidney failure. While the causes and effects of their vulnerability to adult-onset diabetes are complex, high consumption of legumes in the diet is known to protect them from dangerously rapid rises in blood glucose levels after meals. Both cultivated beans and mesquite seeds have been suggested as the bases of special diets to reduce blood sugar and cholesterol levels in obese diabetics.

Further, native desert foods such as beans, mesquite-seed gum, prickly-pear pads, and plantago seed have all been proven effective enough in controlling blood sucrose levels to reduce or eliminate the need for insulin shots for diabetics. Ironically, these very foods are those which have fallen out of the desert people's diets at the same time that diabetes has become more prevalent among them. It is sad but true that the people once nicknamed the Bean Eaters may now be suffering for the lack of beans in their diet.

The winter following my visits to the Romero field, I had a chance to climb to the upper edge of the watershed that feeds the Suvuk valley. With my infant son Dustin in a pack on my back, I climbed with a group of desert campers to the top of Sierra Pinacate and gained views of the entire area from which the valley collects runoff. Along the way, we came upon a saguaro cactus clothed in a mat of climbing vines, as if dressed for the cool of winter. I did a double take: it was the little wild bean, come up again with the winter rains! Kneeling down at the base of the saguaro, I could see how its vines had withered and senesced as the late fall drought set in. Then an early winter rain in the absence of frost allowed them to persist, sprouting again near the base. The new flush of vines zigzagged up the saguaro and quickly zipped into flowering.

A little miracle for a desert ephemeral, I thought. To be alive three months, almost die, then come back again for four more. It's not exactly a resurrection, but close to it. For those of us who are mortal, it's not a bad thing to have happen. It seems these plants have been blessed. Every time a drought comes now, I remember those plants, and I pray. Pray for the return of the bean.

He presented himself at the table…reached down, and his testes turned into chile pods.
He began to sprinkle their spice into all the foods.

For the Birds:
The Red-Hot Mother of Chiles

CHILE, they believed, "is the greatest protection against the evils of sorcery." A Tarahumara Indian confided in Wendell Bennett that "this plant, used ceremonially and privately, is thought to drive away the approaching sickness. The man who does not eat chile is immediately suspected of being a sorcerer."

Somehow, the first Catholic missionaries who tasted this New World spice did not feel as though they were being protected from evil. On the contrary, Padre Ignaz Pfeffercorn, a Jesuit transplanted from Germany to the Sonoran sierras in 1756, could well recall the shock of his initial encounter with chile sauce a quarter century later: "After the first mouthful the tears started to come. I could not say a word and believed I had hellfire in my mouth....It is...bitingly sharp...yet it is *manna* to the American palate and is used in every dish with which it harmonizes."

Hellfire or manna? For many Native Americans, chiles were gifts of the gods, as indicated in this creation myth fragment from the Cora Indians of Mexico's west coast, taken down by a Franciscan in 1673:

> ...The Maker created a man and a woman. The man was called Narama, the woman, Uxuu. He put them in a place with many fruits and minerals, but afterwards cast them out. Then, Narama began to sweat, and his sweat was changed into salt. The Maker chose him the patron of salt, mescal, and chile. As for Uxuu, He made her matron of all the seeds and fruits of the summer, and of watering the earth with rain. Other creatures peopling the earth were assigned to be the nurturers of additional foods, vegetable or animal.

123

A few days after having made these arrangements, the Maker invited all these people to a fantastic fiesta. He set a table in the middle of the earth, and each creature brought the foods entrusted to them, to share. Narama was among the last, and he came naked, covered with salt. After everyone was already seated, he presented himself at the table, took salt from his face and sprinkled it upon the foods. Then he reached down, and his testes turned into chile pods. He began to sprinkle their spice onto all of the foods.

This crude action annoyed all the other patrons, who angrily scolded Narama. To this, he replied that if the others could provide the fruits, fish, fowl, seeds and vegetables that were the basic staples of the fiesta, why could not he provide something that these foods needed to be truly tasteful? He declared that there was nothing so necessary as salt and chile. If they would just try the food both with and without these ingredients, they would know that in their hearts. They ate, and not only became satisfied, but enthusiastic.

For the Cora, as for their kin in the Uto-Aztecan language family to the north in the Sonoran Desert, the original chile was also the most beloved—the wild chiltepin or bird pepper, *Capsicum annuum* var. *aviculare*. Unlike most wild progenitors of crops, which are now looked upon as worthless or inferior by farming people who cultivate their domestic descendants, the wild *Capsicum annuum* has fallen from neither grace nor use. The Papago sometimes refer to it as "I'itoi ko'okol," suggesting that it has its place with I'itoi "at the beginning," rather than being something that Coyote spoiled later on, as he did with most wild relatives of crops. Although domesticated chiles were apparently not grown prehistorically north of the present day U.S./Mexico border, the little wild chiltepin was likely used for centuries in the zone from southern Arizona to the Big Bend of Texas. Padre Pfeffercorn knew this shrub by sight, for it grew along the trails he traveled around Cucurpe, Matape, and Ati. Pfeffercorn compared the plant to the big-fruited domesticated chiles, which were already known in Europe as "Spanish peppers," being among the first economic plants that Columbus took back to Europe from the West Indies:

A kind of wild pepper which the inhabitants call chiltepin is found on many hills. It grows on a dense bush about an ell in height and is similar in shape and size to the thick juniper berry, except that when it is ripe, it is not black, but all red, like the Spanish pepper.... It is placed unpulverized on the table in a salt cellar, and each fancier takes as much of it as he believes he can eat. He pulverizes it with his fingers and mixes it with his food. The chiltepin is the best spice for soup, boiled peas, lentils, beans and the like, where the Spanish pepper cannot be used. The Americans swear that it is exceedingly healthful and very good as an aid to digestion, a contention more easily believed than the claim that Spanish pepper is cool and refreshing.

Chiles do stimulate the flow of saliva and gastric juices which serve in digestion. They are analgesic, and reportedly relieve gastric flatulence associated with dyspepsia. And all chiles, except perhaps for the innocuous bell peppers, do leave the consumer with an after-sensation of coolness.

This "chilly" feeling may be the key to chile's popularity in the *tierra caliente*. When our mouths bite into chiles, nerve receptors initially release a substance that signals "pain." Although we begin to have the sensation that we have been bitten or burned, the repeated contact of chiles with sensory nerves produces a sustained feeling of numbness. It is not surprising that *kokoli*, the term for chile in the language of most Sonoran tribes, is associated with their verbs for "to hurt" and "to bite." As our nerves respond to this stimulus, our "common chemical sense" is triggered, causing a cardiovascular reaction which in turn produces perspiration. As we begin to sweat, evaporation on the surface of our skin makes us feel cool in comparison to the surrounding air. In arid lands where shade is scanty, this gives "desert rats" a bodily sensation of coolness that is inaccessible to them without remaking their entire environment. It is no wonder that many Sonorans have developed a dependency on chiltepines, popping them into their mouths like peanuts, to create a sort of internalized air conditioning.

Turn-of-the-century cowboy Jeff Milton was one man who kept an "internal cool" thanks to chiltepines. Unfortunately, this addiction once cost him a baleful of money. Whenever Milton rode the Sonoran Desert, from the Ajos to the Guaymas shoreline, he would pick any wild chiles he found and stash them in a silver snuffbox that was always close at hand. Though not obvious at first to fellow travelers, Milton kept on his person a month's supply of this canned fire. One time, the snuffbox was noticed by a Bostonian who was riding with Milton to visit a Sonoran mine that Jeff had offered to him for $20,000. The morning before seeing the claim, Milton was making a cowboy breakfast when the visiting mining engineer saw him slip some chiltepines out of the snuffbox, to crumble over his own plate of eggs. As Jeff later told J. Evetts Haley, the East Coast tenderfoot had never seen such a red powder before:

> "Mr. Milton, what's that?" inquired the mining man with the commendable curiosity of the scientific mind and that perfect willingness to ask questions that marks the tenderfoot.
> "Water coolers," said Jeff.
> "Do they really make the water cool?" pressed the tenderfoot.
> "Quite cool," answered Jeff, as he worked the fragments into his eggs.

"Where do you get them?"

"Grows wild."

"Isn't that remarkable," observed the mining man, "that nature, here in this terrible desert, produces something that actually makes water cool...."

After several hours of riding hot and dusty trails toward the mine, they finally approached a water hole just below the claim. The weary mining man was about ready to drink from the tank, when he turned to Jeff and said,

"I believe I'll try some of those water coolers. How do you use them?"

"Just chew'em and drink," said Jeff, fishing out his cap-case.

Taking three or four, the man went down to the water tank while Jeff hobbled the horses. When Milton finally called down to the man to go up and look at the mine, he growled back, "Not on your life! I wouldn't look at a mine with anybody who would treat me like that!" As the Bostonian burned with the heat of the chiles in his head and stomach, Jeff quietly answered, "very well, sir," and rather than show him the claim, he accompanied the Bostonian back to Nogales with no further mention of the deal.

"Those three chilipitins cost me $20,000," Jeff recalled later in his life, for the mining claim, although good, was never worked nor sold to anyone else.

Wild chiles are seldom so costly today. Yet their value in U.S. Indian trading posts and Chicano-owned urban markets in the Southwest has risen from $15 a pound in 1977, to $32 a pound in 1984. Sold in ounce or half-ounce packets, they run $1.10 to $1.50 more per ounce than domestic chiles on the same shelf. An ounce of chiltepines is nothing to take lightly.

Yet the chile industry typically glosses over the great value placed on them. It attributes their high price to the extra time and labor taken to harvest them from the wild, and year-to-year unpredictability of their supply. For those who think a chile is a chile, a chiltepin is just another spice. It contains the same aromatic volatiles useful in flavoring foods, and is incidentally rich in vitamins A, C, riboflavin, fiber and sodium. Yet their supply is limited in relation to demand—a demand so strong that in years when the USDA plant inspectors won't let Mexican chiltepines enter the United States due to supposed insect infestations there, they come across the border as the contraband cargo of a few smugglers who immediately sell out all they have to offer. I know of no cultivated Mexican chile that is "pulled" across the border by a demand of equal strength.

Wild chiltepines must have more of what makes chiles holy than your normal, average, everyday farm-dwelling green or red pepper. This spiritual essence of chile is an odorless, colorless, flavorless non-nutrient that a chemist named Thresh first crystallized and described as *capsaicin* late in the nineteenth century. Thresh correctly guessed that this fat-soluble compound is structurally similar to vanilla. By the 1920s, when Nelson first artifically synthesized capsaicin, chemists realized that any of a number of acid amines with basic vanillylamine units could stimulate pain receptors in the human mouth. Wild chiltepines have as much as four times this pungency principle per unit weight than do larger, domesticated chile varieties. In the definitive survey of the most pungent varieties of the chile genus, wild Mexican chiltepines topped even the Japanese *santaka,* the fire-breathing dragon of the introduced Asian chiles. Human senses can detect capsaicin in dilutions of one part in 15 million, and chiltepines have as much as 2,600 parts capsaicin per million of them. From a quick calculation, you can project that a bite into a chiltepin is 39,000 times more powerful than what it needs to be for your taste buds to tell you that you are eating a chile! In short, the chiltepin, as progenitor to most cultivated chile varieties, is the hottest mother around.

Oddly, once scientists figured out what makes chiles hot, they didn't immediately go on to ask the next question: Why are they hot? To say it another way, what is the adaptive advantage of having pungent fruit? In an evolutionary sense, have red-hot fruit contributed to the long-term reproductive success of the chile clan?

Students of coevolution suggest that "the function of a ripe vertebrate-eaten fruit is to get the seeds into the right animals (for dispersal) and keep them out of the wrong animals." To accomplish this, many members of the nightshade family discourage the "wrong" animals by producing alkaloids such as solanine, nicotine, atropine, and scopolamine that are in levels sufficiently high to be toxic to many vertebrates. Deadly nightshade, jimsonweed, tobacco, and even immature tomatoes can produce such effects. Some invertebrates have evolved tolerance and even attraction to certain levels of these solanaceous glycoalkaloids. Oddly, chiles don't have enough of these alkaloids for even a specialist in solanaceous plants—the Colorado potato beetle—to recognize them as being suitable for oviposition and feeding by adult and larval beetles, even though chile plants can hypothetically support their growth. With the absence of these alkaloids, chiles may have evolved another strategy for partial protection from the "wrong animals" and attraction to the right ones.

Capsaicin is not toxic *per se,* but it may be ferocious enough when it hits sensitive stomach linings to discourage certain animals from eating the fruit. We suspect that an animal which finds the burning sensation of excreted chiles uncomfortable can probably learn to avoid them if posed with the problem frequently enough, and given other food choices. We know for sure that rabbits fed diets that contain considerable amounts of chiles develop stomach ulcers and cirrhosis of the liver. Rabbits and other small mammals have teeth and a digestive tract that will probably destroy most chile seeds, rather than let them pass through relatively undamaged so that they may germinate. Since such small mammals cannot "see red" in order to distinguish these fruit from other, less caustic ones, wild chiles evolved a chemical signal to urge them to stay away.

On the other hand, birds can see red and are attracted to a variety of red fruits. Many tropical birds receive much of their carbohydrates, water, vitamins, and certain minerals from eating these red fruit. They, in turn, have a digestive tract that chemically and physically softens the seedcoat of these fruits without effectively damaging the seed, thus encouraging their germination. In fact, certain seeds will suffer retarded germination if they do not pass through a bird's gut.

Wild chile seeds appear to fall into this category. Germination of freshly harvested and dried seeds is so infrequent and haphazard that scientists have devised several chemical treatments essentially to mimic what goes on in a bird's gut, as a way to increase percent germination when they want to grow wild chiles. Wild chiles are so strongly associated with birds that many of the common names for them refer to this relationship: bird pepper, pico pajaro, pajaro pequeño, and so on. As crop-evolution expert Barbara Pickersgill has observed, they are "dispersed by birds [that are] attracted to the bright colour of the exposed fruits and seen feeding avidly on the flesh of even the most pungent varieties."

Thus chiles are pungent enough to discourage consumption by certain animals that would likely destroy the seed, but attract a variety of tropical and arid-subtropical birds that go where chiles can grow. In the borderlands, wild chiltepines are often found in canyons, growing within the protection of wolfberry and hackberry canopies. Red feathered birds such as cardinals and pyrrhuloxias likely left their chile-rich droppings there while they were pursuing the bright, carotene-rich fruit that these shrubs offer. Vagrant birds not only disperse these red fruit from canyon to canyon as they wander, but they also drop the scarified seed, enclosed in a pellet of fertilizer, into a suitable site for germination.

Man also disperses, pelletizes, and informally plants chile seeds as he travels along, as attested to by the many trailside chiltepin bushes in the barrancas of the Sierra

Madre. In arid valleys in Tamaulipas, wild chiles were a dominant component of human pellets as much as 8,000 years ago. Yet our relationship with chiles historically puts us someplace between birds and bunnies. We have served as a dispersal agent for even the hottest wild *Capsicum,* but typically we've worked to dilute their strength in order to keep our stomach linings from being burned out. Through man's selection over the centuries, chiles have gradually evolved into domesticated forms that have more bark (or at least more flesh) than bite. Since Mexican Indians selected chiles for larger fruit size, they have evolved into forms that are eighty times heavier in dry weight than a wild chiltepin, with only about ten times more seeds. In other words, the "package size" has increased more than the number of dessiminules it carries, and the capsaicin content per package has been spread thinner. Capsaicin appears to be largely concentrated inside the fruit, in the placental tissue to which the seeds are attached. This tissue probably makes up relatively more of the fruit weight of a tiny chiltepin than it does of a Big Jim or jalapeño. In addition, humans have occasionally found, and saved the seeds of, wild chiles that express the recessive gene which lacks capsaicin. These "sweet peppers" would likely not be as attractive to birds. But what bird could swallow or carry a big quarter-pound bell pepper anyway? They are not easily deciduous from the rest of the plant as chiltepines are when they are ripe, nor do they ripen as immediately. They are in a prolonged immaturity, staying green and fleshy for many more days than a wild chile would ever dare to.

The domesticated chiles are mostly pendant, rather than being erect on the stem in a position so that birds can reach them. Whereas chiltepines ripen quickly and stick out above the foliage like sore thumbs, domesticated *Capsicums* like bell peppers hang to the ground below the plant's foliage, like a silicone-injected monster too awkward to behave properly.

Birds are not a major pest in bell-pepper fields. They have little to do with such freaks of nature, or better, freaks of nurture.

It is something of a biogeographic fluke that wild chiles still exist as relics as far north as Papago country. Summaries of the plant's range typically refer to it as being limited to the tropics, and rarely show any populations reaching into the United States. Locals know that it is commonplace in south Texas and in Florida, but those localities are mostly humid and subtropical in climate. And yet, botanists have known for decades that there is a wild chile locality in Arizona's Baboquivari Mountains, though the herbarium specimens have been erroneously referred to as *Capsicum baccatum,* a South American species, rather than being correctly labelled *Capsicum annuum* var. *aviculare.*

Local folklore, however, retains knowledge of several other sites in Arizona, a couple of them too arid to be called tropical by any stretch of the imagination. Chiltepines reach the far western edge of the Papago Indian Reservation, on the slopes of the Ajo Mountains, where they associate with saguaro and organpipe cactus, limberbush, and their old friends hackberry and wolfberry along washes. This locality, well known to many Western Papago, receives fewer than twenty-five centimeters of rainfall annually, where evaporation is at least six times that. Chico Bailey, a Papago from nearby Pisinimo, recalled that ten quarts of these chiles could be harvested after a good rainy season. To him, they were not an edge-of-the-range oddity; they have been there "since the beginning."

Another site, a few kilometers from old Indian settlements along the Santa Cruz River, is at a latitude and elevation that make it too cold to be considered tropical. Indian, mestizo, and Basque families have long made forays into Rock Corral Canyon near Tumacacori, picnicking and picking chiles. Our friend from the eighteenth century, Padre Pfeffercorn, recorded that the name Tumacacori meant "pepper bush; place where the little round pepper is found in abundance." This has seemed preposterous to some historians, who were not aware that chiltepines are locally present. Yet in archaic Papago, a little round chile would be called *aritu tum kokori*, or a conjugation thereof that may be even closer in sound to our present-day Tumacacori.

These little outlier populations show a degree of frost resistance seldom found in other *Capsicum annuum* populations. I have collected their seeds for gene banks, hoping that someone may eventually find other useful traits in them, such as the resistance to certain viruses that have already been transferred into a few jalapeño cultivars. Ten strains of virus severely damage the commercial chile crop of Mexico and the U.S., sometimes severely infecting all the plants in a field and causing crop failures for an entire valley of production. Chile pathologist Ben Villalon has found resistance to several of these virus strains in wild chiles, but individual wild chile populations tested exhibited resistance to different virus strains. As islands separated from the main stream of wild chiles running through Mexico's Sierra Madre, Arizona's chiltepines may offer unique sets of genes for plant breeders wishing to decrease the vulnerability of the commercial chile crops.

In the Sierras, another threat, similar to that facing wild agaves, has affected numerous wild chile stands over the last several decades. The demand for chiltepines as a spice has escalated on both sides of the border as the Spanish-speaking population has grown. Currently, about fifteen metric tons of dried, ripened chiltepines are wild-harvested out of Sonora alone, and perhaps the same quantity is gathered out of adjacent Chihuahua and Sinaloa. Ranchhands and subsistence farmers take a few weeks off in late summer and early fall to move up from the valleys into the sierras where the chiles form much of the shrub cover. Buyers come around in trucks from the cities and purchase the wild spice for the equivalent of four to six dollars a kilogram. This is cash in the hand at a time of the year when savings have dwindled, and when there are bumper crops, it works out to be good daily wages.

But drought years are frequent enough to make the yield unpredictable. As the buyers begin to see from the first few weeks' harvest that they will have trouble meeting their customers' demands, they offer as much as a dollar and a half more per kilo, and the harvesters become more desperate to harvest the remaining chiles.

The result is that gatherers compete for chiles in the same hills, busting through a stand, breaking whole branches off to skim a few chiltepines into their bags as fast as they can. Many of the wild chile bushes are on communally managed *ejido* lands, where people realized that damaged plants might diminish future economic yields but did nothing about the problem until recently. In the past few years, *ejiditarios* in east-central Sonora have voted to fine anyone caught breaking branches off chiltepin plants during harvest time; fruit must be picked individually.

A quarter of a century ago, ethnobotanist Howard Scott Gentry observed an increase in plant damage as a result of the first chiltepin exports northward across the border; he prophesied another solution to the problem:

> Recently the natives of southern Sonora have started collecting the fruit for export to the U.S. Their method of collecting is highly injurious to the plant. If commercial exploitation of the plant is successful, it is probable that the great majority of plants will die under persistent breaking, and what has been a common plant will become rare. Or perhaps it will be cultivated.

"Perhaps we can bring chiltepines into field cultivation," mused Alfredo Noriego of the Costa de Hermosillo at about the same time. A native of Sonora, Noriego knew that chiltepines in home gardens grew fine on the coastal plains away from the mountains, though they were slow to grow the first year after the seeds germinated. He would occasionally mention this idea to his sons, who kept it in the back of their minds, but who continued on with their more conventional agricultural activities—groundwater-irrigated cotton, wheat, corn, and garbanzos.

Then, about the time the old man died, another reason arose for considering chiltepin cultivation—the escalating costs of pumping groundwater. Noriego's father, killed by Yaquis in 1920, had been the first farmer on the Hermosillo coastal plains to pump water mechanically from the underground aquifer. First using a steam pump bought from an American in 1906, this pioneer opened to cultivation an irrigation district that now covers 118,000 hectares, and which became part of the great Sonoran breadbasket by the 1950s.

Yet when the first Noriego tapped into coastal groundwaters, they were sweet, at a depth of forty meters. Today, owing to decades of pumping quantities of water that exceeded annual recharge, his grandsons bring up somewhat salty water from a depth of one hundred meters. Saltwater intrusion underground has already forced the abandonment of miles of farms between the Noriegos and the coast. Of the 800 million cubic meters of groundwater extracted in their irrigation district in a recent year, a 450 million cubic meter deficit in the aquifer was created because extraction so greatly exceeded natural recharge. Water levels have dropped at the same time that electrical costs per foot of lift have risen. The Noriego grandsons simply cannot afford to irrigate the same crops with as much water as their grandfather or father did.

One grandson, Alfredo Junior, reconsidered his father's chiltepin scheme, guessing that such a hardy plant would not require so much irrigation to produce an economic crop. He overcame the first year's slow growth by starting plants from cuttings taken from three transplanted wild plants. The cuttings not only rooted and grew rapidly; they would sometimes begin to fruit after just a few weeks in the greenhouse. Transplanting thousands of these rooted cuttings out to a field, he put them to the acid test, and they passed. On six irrigations a year, or one a month from April through September, Noriego's chiltepines produced enough fruit for him to be able to market hundreds of kilograms of them their first autumn. Together with his brothers and friends, he is working to solve other agronomic problems. If insects and diseases do not thrive in their dense plantings, within a few years their production may eclipse the quantity that is currently harvested from the wild. Perhaps that will take some of the pressure off wild populations as the cost of seeking out remote stands of chiltepines becomes less than their economic return. Perhaps there will be more left for the birds.

Because I had heard that chiltepines have been used in the treatment of earaches, and as a way to wean babies (by putting chile powder on the mother's breasts), I wondered if they were actually classified as a medicine by Mexican people. When I once asked a Sonoran woman if chiltepines are a food or a *cura,* she frowned, then looked at me as though my categories didn't elucidate anything at all. "We eat them here in Babiacora, but we use them more to preserve food [as an antioxidant] than as a food in and of themselves. And they are not really a cure, but if you eat them now and then, you won't get sick."

This view of chiltepines as a preventer of illness reverberates back through history, and back into the most remote reaches of the sierras. Ethnobotanist Robert Bye has observed that their use in so-called Tarahumara curing ceremonies is not really to rid someone of a current affliction, but to prevent maladies potentially caused by future witchcraft.

Such witchcraft is caused by a *sukurame* sorcerer who uses a special bird called a *disagiki* as a pathogenic agent to transmit illness. He is the only one who can see the bird, which is no bigger than a finger tip but lives on meat and tortillas.

It flies into houses crying "Sht! Sht!", and then eats your food or shits on
you. The only way to prevent its coming is to throw chiltepines
into the air and eat some yourself. This bird is
like no other birds. More like evil people
than like its feathered kin,
it cannot stand
chiles.

FALL

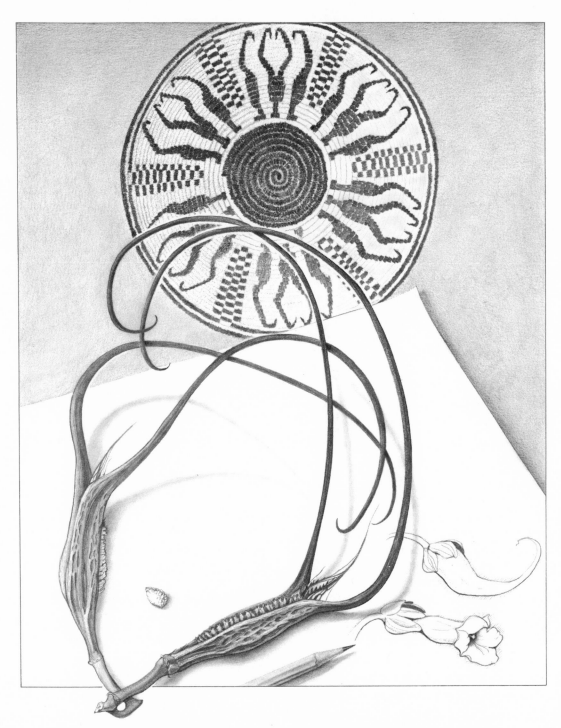

"I can see the whole design as I am going along, weaving it, just like I am weaving into it things that I have gathered from here, where we live, to make it real."

Devil's Claw:
Designing Baskets, Designing Plants

"CURIOUS among vegetable growths of the new world, and one which is seldom seen by man," wrote Harry H. Dunn, "is the rootless cactus of the California desert." The July 1908 issue of *Technical World* featured a photo of this fantastic desert growthform, accompanied by the following remarks from Harry:

> The plant, a round, compact growth, rolls about the level floor of the desert for some eight or nine months of the year, tossed hither and yon by the winds which blow with fierceness over all of California's sand plat during those months.
>
> At the coming of the rains, or rather, the cloudbursts, which sweep the desert in its springtime, this cactus takes root wherever it happens to have been dropped...and immediately begins to put out all around it small shoots, which in turn become cacti, exactly like the parent.
>
> When the damp season is over these roots shrivel up and finally fall off the parent cactus...[which] dying from the constant sapping of the circle of young ones around it, leaves this circle a hedge of thorns. Such rings in sheltered parts of the desert...have resulted in endless speculation by botanists until the true reason was discovered by the bringing of a few plants to the coast experiment stations by travellers who had crossed the deserts.

When Harry H. Dunn's "true reason" appeared in print, the crusty old botanists in residence in the West had a merry time with it. For the "rootless cactus" he had described was not a whole plant at all.

It was instead a hooked-together cluster of the dried fruit of the devil's claw or unicorn plant (*Proboscidea*). And *Proboscidea* is not a cactus, but a member of the *Martynia* family. In fact, it is more closely related to sesame than it is to true cactus!

The editor of the journal *Plant World* observed that "the photograph accompanying this unique sketch represents a bunch of the fruits of the unicorn plant…and the reckless disregard of truth displayed by the author excites admiration. The actual history of these fruits, their formation, structure, ripening, and transportation by animals, the important part played by the fiber derived from them in the textile work of the Indian…furnish facts which for novelty and interest far surpass the efforts of Mr. Dunn's imagination."

Harry had done little wrong, really. He had simply portrayed a plant out of context, out of season, with few clues to its role in the desert environment. What he had guessed was "rootless," Western botanists knew was part of a plant with roots responsive to the poorest of summer rains and slightest of desert runoff.

These Western botanists knew too that the various species of devil's claw were rooted culturally in the Southwest. Virtually every tribe in the American Southwest and northwestern Mexico used them in one way or another.

The uses of various species did vary, and certain ones were more restricted culturally or geographically. The huge underground tuber of the yellow-flowered *Proboscidea altheaefolia* was formerly eaten by a group of Seri Indians which once spent much of its time in the dry interior of Tiburón Island in the Sea of Cortez. They would peel the bark off this orange-red perennial root and eat the outer portion, just under the bark, without cooking it. The bitter, inner pith would be discarded. Available at times of the year when other food plants were unproductive due to drought, Sonoran cowboys occasionally dug up these roots to feed starving cattle.

The use of the annual devil's claw, *Proboscidea parviflora*, may be rooted even further back in time. The dried bony fruit of annual devil's claw are found in Exhausted, Cordova, and Ventana cave sites in the Southwest, associated with cultural materials ranging from A.D. 300 to late prehistoric times. These durable capsules all have rather short "claws" or curvilinear appendages that splay out when the maturing fruit sheds its green fuzzy skin and begins to split open, dropping seeds. The seeds and even the very immature fruit were sometimes cooked, though more frequently, Southwestern Indians simply chewed on the raw seeds of devil's claw.

Yet the claws themselves provided the major products of this plant—fiber splints woven into basketry. Devil's claw is found woven into baskets in caves within the upper Gila River watershed at least as early as A.D. 600. By the 1930s, over twenty-five distinct culture groups in the Southwest were known to have used devil's claw in their coiled basketry.

"On the Third Day, Great Spirit gave to each tribe a basket," an old Papago man told Harold Bell Wright decades ago,

> And when all the women were making baskets, I'itoi saw it would be best for them to mark their baskets that they might know to whom the different baskets belonged and for what each was to be used. So Great Spirit took some seed pods of the plant 'ihuk—which we call the devil's claw—and showed the women how to weave the black fiber of 'ihuk into their baskets so that each pattern would be different, and by the patterns baskets would be known.

A warm wind blew through the ramada, jostling the discarded, stripped devil's claw at Winona's feet. One of her feet had a cord looped around it, which ran up over a saguaro rib that was part of the ramada's covering. It ran back down to the lip of a basket suspended from a mesquite beam. Whenever Winona tapped her foot, the baby in this makeshift crib would be rocked gently. The light wind helped sustain this motion.

Winona would hum for a while as she unhooked devil's claws from a hoop of a hundred or so on the bed next to her. She put them in a large bowl of water to let them soak. Then she would take an already moistened one, and dig her awl in under the black fiber at the juncture of the claw with the body of the fruit. She would stop humming long enough to take hold of the fiber splint with her teeth—while rotating the claw with both hands—to peel the fiber slowly back up toward the tip of the claw. Setting the stripped splint in a smaller bowl of water, she would begin humming again.

"Are these for a basket that you have already begun to weave?" I asked.

For a minute, she didn't answer. We both looked out, down the hill from the ramada, where a dust devil was spinning across the wash, whipping plant debris up into its funnel. It passed.

"Oh yes, this is the start of the basket right here," she said, taking a small loop of woven yucca, beargrass, and devil's claw out of a pillowcase next to her. "It is for the baby, so that she may have some kind of thing that I made for her to be with her all of her life. My mother made me a big basket too when I was small, but a few years back a drunk stole it to sell it to get money to buy more beer...."

She stopped speaking for a moment, long enough to strip another claw with her teeth. She began again: "But this basket, we'll protect and keep for her until she has children of her own. It will be special. I gathered the yucca and beargrass myself last week. And we grew the *'ihuk* this fall, over there at the field...." She pointed her chin out toward where the dust devil had been, down on the floodplain, where her husband's family had kept fields for over a century.

"This basket will have a lot of devil's claw in it. It is a special one because it is the kind that I dreamed."

"You dreamed it?"

"*Heu'u.* Yes, when I first began to learn how to make the baskets, I never did finish one. Then my mother told me just to wait until I dreamed a basket design that I could remember, and that would be my own to do from then on. I dreamed one that took a long time to make the first time around, and gave it to my godmother who still has it. But now it doesn't take so long to do—I can see the whole design as I am going along, weaving it, just like I am weaving into it things that I have gathered from here, where we live, to make it real."

After talking a while longer with Winona, I asked if it was okay if I walked down to the field.

"Go ahead," she said.

"I'll bring you more *'ihuk* if I see any," I replied.

"That will be fine."

Their field is on the Sells Wash floodplain. However, it received its runoff from a small tributary that spreads out into many braids just before it reaches the big wash. I walked down off the hillside where a few scattered houses are perched, high above where any floods could reach. They have a small shelter down at the field too, to keep their cots in during the growing season, when they like to sleep in the field to keep coyotes from eating the harvest. I walked down across the bursage and burrobush flats, past this fieldhouse, and into the field of dried weeds.

Winona's father-in-law had already harvested the remaining beans and corn a few weeks before. But on the edge of the plowed area of the field, in little circles of dirt cleared of weeds by a hand-held hoe, dried hollow stalks of devil's claw stood, twenty to forty bony claws clinging to each stem. Winona and her mother-in-law had scraped these circles clean, and had planted a few white seeds in the middle of each circle at the same time that the men were plowing the main part of the field. Here, the floodwaters crossed the devil's-claw plot before they reached the more orderly squash, corn, and bean plantings. The devil's claw were kept on the poorer ground on this upstream side, leaving the best earth for the food crops, even though the family did not have to depend upon the food supplies they grew themselves, as they had once done.

As I gathered up the claws, hooking them into a circle so that I could add on others later to form a hoop like the one Winona had been working from, I thought about how different the field had looked in late August when I had last visited.

It had been hot and humid even early in the morning, as if the plants and ground were giving off the warmth and moisture they had accumulated, even before the sun was very high above the horizon. Insects splashed up out of the foliage as I walked through the rows just after dawn. I came to the devil's claw plants at the field's edge, and was amazed that they already had small fruit developing not much more than a month after planting. The smallest fruit looked like fuzzy okra hidden under the broad sticky leaves of the plant. As they mature, they elongate, until the fiber beneath the green fuzzy skin gets hard and begins to curl. The skin breaks open along a seam-like suture and is shed, leaving a black, bony capsule to dry in the sun.

As I knelt, testing the tip of a developing claw to see if it was nearing maturity, I noticed a small bee fly into the corolla of a devil's-claw flower. I quickly enclosed the flower in my fist and held it until I could put it in a plastic bag I had in my pocket. The bee was captured in the bag, and soon transferred into a sealed jar.

The bee turned out to be *Perdita hurdi*, a solitary bee known to pollinate the big yellow-flowered perennial devil's claw, *Proboscidea altheaefolia*. The female bee lands on an unopened flower, and on the underside of the corolla, she cuts open a hole through which she enters to collect pollen. After four or five minutes of gathering pollen in the unopened flower where neither the nectaries nor stigma are yet functioning, she leaves it to seek nectar in an opened flower.

Entomologists Hurd and Linsley have observed that male bees that have already imbibed nectar from open flowers sometimes rest inside the flower after drinking, and perhaps wait for female bees to visit. They note that

> since it is these males that pounce upon the pollen-laden, nectar-questing female and copulate with her as she crawls into the open flower, it would appear that her arrival is anticipated. In several instances during this mating commotion, we observed the pollen-laden scopa to brush against the stigma and thereby presumably affect pollination....If indeed the nectaries do not become functional until the flowers open, this then would appear to be an exceptionally fine mechanism to

insure cross-pollination by forcing the pollen-laden female to visit an open flower and, incidental to that quest, deposit pollen upon the stigma.

Yet what was *Perdita hurdi* doing in a planting of annual devil's claw, since entomologists had searched for it in many other parts of Arizona and never found it on *Proboscidea parviflora* in the wild? Was there something about the density of this planting that made them attractive? Or was there some way that these flowers were more like those of the perennial devil's claw?

The flowers in this Papago planting and others do appear different from those of truly wild devil's claw. They are more robust, with a larger opening, closer to the shape of the perennial. In color, the flower of the devil's claw that Papagos cultivate is more often pale white rather than reddish-purple, like the majority of wild *parviflora* corollas in Arizona. On a pale background, the yellow stripes are perhaps more prominent, attracting the bee like the yellow corollas of the perennial do. Peter Bretting has found that the style and anthers are also longer, but no one knows if this oversized flower produces more nectar and pollen relative to those of the annual devil's claw.

The bees may sense something that botanists have recently confirmed: the plant cultivated in Papago fields is not exactly the same as the wild annual devil's claw in the Sonoran Desert. Something has happened to it, more than its being grown on good soil with supplemental water. Plant seeds of wild devil's claw under the same favorable conditions, and they still do not get as robust or take on all these exaggerated characteristics.

By late fall, the difference is even more evident. I accidentally picked up a wild devil's-claw fruit while walking across the wash on my way to the field—it hooked around my ankle, tagging along. When I reached the dried stalks of Winona's plantings, I picked up a cultivated claw, pulled the other off my ankle, and compared them.

The body of these dried fruits was about the same size and shape. But inside Winona's cultivated ones, the seeds were white, while the one from the wash had black seeds, as do all truly wild devil's claw.

Then I compared the claws themselves—that's where the big difference lies. The wild ones from the wash looped up in a curve no longer than the distance from the tip of my thumb to that of my index finger, about seventeen centimeters. The one with the white seeds from Winona's planting curved up more delicately, stretching out more than twenty-eight centimeters, dwarfing the other. It appeared more supple and flexible. These, I realized, were characteristics that Winona and other basket weavers liked. For every claw they stripped, they not only received longer fiber splints with which they could make more accentuated designs, but also the splints were easier to coil tightly around the beargrass. The truly wild devil's claw looked tough and stubby in contrast.

Botanists now agree that these differences are significant enough taxonomically to distinguish the white-seeded form of devil's claw sown by Southwestern Indians from other forms. Peter Bretting recently named this Indian-cultivated variety *Proboscidea parviflora* var. *hohokamiana,* to indicate its presence today in the land occupied prehistorically by the Hohokam culture. It is now recognized as one of but a handful of wild species domesticated north of Mexico by Native Americans—the majority of other domesticated plants historically cultivated in the United States were originally derived from regions beyond our present-day borders.

Domestication: bringing a useful organism into the human household, and making it increasingly dependent upon our care. In a technical sense, domestication means recurrent sowing of selected seeds, and protection of the resulting plants. By planting seeds with characteristics that are rarely found in wild populations, and encouraging a greater frequency of these characteristics in an "artificial" population, this population diverges from those in the wild. Indians did not have to "breed" plants such as devil's claw by manually transferring pollen from one plant with desired characteristics to another. By repeated sowing of seeds maturing in a cultivated environment, there is automatic, unconscious selection for certain characteristics such as quick germination of the white-seeded types. By saving the seed of variants that they preferred, and placing their seeds where their progeny could freely outcross with one another, they gradually changed the frequency of expression of other desired genetic traits. Generation after generation, recurrent selection and weeding out of less useful plants increased the abundance of plants with long, flexible claws. What were once infrequent variants in wild populations are now traits that dominate field populations—and these useful traits can all be found combined in the same plants! What has happened to devil's claw in the Southwest is a process similar to that which happened long ago to all the food and fiber plants upon which modern agriculture is based.

Yet when did it happen for devil's claw? Where did it occur? And as is asked in most mystery stories, "Who done it?"

As of yet, there are no firm answers upon which scientists have agreed. But the answers may be closer to home than scientists have suspected.

When the Forty-niners came through Arizona and Sonora on their way to seek California gold, they became dependent upon their stops at Indian rancherías for acquiring new supplies. In addition to letting their stock out to pasture and water, they often bought food and containers in which to carry it. John Bartlett, the U.S. Boundary Commissioner around this time, was particularly impressed by Pima and Maricopa pottery and baskets. He marveled that the typical Pima basket was "remarkably well made of willow twigs, and [woven] so close as to be impervious to water." What he sketched, but failed to describe in his writing, was that the Pima baskets had dark designs of devil's claw that contrasted with the pale background of willow splints. The core or base of the baskets he drew had the black color that only devil's claw provided to the O'odham. What's more, Pima and Papago elders now say that devil's claw was formerly preferred as the base of utility baskets, since it wore down much slower than other basketry fibers.

With this quality of product, and an expanding market, baskets soon became more than simply a utility item used in their own households. Papago and Pima women, and later those of other tribes, soon began to make more baskets for sale to Anglo- and Mexican-Americans than for their own use. At first, perhaps, these were exclusively utilitarian items—it is said that tight-woven Papago baskets were once used like buckets for milking cows in the early days of southern Arizona's dairy industry! But with the coming of the railroads, mining, and ranching to the Sonoran Desert, there arrived in Tucson and other desert towns wealthy people willing to buy these crafts purely for their aesthetic value.

Another change occurred in the second half of the nineteenth century. As Anglos brought unprecedented numbers of cattle to southern Arizona, the devil's claw once gathered from plants out on the open range diminished in abundance. Livestock, particularly during drought years, will consume nearly every herbaceous annual within their reach. Devil's claw was not the only useful plant to diminish in numbers. A number of other wild resources that the Papago and Pima relied upon became so scarce that to survive, they had to increase sales of whatever products they could muster in order to buy sufficient food. A common sight in the late 1800s was that of a wagonload of firewood, baskets, and pots being driven into Tucson by a Papago family that had been traveling one or two days from the west. The River Pima, having had their irrigation water usurped by Mormon settlers at Florence upstream on the Gila, were forced to pursue similar options.

Perhaps it was during this time that O'odham women first began to save seeds of the devil's claw that they had to search long and hard for out on the range. Rather than simply chew on the seeds that fell out of the claws they were processing, they gathered up the seed, or protected plants that volunteered near the ramada where they wove baskets. Where hedgerows and barbwire were effective in keeping cattle out of fields, they realized that sowing seeds of devil's claw within those protected areas would insure that the plants would not be devoured. Gradually, women began to sow their own plots of saved devil's-claw seed on the margins of the men's plantings of food crops, or around family quarters from which livestock was excluded.

Women. A few archaeologists have casually speculated that women may have been originally responsible for bringing a large number of plants into cultivation, particularly ones which have multiple products including medicines and fibers. Yet this notion has been obscured by scholars' persistent use of terms such as "plant husbandry" and "plant/man coevolution."

In the case of devil's claw, it appears that women were not only the ones to use the plant, but also the ones to select and sow its seeds. Plant *wifery* is the only term appropriate.

As devil's claw seed became increasingly important as something to save rather than to snack upon, some interesting womanly lore developed. Among the Pima, young girls were told not to eat the seeds of devil's claw unless they wanted to bear only boys as children. Among some Papago women, a spicier seed-eating taboo developed. Teenage girls were told that if they ate devil's-claw seeds, their pubic hairs would stand up like the bristly fibers that are found between the two devil's claw appendages. Whether adhered to or not, these tongue-in-cheek warnings underscore the relationship between devil's claw and women.

These O'odham women have good eyes for the variation within a devil's claw population. I once walked through the runoff field near Winona's house with her mother-in-law, a frail old woman who still retained sharp vision. She had been holding on to my arm for balance as we went along, but all of a sudden gave me a nudge with her elbow.

"There, *waik daika, Hegai 'ihuk*," she pointed.

"What?" I asked. "Four what on that plant?"

"Four of those hooks on the same one." She pulled off a green, maturing devil's-claw fruit from the plant next to us. It looked the same as all the others to me at first glance. Deftly peeling back the green fuzzy skin, she exposed the bony fingers that had not yet twisted apart. There were four, not the usual two claws.

"We say that they are twins on the same one. Most women don't like it, hoe them out if they see them in their fields. They say it will make them have twin children, keeping them around. Me, I don't care now. My husband's a *makai*, a medicine man. Twin boys anyway, long ago. He has good fields, give me twin boys, always fertile here. But those twin *'ihuk,* they come up all the time here."

Her comments hadn't quite sunk in. I asked naively, "Well, if those other women can get four splints, not two from the same *'ihuk,* isn't it better to plant those than the regular kind because they can get double the amount of material for their baskets?"

"They don't want twins," she said. "What they want is the long ones, those *ge'eged 'ihuk,* so it is from those that they save the seed." She walked on.

I watched over the next few years, whenever I was around a woman preparing the devil's claw splints, to see if she saved any particular seed. Sometimes she would sweep up all that had fallen to the dirt below her, and these were kept as a backup supply. A backup for what? For specially kept seed from extra long, dark, flexible claws, often set aside in a pretty jelly jar or marked box. These were inevitably white seeds, not the dark black or charcoal gray of the wild types. Perhaps early in the history of cultivation of devil's claw, a woman noticed that a plant with fairly long fruit had seeds lacking the color pigment of the others. Saving these, and planting them apart from the others, she continued to select for even longer claws. Today, these white seeds have higher germination rates than wild types, and perhaps germination inhibitors were selected out of this strain fairly early. When later intermixed with claws containing black seeds, she could use the white color as a marker of those which consistently produced longer seeds. I speculate that neighboring women eagerly sought to borrow or trade for these seeds, and that once the word got around of their availability, they spread like wildfire.

Amazingly, that wildfire spread way beyond the Papago and Pima country to dozens of other tribes within a few short decades. Peter Bretting's fine bio-geographic analysis of seeds provided to him from various tribes suggests that the white-seeded devil's claw is most morphologically similar to the wild types in southern and central Arizona. For tribes like the Havasupai who now have both white and black seeded types, it appears that their white seed type is more like the southern Arizona wild type than their own local wild type. Although not proving diffusion through tribal trade networks, such evidence strongly suggests that superior strains of devil's claw were passed from hand to hand.

Most astonishing is that within the last century, the white-seeded domesticate was traded even beyond the natural range of wild devil's claw. Again, the potential for basketry sales to newly settled Anglo-Americans appears to be the driving force. We know from Edward Palmer's notes among the River Pima that in the decades after the Civil War, they were trading both devil's claw and basketry to Colorado River tribes, some of whom were then congregated at Fort Mohave. From there, it may have spread to several California and Nevada groups, as this 1941 note by Edmund Jaeger suggests:

> Devil's claw was introduced into Death Valley eighty years ago by a brother of Hungry Bill, a Shoshone Indian, who visited Fort Mohave and found the Indians there making black patterns in their baskets from fiber from the fruits. He procured seeds and planted them in Johnson Canyon; the plant still flourishes there.

Several families of Death Valley Shoshone eventually settled at the Wilkerson Ranch on Rawson Creek, California, eighty kilometers north of Death Valley and nearly as far north as San Francisco Bay. In a small booklet on California basketry

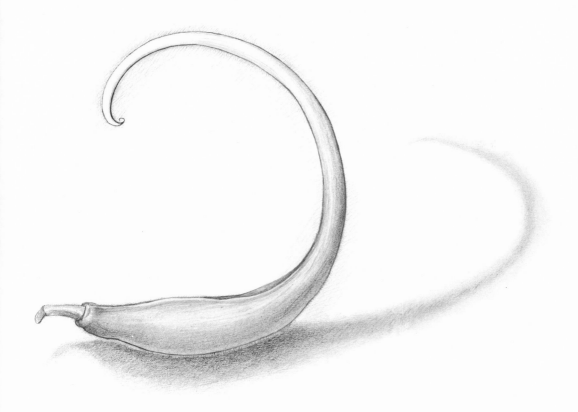

from the 1960s, the staff of the San Bernardino County Museum noted that two Shoshone families there, "the Hunters and Buttons, cultivated this black-seeded annual in their gardens."

Fifteen years after a devil's-claw fruit was collected by their museum staff, I sent the San Bernardino Museum a letter requesting a loan of this material. To my surprise, the fruit they sent contained white seed—the botanist whom they earlier asked to identify it simply told them that it was known as *Martynia parviflora,* a black seeded annual, never bothering to look at the seeds inside.

To my greater surprise, two seeds from the many inside germinated. They too produced white seed, and other traits of a true domesticate. Seven hundred fifty kilometers north of the River Pima, the white-seeded devil's claw had found a new home.

With the many new ways in which Indian tribes today have become linked as never before—boarding schools, powwows, peyote rites, and intertribal crafts fairs—devil's claw and its use in basketry is still getting around to new spots. The Hopi have long known wild devil's claw as *tumo'ala*—a plant once left in fields to produce sympathetic magic. Its zigzag shape is said to bring lightning, which in turn brings rain, which may then bring good crops. Any field weed which might result in such good works was spared the hoe.

But now, at Lower Moenkopi, there exists a more aggressive devil's claw, said to be introduced from the Kaibab Southern Paiute, who in turn received it from the Moapa Southern Paiute. It has white seeds.

It may have been seeded there by Kaibab Paiute who were allowed by the Hopi to collect the wild *tumo'ala* which they used in their baskets. The Hopi had no such use for it. Now, with the newer kind of devil's claw spreading in their fields, and wrapping their claws around everyone's ankles, some Hopi farmers are beginning to weed it out whenever it appears on their land.

Edna Dallas, an expert Hopi basket weaver, had another idea. She had seen the Pima and Havasupai women weave with it at intertribal crafts fairs. Having mastered the arts of making Hopi dyed, twined wicker plaques, and plaited "ring" sifter baskets, as well as Ute/Navaho-style close-coiled wedding baskets, she decided to try her hand at devil's claw designs. After gathering the devil's claw in her field, she began to soak them. In a few weeks, she had the first Hopi-made coiled basket with a black devil's claw design.

Squash blossoms. Shields. Snakes. Swastikas. Seven-pointed stars. Mazes. Tur-tlebacks. Trees of Life. Camels. Circus animals.

From the Western Apache to the Chemehuevi, from the Papago to the Tubatulabal, tribes have come up with a variety of designs using devil's claw as their means of expression. Some mandala-like patterns are held in common by several tribes, but more often than not, you can tell one group's baskets from another's without much scholarly analysis.

Whether the women say they dreamed the pattern or "made it up," whether handed down from a grandmother or pulled out of an old ethnography book on their people, the designs speak to us as differently as languages do. Even stars executed by White River Apache and Papago women burn in your mind in different ways—one multi-layered and shimmering, the other, more symmetric, sturdy and constant.

Somehow, domesticated devil's claw spread to more than three dozen Indian villages in a five-state area over less than a century's time. Rather than make cultures more uniform as most technological introductions have done in the last few decades, its use has enabled a diversity of distinct forms of expression. It has resulted in more than just patterns to tell tribes apart from one another, as the

Papago story suggests. It has given individuals like Edna Dallas a chance to

innovate, to do something a little different from the cultural norm,

but something still appreciated for its own beauty. And it

may be through such innovation, playfulness

and skill, that any culture renews

itself, renews its

health.

He had already buried the badger claws once, and the river had begun to rise toward
them.... Trudging through the knee-deep mud, he blew seeds from his mouth
to be scattered by wind and draining water.

F EW men knew how to use the badger claws to make the river banks cave in. He had already buried the claws once, and the river had begun to rise toward them, digging, imitating the badger. Here, on the main channel of the Río Colorado, the banks crumbled. He had found the three claws and was moving them back, away from where the floods had reached yesterday, hoping that the waters would rise even more, following the claws. As the river continued to fatten this June, leveling and saturating the ground, he would keep it digging toward the buried badger claws. Then, when the floods subsided in July, he would begin to plant the *shimcha* grain there, on the newly watered, fertilized mudflats.

He knew not what the other Yuman-speaking peoples did, but among his band, he was one of a handful of men that went to the effort to obtain the claws, to plant this grain. His motivations were simple. His children loved the taste of the sun-dried cakes made from the ground *shimcha* grain. He himself preferred to have them now and then as a change of pace when their diet grew monotonous.

So he took the time to purify himself to be worthy of killing a badger. For four days in early June, he had not eaten nor coupled with his wife. Waking before daylight, he would go to the river channel, swim and wash his hair, to return before the others rose. He stayed away from where the women gossiped over their grindstones, and sat quietly at the margins of the camp throughout the day.

The fourth evening, an elder gestured to him to go. He left camp, to return to a badger hole he had spotted not too long before. He kept a club poised in his right hand and probed the den with a slender, curved stick held in his left. Dirt fell from the roof of the tunnel into the den. Confused, the badger lumbered out. In a moment it was dead, skull cracked at the neck. Three claws were cut off the front feet.

Now, a good place for planting *shimcha* could be assured. He looked out over the inundated flats, imagining what it might look like in another three months: thousands of long seedheads, golden, nodding in the sun.

What the migrating birds did not bother, he would harvest. He would work through the stand, rubbing dried-out seedheads over pottery pans. His wife would parch the harvest, loosening the chaff and roasting the grain, then winnow away the refuse. She would grind some of the grain fine, like pinole. Part they would give to relatives, who would soon come to camp and gamble with them. Part they would keep for periodic use, storing it in huge bird's nest granaries. These enormous baskets would be lifted to the tops of storage platforms, secure from floods and wild camp robbers. And part of the harvest he would save as seed for planting. He would weave willow splints into a *sawa* basket, shaped like a bulging bag, fill it with seeds, then stitch it shut. This he would hide in a place safe and dry, for future sowing.

Centuries passed.

It held the odor of wild animals. The young Cocopa Indian men were uneasy. It was a cave high in the Trigo Mountains, above the east bank of the Río Colorado. Haskell Yowell had found the cave while prospecting, and thought that the bat guano which filled it, or something else hidden inside it, might have economic value. He and his brother Dudley had driven north from Yuma twenty-eight kilometers, then up into the range as far as the road would go. From the road, up to the cave, they rigged a little trolley to carry down the slope whatever was worth pulling out of the cave. Then, with gunnysacks and spades in hand, they all climbed to the cave mouth and smelled it. They stood outside the cave for a minute, sharing a cigarette. The Indians spoke quietly to one another in a mixture of Spanish and Cocopa.

"Well, go ahead, boys," one of the Yowells said. "That bat dung, there on the floor, let's bag it up. If we don't find anything else here, at least we can use some of that as fertilizer back on the farm."

A half meter of guano disappeared into the gunny sacks. They scraped the floor of the front of the rock shelter clean, then moved back into more cramped space. An inner chamber, perhaps five meters deep and ten wide, was nearly filled with guano to its ceiling. They shoveled out layer after layer, filling one sack after another. As their spades reached toward the inner chamber floor, one of them nudged something spongy. They stopped.

"What's that?" asked Dudley. "Here, give me that shovel."

As they scaped the guano loose, he could see that it was straw wrapped around some object. Peeling back this covering of slender grass stems and leaves, they found a plump, twined-woven bag. It was stitched shut.

Bringing it out into full light, Dudley loosened the bag's stitching. He tipped it, and a stream of golden grain spilled onto the ground.

"Why, look at all those seeds! It's jammed full of them! Must be at least a pound packed in there!"

"You boys know what they are?" Dudley queried.

They shook their heads faintly.

"Well, it don't look like anything that grows up here."

"C'mon, let's tighten these stitches and close it," Dudley deliberated. "I want to get this to the state archaeologists, to see if they've ever seen anything like it before. Let's get digging again, see if there's pots or arrows or anything else under there. If you hit anything, stop, and we'll take a good slow look at it."

No other artifacts were found in the cave or in any other caves nearby. Haskell and Dudley eventually mailed the bag and its contents to the Arizona State Museum in Tucson to learn of its antiquity and identity. Museum curators found a similar, modern bag made by Yuman Indians in their collections and sifted through the seeds. In addition to the golden grain, they sorted out seventy grams of seeds of green-striped cushaw squash, and about the same amount of three different kinds of tepary beans. The grain itself weighed three quarters of a kilogram, and a sample of it was ample for radiocarbon dating. Though still appearing to be in a perfect state of preservation, the seeds were estimated to be 603 years old, plus or minus 140 years.

So they tried to figure out what this grain was that filled the bulk of the woven bag.

Most of the 2-millimeter-long seeds, golden to cream-colored, roundish and shiny, looked like a grain that the Indians were once said to have sown and eaten. It was called *Panicum sonorum*, the Sonoran panicgrass or millet. Just before the turn of the century, several delta explorers noted that the Cocopa and nearby tribes grew and ground it, making cakes, gruel or mush. Another panicgrass, smaller, darker, more slender in seed shape, was found in the bag among these domesticated grains. Perhaps it was a wild form of Sonoran panicgrass that spontaneously came up as a weed in their plantings, or a closely related species. The Indians had once spoken of a spontaneous panicgrass, more bitter in flavor, harder to thresh than the form they usually had sown. Yet most of the seeds in the bag were cleanly threshed, with hardly any chaff left in the whole cache.

Great care had been taken to clean and store this grain. By whom? Why?

The grain of the Trigo Mountains cave cache revealed little else. The tepary beans, however, spoke to Dr. Lawrence Kaplan, who compared them to many other collections. The only historic Indian community known to grow both kinds of dark-colored teparies found in the cave was the Cocopa band that now lives around Somerton, Arizona.

When the Cocopa men went back to the ramshackle houses where their families lived near the border, they still had the bagful of seeds on their minds. They mentioned them to one elderly man, an invalid with an amputated leg.

"Seeds? We used to harvest many kinds of grasses on the delta, some of which we would plant there. But the river is different now. They have dammed it upstream. It has gone into their ditches. The floods don't flow the same way anymore, so those grasses can't grow."

But these grains. They must have been special. The guano miners tried to describe them to the tired old man.

"Who knows what they were? We'd have to hold them, taste them to know. It's been years since our people harvested those things. They're gone. It's too bad Sam Spa is not living among us anymore. He would have known. He's gone too...."

Sam Spa died in 1951 at the age of seventy-seven. Although of mixed ancestry—Pai Pai, Diegueño, and Mountain Cocopa—he grew up among the Kwakwarsh Cocopa band below the Río Hardy–Río Colorado confluence. For his first dozen years, he was immersed in the life of the delta. In his last dozen years, he recalled those days to a young student out of Harvard, William Kelly. His recollections had a tragic undertow to them. He remembered a river, a culture, and a riverine agriculture that had already been broken, dammed off, and invaded.

Sam Spa become a man amidst mudflat fields of *shimcha* that extended for more than eight kilometers along the channels of the delta. A patchwork of five plots, each one sown by a different man, edged the channels. The plots were up to 500 meters wide, and might take each man six days to plant, for the work was tedious and tricky. Young boys could hardly help with it.

The difficulty was that the panicgrass came up thickest if sown by hand. The planter needed his limbs to balance himself, to hold walking sticks to help pull him forward through the mud, to steady his footing or to lift himself up if he fell. The seeds were therefore blown from his mouth, and scattered by the wind or draining water. These seeds for planting were carried in a gourd hung around the neck.

After planting, the Cocopa men would remain nearby, fishing or weeding amaranth greens out of tepary and corn fields, while the women gathered the all-important mesquite beans and other wild plants. The Cocopa hardly weeded the panicgrass fields compared to those of other crops. Floodwashed panicgrass fields, Spa recalled, seldom had as many weeds as the more permanent plots of ditch-irrigated beans, grains, or cucurbits. Some wild panic, sour to the taste, may have come up as a crop mimic among the domesticated *shimcha*, but this they could have accidentally sown themselves. Or the droppings from last year's harvest could have volunteered. The Cocopa had little time and no reason to bother with them. They soon had to leave for the mountains to gather upland plants, and would return just before the crop would be ripe.

In October, as they trailed back to the delta, the river volume was only a sixth of what it was when the badger claws were left in the banks during June. Side channels had dried up. The mudflats were deeply cracked in some places. In the sandier loams where the panicgrass had been sown, the top few inches were dry to the touch, and shallow-rooted wild plants had begun to wilt.

The panicgrass itself had several tillers as well as a meter-high main stalk to support. All its energy was being shifted to the filling of the grain. As many as 2500 grains per plant were fleshing out and drying in the still-hot autumn sun.

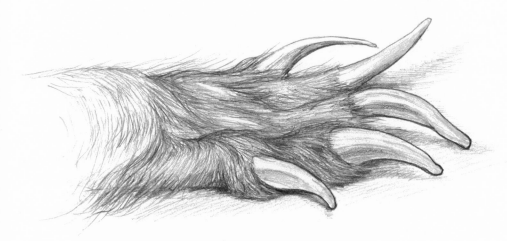

Sam Spa remembered that one man's *shimcha* harvest might fill a small bird's nest basket, roughly sixty centimeters tall and the same in diameter. Other Cocopa recalled yields at least six times that per plot. Alice Olds said she knew of a *shimcha* field that supplied thirty-five to fifty-five kilos of grain for her family one year. It was not their mainstay, but with grains containing around twelve and a half percent protein, *shimcha* was probably a fine addition to their seasonally variable diet.

The Cocopa was not the only Colorado River tribe that planted panicgrass as part of its flood-recession agriculture. When Hernando Alarcón made the first European contact with several Yuman-speaking peoples in 1540, he observed that "these people have, besides their maize, certain cucurbits and some grain like millet."

The comparison of Sonoran panicgrass to millet is fruitful, for this Old World grain is also a *Panicum* with similarly shaped grain. In certain of the Yuman tribes, it was said to have been scattered along the lower Colorado by the god Kumastamxo. Sonoran panicgrass cultivation did extend north beyond the Yuman speakers, into the Río Colorado floodplain territory of the Chemehuevi, north of Parker, Arizona. In 1904, desert scientist Robert Forbes boated down the Colorado, and found that the Chemehuevi had an agriculture at least as diverse as that of the tribes downstream:

> The Indians, especially the Chemehuevis, who are at present the most successful farmers on the river, grow beans, cowpeas, watermelons, Turkish winter muskmelons, martynias [devil's claw], a soft maize easily ground in their metates and maturing in about seven weeks, a black sweet corn, winter squashes, pumpkins, a little wheat, barnyard millet and a seedy grass, *Panicum sonorum,* useful for both grains and horse forage....Grass and millet seed is sown in the soft mud as soon as the river subsides, a method strikingly similar to that employed by the Egyptians in sowing their great forage crop, Berseem, along the Nile.

This crop diversity was soon to disappear along with the natural diversity of the lower Río Colorado. In retrospect, it is hard to underestimate the extent to which the lower Colorado was a vortex of life more powerful and productive than anything else between the Continental Divide and the Pacific Coast. Yet we know from naturalist Aldo Leopold that its richness was once so stunning that he could not emotionally bear to return there after the river had been starved by dams upstream. His account of a 1922 canoe trip through delta lagoons, already after the river had partially healed from the first few modern engineering operations to hit it, describes a calm before the storm of more pervasive assault:

'He leadeth me by still waters' was to us only a phrase in a book until we had nosed our canoe through the green lagoons....At each bend, we saw egrets standing in the pools ahead, each white statue matched by its white reflection. Fleets of cormorants drove their black prows in quest of skyward in alarm....All this wealth of fowl and fish was not for our delectation alone. Often we came upon bobcats...families of raccoons...[and] coyotes. All game was of incredible fatness. Every deer laid down so much tallow that the dimple along his backbone would have held a small pail of water.

The origin of all this opulence was not far to seek. Every mesquite and every tornillo was loaded with pods. There were great patches of a legume resembling coffeeweed [*Sesbania*?]; if you walked through these, your pockets filled up with shelled beans....The dried-up mudflats bore an annual grass, the grain-like seeds of which could be scooped up by the cupful....

If the grains of the annual grass which Aldo Leopold scooped up were by happenstance Sonoran panicgrass, he may have been the last scientist to see it growing in the Colorado River watershed. The river had already undergone dramatic changes in the two decades prior to Leopold's visit, but those which were to occur in the next two decades bordered on being irrevocable. For the Cocopa farmers and for the panicgrass seeds dependent upon the rich floods of the delta, their world was drying up.

They had always responded to the uncertainty of delta life, but this time, the scale of change was devastating. For the four centuries prior to 1890, the Río Colorado would meander from one side of the floodplain to the other. Yet it generally followed the same course between Yuma and the Sea of Cortez. Yields of crops fluctuated with the amount of runoff issued from the watersheds, but the delta's subsistence resources for the Cocopa and their neighbors remained rich. In addition to their range of crops, the Cocopa could draw upon fish, fowl, and wild stands of plants such as mesquite and Palmer's saltgrass. They had even gone to work for Fort Yuma riverboats between 1852 and 1877, only to return to delta farming and foraging when the railroads economically displaced the river transport.

By the 1890s, there remained at least 1200 Cocopa on or near the delta, but around them, a population of recent arrivals was becoming more evident. These Anglo-Americans were confident that they could organize themselves to engineer the great river into a series of ditches that would turn the Salton Sink into the Imperial Valley Irrigation District. The Cocopa and others had never tapped the river's "potentialities of production" that were "beyond any land in our country which has ever known the plow." The Imperial Valley boosters were sure that in the West, water is power. In a 1900 *Sunset,* they prophesied that "whoever shall control the right to divert these turbid waters will be the master of this empire."

Cocksure that they could control the Río Colorado, they began a flow of water into the Imperial Valley in June 1901, which ignited a land boom. Yet their canal headgate at the river was poorly placed for remaining free of silt and diverting sufficient water toward the below sea level areas of the old Salton Sink. In 1902, 1904, and 1905 new canals were dug. The more successful placement of the 1905 canal, combined with a spring of heavy rains in watersheds upstream, enabled the Imperial Valley developers to become the greatest overachievers of river diversion in the history of the West. By August 1905, the entire flow of the Colorado was washing a kilometer wide across the Imperial Valley, draining down to where prehistoric Lake Cahuilla once stood. As the Valley gained the Salton Sea, the Cocopa were left high and dry on the old delta.

Cocopa problems didn't stop when the riverbank was finally patched in February 1907, allowing some flow to return to the delta. The Wi Ahwir Cocopa had already begun to move to Mexicali when their habitat had been starved by the diversion. With the building of the Laguna diversion dam twenty kilometers above Fort Yuma in 1909, floods on the delta were decisively lessened, and the river never returned to what had been its main channel in previous decades. This forced the Hwanyak Cocopa who had remained in the midst of the delta to abandon their homes and resettle in Somerton, Arizona, and in San Luis del Río Colorado, Sonora.

Thus when Aldo Leopold canoed the delta lagoons in 1922, it was depopulated and degraded compared to what it had been in decades and centuries before. The evening-out of the river volume had allowed the establishment of introduced plants that may have been no more than scattered, inconspicuous seedlings from his canoe. These plants, known as salt cedars or tamarisks, were introduced from the Old World as an erosion-control plant. They rapidly began to colonize areas of reduced flow on the lower Colorado, and within decades became established hundreds of kilometers upstream on the Gila as well. Their rapid spread during the late 1920s probably reduced habitat available for the germination of panicgrass.

As the Great Depression hit America, a permanent depression hit the Cocopa, and with them, cultivated panicgrass. The Vacanora Canal, completed in 1929, established a channel for delta drainage that has persisted ever since. It was kilometers away from the old panicgrass fields. By the end of the 1931 drought, the old fields were bone-dry, since no summer rise in flow occurred that year at all. Then, with the completion of Hoover Dam in 1935 and Parker Dam in 1938, the river became so tamed that both Mexicans and Arizonans felt confident enough to begin to level and develop the delta for their own purposes. Scientists Edward Castetter and Willis Bell were soon to realize that these dams would in most years eliminate the remaining river overflow and make the practice of ancient flood-recession agriculture on the delta virtually impossible. Though they asked to see panicgrass fields during their fieldwork on the lower Colorado in the 40s, seeing a handful of seed in Yuma was the closest they came.

At the same time, the Cocopa were being swallowed up by those who had come into their homeland to practice "modern agriculture." An ejido farming cooperative was set up for the Baja California Cocopa by the Mexican government in 1936, but mestizos had completely taken it over by 1943, and many of the Cocopa who had at first participated in it moved to Sonora. There, they watched as San Luis del Río Colorado grew from its 1921 population of 175 people, to 4079 in 1950, to more than 50,000 by 1970. The binational Cocopa population dwindled to half of what it was prior to the disruption of the delta.

In the abstract terms of human ecology, the Cocopa had lost their traditional ecological niche. By 1970, nine out of ten Cocopa men in the U.S. were unemployed. Their meager reservation lands near Somerton were often leased out, so that few grew any food for direct consumption by their families. The foodstuffs that they received as government aid, conceded food scientists Doris Calloway and June Gibbs, were of "dilute nutritional quality." On their modern diets of snack foods and groceries purchased with food stamps from minimarkets, contemporary Cocopa lack vitamins A, B-6, C, panothenic acid, calcium, and iron. There are high incidences of liver, kidney, gall bladder, and respiratory diseases among them, as well as an unusual frequency of colitis, gastroenteritis, rabies, tuberculosis, and trachoma for a human population in a "modern country." The inactivity resulting from these ailments reinforces obesity, which in turn aggravates the extremely high expression of diabetes among adult Cocopa. As if ill physical health weren't enough, alcoholism and suicides frequently take their toll in the American Cocopa community.

The Mexican Cocopa communities are perhaps as poor, but they retain some traditional activities such as fishing to a greater extent. Nevertheless, they too live between a rock and hard place in the most marginal areas of the valleys of Mexicali and San Luis. When we visited the El Mayor Cocopa in 1983, almost the entire floor of their village was under water, with only hillside houses and those upon stilts remaining intact. They had no land that could be cultivated, since most everything below the cliffs had been flooded for months. The dams built upstream half a century before had accumulated so much silt in their reservoirs that they had become worthless for containing floods of any size. Thus water was let out over the dams, inundating what was left of Cocopa country.

We showed middle-aged Cocopa men and women specimens of panicgrass. For most of them, it was an historic oddity. One older women, though, asked for a few seeds to examine. She ground a few grains between her teeth.

"*That* would be good grinding, good flour, good food...." She tucked the other seeds into her apron pocket. Ancient seeds had returned to her community, but there was literally no place to plant them. The exotic salt cedars would again infest the mud flats as soon as these once-in-a-generation floods subsided.

William Kelly called them "the scattered descendants of a once powerful people who, from earliest known times...occupied the rich delta country of the Colorado River." For decades, there has hardly been an opportunity for this scattering to reseed itself on the delta.

What happens to the human spirit when that which once gave it productivity and meaning is cut off, disrupted upstream? A *Look* reporter recorded the uninterested Cocopa responses to the promise of new opportunities and adequate housing from a BIA bureaucrat. A fourteen-year-old Cocopa boy reiterated to his grandmother that she might get a new house.

"When?" she asked.

"Maybe two years," he replied.

"Oh, I die before then," she said. "Sometimes we feel we're already dead."

As Sonoran panicgrass was dying on the delta, the Depression was forcing out of business a number of the southern California vegetable growers who had responded to the irrigated land boom during the previous decades. The hard times which followed in the United States forced a change of plans for one southern Californian. And it was he who was soon to find a refugium of panicgrass left 800 kilometers south of the delta, in the barrancas of Chihuahua.

A family by the name of Gentry lost most of their California cantaloupe business as the Depression unraveled the financial supports for farmers. The two young Gentrys, after seeing their farming future crumble, considered college. With the family's financial position weakened, but both of them hard workers, the Gentry brothers resolved themselves to taking turns, one working packing fruit and vegetables while the other pored over the textbooks.

One of these brothers, Howard Scott Gentry, extended his interests beyond agriculture to biology and to the natural and cultural history of northwest Mexico. He came under the influence of the great geographer Carl Sauer at the University of California at Berkeley. Sauer and anthropologist A. L. Kroeber had each traveled down to southern Sonora in 1930, "rediscovering" a Uto-Aztecan-speaking tribe which they called the Varohio. These scholars must have immediately seen in Gentry a perceptive student tough enough to endure fieldwork in the back country with a minimum of institutional support. They encouraged him to visit this tribe in the canyon country above Sonora's coastal plains. With his savvy for biology and experience in farming, perhaps he could learn more of the Varohio plant lore and subsistence skills which their own brief visits had not been able to decipher.

Gentry found something quite different from the winter rainfall-dominated open desert he had known in southern California. He journeyed upstream from the southern edge of the Sonoran Desert, through a Sinaloan thornscrub transition, into the Short Tree Forest of the barrancas of the Sierra Madre. These subtropical deciduous forests covered an "endless series of ridges flanking their mother sierras," in a topography so complex "that a traveler scarcely knows just where he is hidden or from which direction the tortuous trail has brought him."

There, in the barrancas where cardon and old man's cactus abound, where thick-trunked pochote trees dangle cottonlike kapok from their branches, where lianas, orchids, and epiphytic bromeliads tangle, Gentry went to camp and hunt for plants and animals with the least-known tribe in northwestern Mexico.

Other than Gentry's ethnographic notes on these Indians, now known as the Warihio, there has been little published on their culture or agriculture. Numbering around 2000, they speak two dialects of a language closely related to that of the Tarahumara, the mountain tribe that is the second largest in the Uto-Aztecan family. They have maintained certain traditions which the more vulnerable Mayo and Piman tribes to the south, west, and north have long abandoned. While many of them have visited or worked in the coastal plain cities of Navajoa and Obregón, their life in the foothills and barrancas is one in which ancient subsistence skills have still retained their usefulness in the twentieth century.

Occasionally, Gentry would go with a guide and perhaps a pack mule or two into the remote headwaters of the Río Mayo watershed. On one such trip in September 1935, Gentry came upon a handful of houses stuck out on a steep projection in a deep barranca. This was the ranchería named Sahuacoa. There, elderly Warihios let him collect a rare grain plant that others had told him of—*sagui*. He soon realized that this was the same cereal that Edward Palmer had collected from Indian fields on the Colorado delta decades earlier—*Panicum sonorum*. His notes, jotted down while the Hoover Dam was placing the headstone on the grave of panicgrass cultivation in the U.S., give the sense that here that was something very valuable indeed:

> It is planted in the milpas or in the small gardens and like weywi [grain amaranth] is valued as a pinole or prepared and eaten in the same way. While generally known to both the Warihio and the barrancan Mexicans, it appears to be quite scarce and its culture is being lost. I found it only upon one occasion, tended in the small milpa of an old couple in Sahuacoa, near Guaseremos. They had only a few dozen plants, but sold me a few entire plants for samples. The plants were about 1 meter tall with large panicles of seeds just beginning to mature in late September. Like the corn, they had germinated in June with the first summer rains and would therefore require some 90 days to mature....With weywi and conivari [cultivated *Hyptis suaveolens*] it may have preceded maize in the Warihio culture...."

When I first spoke with Gentry about Sonoran panicgrass, it was more than forty years after he had pressed twelve robust plants from that milpa to make dried herbarium specimens. In the intervening period, he had worked for twenty years as the USDA's principal plant explorer collecting viable seeds from around the world for government genetic-conservation programs. He had thought about *sagui* many times since, he said, with a sad look in his eyes. He had collected herbarium specimens of a rare plant, but unlike his habitual activity later in life, he had not worried about obtaining any viable seed. The seeds on the herbarium sheets were now dead.

"I've always wondered if those Indians back in the barrancas still have seed of that domesticated *sagui*. Young man, if you ever travel down into the Río Mayo, be sure to tell me you're going beforehand. I want to give you directions on how to get to that Rancho Sahuacoa."

If young Howard Scott Gentry had felt challenged by the Sauer and Kroeber suggestion to visit Warihio country, a few of us in Tucson could hardly stand still long enough to make plans to visit Sahuacoa. For a combination four-wheel-drive and mule trip, I had no trouble enlisting Barney Burns, who already knew the region from his studies of tree-rings and traditional crafts, and Tom Sheridan, an ethnologist who doesn't feel comfortable unless he's in backcountry Sonora. Barney and I had already spoken with Warihio farmers at an all-night pascola dance near Buropaco. Yes, they knew *sagui,* though none of them personally grew it. Yes, perhaps someone still did, "mas allá," back in the sierras. That was all the extra encouragement we needed.

In early autumn of 1978, Barney's Scout brought us into Alamos, Sonora, in the middle of the night. Leaving around noon the following day, we hightailed it for the sierras, across the Río Mayo, up the switchbacks of the Cuesta de Algodones, to reach the pine forest on the Sonora-Chihuahua border—just in time for a nightful of rain. With the arroyos running, we were unsure how much farther we could drive. It turned out that we were just a short distance from the Byerly Ranch—the part-time home of an English-speaking European immigrant whose father had started an experimental orchard back in the sierras. His men directed us to nearby El Limón, a mestizo village where we rented mules and gained the help of a young guide who wanted to visit his aunt in Guaseremos.

When our group left early the next morning, knapsack stuffed with seedbags and a plantpress strapped over the mule's ass, I quickly came to realize why panicgrass may have had a chance to persist here. For every horizontal kilometer of distance, we had to ride five. Sometimes ten. The switchbacks wound us down a seemingly endless slope, we splashed across a meter-deep stream bubbling with rapids, and then started the climb up to a ridge that always seemed beyond our reach. In land like this, how could cash crops replace ancient ones? Who would ever have the endurance to carry their harvest out through such terrain? The Colorado delta, though once considered inaccessible, was at least flat. Once it had been drained, modern agriculture quickly made its inroads. Back here, it would be hard to find more than ten contiguous flat hectares within a fifty-kilometer stretch. What fields we saw were patchily placed, slash-and-burn milpas on 30- to 45-degree slopes. Each was an ideal island within which to preserve crop genetic diversity, for each was situated differently in terms of elevation, slope, aspect, and distance to others. Throw in the various house gardens where Warihio families still raised chia-like conivari, native tobacco, and amaranth, and we could see that the barrancas still harbored a diversity of habitats in which native crops could thrive.

Yet what we didn't see was panicgrass. It had remained as a minor crop, but farmers simply did not sow it every year. We learned that it grew best in the ashes of freshly torched, first year slash-and-burn milpas. We learned that Warihios attempted to rogue out most of the hairy, darker-seeded weedy plants, preferring the sweet taste of the domesticated *sagui.* They would harvest the mature plants by cutting the seedheads free with knives or sickles. These are placed on woven mats to dry in the sun, and then are rolled over with a smooth-sided stone to loosen the grain. The wind-winnowed cereal grain is later ground for tortillas, tamales, and atole, as well as the pinole which Gentry had reported. Yes, they still ate *sagui* foods, but didn't have any seed on hand for planting. No, they had no mature living plants to show us.

At Sahuacoa, the old couple which Gentry had met had long ago passed from the scene. Houses and garden fences were in a state of deterioration, sliding down the slope.

Yet not far way, at Guaseremos, both panicgrass and grain amaranth were still occasionally grown by a sizable, healthy Warihio farming community. We visited the family of our quiet teenage guide. He whispered something to his aunt. She went into the house, and returned with a bag holding half a kilo of seed.

The seeds within that bag have prospered. In a 1980 growout by Pat Williams of the U.S. Soil Conservation Service, more than thirty-five kilos were produced in a small plot—a yield equivalent to 440 kilograms per hectare. Looking out over the dense stand of nodding seedheads, I had to smile: they didn't look as though they minded being north of the border again.

But much of that harvest didn't stay north of the border. Anthropologist Eric Powell has distributed several kilos to Warihio villages and ranchos that had lost their supply of seeds. I have taken seed to their neighboring tribes, which historic documents suggest once had a milletlike grain called *sabi* as well. The seed supply has made it into U.S. and Sonoran state seed banks. And a cupful has been given to the Cocopa in Baja California.

In his herbarium in Papago Park, an anomalous chunk of desert stuck between downtown Phoenix, Tempe, and Scottsdale, Howard Gentry held a vial of golden viable seed up to the light. He went to one of his herbarium cabinets, and pulled a half-century-old specimen filed neatly in a manila folder.

"Ho! Old *Panicum sonorum*—there it is." He compared the seeds. "God, those were robust plants in that little milpa at Sahuacoa. Each filled up a whole sheet. Some were more than a meter tall, I'd say. You said you got out from Byerly's ranch clear to Tucson in one day! Pshaw, young man! It must have taken me five! Well, you brought me some seeds! Well, look at that!"

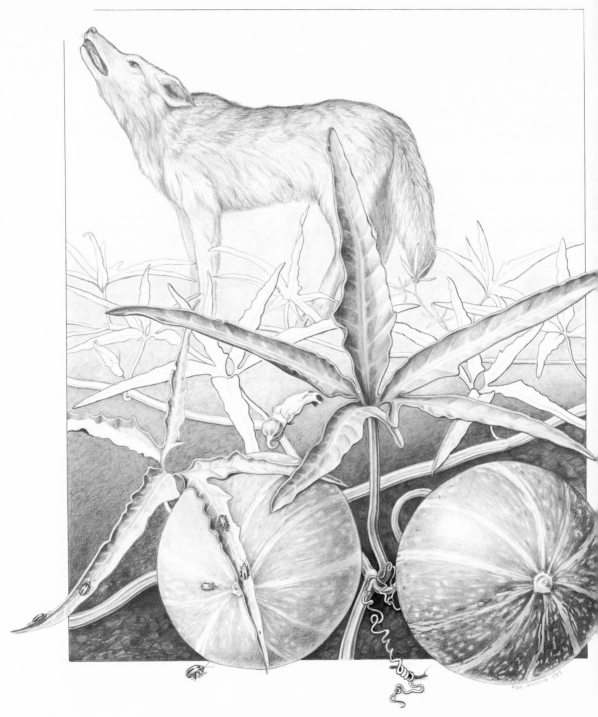

So that old trickster Coyote is even willing to trick innocent babies.
"It's for their own good," Coyote offers.

J UAN Espinosa held up two globular desert gourds in front of his chest. The
Baja California native posed there for a moment, dwarfed by the tall rock
walls of Canyon de Guadalupe, the stone image of the Virgin looking down
upon him.

"Do you know why they call these fruits *chichicoyotas*?" he asked in
Spanish, a quizzical look on his face.

"No, why?" I replied, sensing that his answer might be one of numerous folk
variants. The name *chichicoyota* is used for several species of wild gourds belonging
to the genus *Cucurbita*, as do pumpkins and squashes. This name helps to distinguish them from the unrelated, cultivated gourd, *Lagenaria siceraria*, which is
called *bule* in northwestern Mexico.

"*Pués*," he whispered, tipping his hat back, looking around to see if anyone else was within eye- or earshot. "The women use these when they want to
wean the babies. They just cut the fruits open, and rub a little of the bitter juices on
their *chichis*."

He wildly pantomimed a well-endowed mama in the act of squashing the foul-
smelling gourd pulp all over her breasts.

"Then when the baby tries to suck, he tastes the *amargidad*, and is tricked into
thinking that *chichis* are no good any more!"

Chichicoyota. Trickster breasts. In English, they're called coyote gourds.

So that old trickster Coyote is even willing to trick innocent babies. "It's for
their own good," Coyote offers.

Of course. Everything coyotes do is said to be for someone else's own good....

Cucurbitacins, the foul-smelling chemicals in wild gourds, are the most intensely bitter substances known to humankind. Taste panels can sense the presence of the foetid flavor of these oxygenated tetracyclic triterpenes in dilutions of one part per billion parts water. Accidental consumption of bitter cucurbit fruit has made people nauseous to the point that they simply collapse. Severe stomach cramps follow for three days, and diarrhea persists even longer. Cattle and sheep have died from eating too many wild gourds. A lethal dose of cucurbitacins for a small mammal is scarcely more than a millionth of the animal's body weight.

As wild gourds evolved, perhaps they selected cucurbitacins as a way of protecting their sprawling vines and developing fruit from being devoured by animals. In this manner, grazing animals are discouraged from damaging the plant to the extent that it would not survive to produce more fruit. In all but the most desertified areas, such as the Navajo Reservation, livestock generally avoids the foetid foliage of desert gourds. It is common to see large vines of the buffalogourd, *Cucurbita foetidissima,* or of the coyote gourd, *Cucurbita digitata,* persisting on overgrazed Southwestern ranges where more palatable plants have disappeared already.

There are critters that agree with Coyote that wild gourds' bitter juices are for their own good. They are the Luperini beetle tribe, including striped and spotted cucumber beetles and corn rootworms, all of which can metabolize cucurbitacins without ill effects. Ironically, the bitterness which evolved to repel animals not only serves to attract Luperini beetles, but also turns them into compulsive feeders. These beetles are a thousandfold more sensitive in detecting the exact location of cucurbitacins in plants than are the best chemical assays that researchers have been able to come up with. Once found, the bitter plant tissue is fed upon ravenously by the beetles, which become "trapped" by the spell of the cucurbitacins.

There is usually enough bitterness to go around, since cucurbitacins can be found in seedlings, foliage, fruits, and roots. However, in perennials such as the buffalogourd, the beetles may do more severe damage to new seedlings. Over several years, the beetle population builds up in a perennial stand. Whenever new seedlings volunteer, the beetles jump on them, for they are usually particularly rich in cucurbitacins. Most of the seedlings are gobbled up by cucumber beetles, thereby serving to slow population growth within the shadow of old mother plants. As such, the beetle predation on seedlings may regulate population densities of the gourds, reducing competition for scarce resources such as water. It seems that the Luperinids have coevolved with the bitter gourds, each contributing to the long term maintenance of the population of the other.

Foetid-scented, hard-shelled gourds. In the Sonoran Desert, they are represented by *Cucurbita sororia* in southern Sonora, *C. foetidissima* in the upland transition between desert and woodland, and the *C. digitata* group, centered on the coasts of the Sea of Cortez. All have globular fruit with brittle rinds and bitter flesh. The quintessential cucurbit for most folks is something altogether different: the sweet, soft-shelled, plump-fleshed squash or pumpkin of jack-o'-lantern fame. And yet wild gourds have been served humankind for many more millennia than their mild, watered-down, domesticated counterparts. One might ask how anything so bitter could be of use.

Indigenous medicinal uses of the roots, fruit, and foliage of the wild gourds abound. Perhaps it was the intense bitterness of the cucurbits that tipped medicine men off to the possibility that these plants had the power to kill or to cure. Yet it is not always clear whether the cucurbitacins themselves, or a complex of chemicals in gourds are the active agents. Saponins, steroids, tannins, and organic acids are associated with the cucurbitacins in cucurbit gourds and roots. An extract of the root of wild *Cucurbita foetidissima* induced the contraction of uterine muscles in a manner similar to that of drugs which are used to hasten childbirth. It also increased the degree of contraction in small intestines and caused vascular constriction in coronary vessels of the hearts of small mammals, according to H. C. Ferguson's pharmacognosy studies at the University of New Mexico. Cucurbitacins purified and isolated from plant tissues are known to retard the growth of certain kinds of cancerous tumors, changing the viability, morphology, and respiratory activity of tumor cells.

When Native Americans began to use wild gourds as medicines, they obviously had not had the chance to review the results of empirical laboratory investigations noted in the pages of *Cancer Research* and the *Journal of the American Pharmaceutical Association*. Yet they had their own empirical methods of testing dosages of various plant parts, accumulating data on a trial-and-error basis through time, and distilling this experience into certain folk prescriptions for use of these crude drugs. It is not surprising that there is considerable similarity in the medicinal uses of wild gourds from the tribes of the Sierra Madre Occidental to those of the Sonoran Desert and Colorado Plateau.

If the roots cause vascular constriction, as Dr. Ferguson's analyses indicate, cucurbits probably do affect hemorrhoids, ulcers, pus, and sores on horses' backs as the River Pima, Papago, Cahuilla, Western Apache, Acoma, and Laguna maintain. Their uses in the form of hot aqueous extracts for headaches, chest pains, fevers, toothache, and earache may also be related to their influence on coronary vascular constriction and blood flow. The cucurbitacins may be bitter enough to draw out worms and bedbugs, and are certainly effective as a purge, as Indians from Nevada to Chihuahua well know. The roots may function as a laxative due to the cucurbitacins as well as to structurally related saponins which serve as fecal softeners, if Dr. Robert Bye's interpretation is correct.

One cannot dismiss the medicinal value of cucurbits simply by assuming that people nowadays prefer manufactured, store-bought drugs. In medicinal herb markets across the U.S. Southwest, buffalogourd roots continue to sell for as much as seventy-five cents for a 15-cubic centimeter piece. From a gourd plant more than several years old growing in loose soil, one could harvest root fragments that would cumulatively retail at $150! Mexico's Institute for the Study of Medicinal Plants has already completed preliminary evaluation of gourd roots for pharmaceutical purposes, assuming that Mexico has much to gain in becoming medicinally self-sufficient as the cost of synthesized, highly refined imports continues to rise.

Many rural desert-dwelling people continue to use the undried gourd or the root of *Cucurbita digitata* for soap and bleach when they run out of store-bought soap, or the money to buy it with. When a couple of fresh gourds are cut in half and placed in a small wash basin filled with water, their saponins sud up into a froth that looks as good as any laundry soap foam I've ever seen.

I am less sure about the bleaching agent in the gourds, although Indian women assure me that "it's just like Clorox." One time when I was assigned to assist an Eastern photographer from a slick magazine in obtaining photos of useful desert plants, he asked if we could arrange for a photogenic Indian lady to wash clothes in a large bowl loaded with coyote gourds. We had driven across several reservations that week, and had met numerous families from various tribes, but had not gotten around to a gourd demonstration. Finally, we came to a village where a middle-aged spinster lived whom I knew, and with whom I had talked about the gourds before.

"Could you wash some clothes for me with the gourds later in the day?" the

Eastern photographer asked, wearing a brand-new cowboy hat and an unfaded, indigo-blue pair of designer jeans.

The spinster looked him over for a moment, then said, "Sure, you come back in an hour, and I'll have everything ready." We provided her with some gourds and left, so that the photographer could drop me off at a meeting nearby. He would go and work with her, then meet me in three hours. Or so we had planned.

He returned to the meeting hall after about an hour and a half, looking pale. As he pulled me out of the meeting, I whispered, "What happened?"

"Well I-I-I d-don't know exactly. I returned to the lady's little wikieup or what-ever you call it, and she was dressed to kill, I guess because you told her I was going to photograph her. So I asked her, 'Now, are you going to wash some clothes for me?' and she replied, 'Yessir. Take off your shorts.' 'My shorts?' I asked, confused. 'Your undershorts,' she smiled. 'My undershorts?' and I saw her coming toward me with the bowl of bobbing gourds and suds, as if I was going to...ummn, I don't know what. All I know is that I jumped into that truck as quick as I could, locked the door and took off before that woman could get her hands on my shorts."

"Well," I replied, pokerfaced. "That little Indian spinster was just trying to help you out. Maybe she thought you had some stains in your underwear that she could bleach out for you...."

Nonetheless, there are still diehards who will insist that wild gourds have no redeeming value. While collecting native cucurbit germplasm for Dr. W. P. "Buf-falogourd Bill" Bemis of the University of Arizona, I came across one such stalwart just between Marfa and the Big Bend of Texas. Driving along in my old stepside Dodge pickup on a late August day in 1977, I skidded to a stop in front of a ranchhouse after noticing a huge patch of buffalogourds lined up along the edge of an irrigated pasture of alfalfa. Politely, I went to the door of the ranchhouse, knocked, and when met by an old, tanned rancher, I asked if he would mind if I collected a few seed for some experimental plantings of wild cucurbits in Arizona.

"Seed?" the rancher asked in amazement, tilting his hat back enough to display his two-toned forehead. "Y'all want seed of them thangs?"

"Seed. Yessir."

"You can have more 'an seed. Take the whole damn plants. Git 'em outta here. Take all you want, if y'all are dumb enough to plant them in Arizona. Do you know how hard it is to keep them from sleezin' in on an alfalfa pasture? Do you know that yore jeans smell like some dawg puked up on you for days after just walkin' across them thangs? Son, take ever' itsy bit of them gourd plants, 'cus I don't ever wanna see 'em agin!"

If there has ever been a group of critters that overlook all this bitterness on account of some hidden sweetness, it is the digger bees. These diminutive, solitary bees base their entire economy on the nectar and pollen of wild cucurbits, eating no other food plant's products, either as larvae or as adults.

It is hard to overstate the allegiance that digger bees keep for cucurbit flowers. Male diggers may sleep all night in the withering blossoms. Their female counterparts sleep below the vines in ground burrows (hence the name digger), but wake up earlier than all other bees, beginning to lug around pollen long before the sun rises. When they are not actively pollinating or otherwise active in these blooms, the bees still hang around them. As pollination ecologist Steve Buchmann has observed, "Many times male *Xenoglossa* are neither working flowers for nectar nor grooming or sleeping in the flowers, but can be seen for long periods just hugging the [flower's] style."

In the twilight before dawn between June and October, you can hear bees in the cucurbit patches long before you can see them. They know what they are after. While we smell the rank odor of the vines themselves, the diggers are picking up the more delicate floral scent, the product of no less than thirty distinct chemicals, according to Buchmann. The blossoms open before daylight, and the diggers fly straight and true into their pleasant aroma. Catch a bee in your fist, then hold her in your cupped hands up to your face: you can sense the pollen-and-nectar-laden cucurbit blossoms, for their odor rubs off on the bees as they do their work.

Symbiosis. That's the best way to describe the relationship between gourds of the genus *Cucurbita* and digger bees of the genera *Xenoglossa* and *Peponapis*. These bees have the ability to work the flowers so early in the morning that light intensities and air temperatures are too low for other kinds of bees. In turn, the flowers are highly reflective, helping the diggers spot them even in the poorest light. The anthers of male flowers burst open well before sunrise to make pollen available for early risers. The blossoms also begin to close to exclude late-waking potential pollinators between eight and ten in the morning. Cucurbits produce huge spiny pollen grains that attach easily to these bees' body hairs as the bees groom themselves inside the gourd flowers. Crawling space inside the blossom is form-fit to the shape and size of the diggers. Moreover, Steve has discovered that half of the male flowers' nectar drains down to a groove rimming the bottom of the corolla. This food source can be reached only by bees with tongue lengths as long as those of the diggers.

There are tangible benefits from this reciprocal fine-tuning, as Steve Buchmann's careful observations have documented. The bees draw upon nearly all the sucrose-rich nectar that the male and female flowers exude. This provides the energy-rich fuel for their flying. In addition, a single gourd blossom may produce over 50,000 pollen grains. Steve's lab analyses have found these grains to be of high protein quality, providing the bees with excellent nourishment. Sometimes female digger bees harvest so much pollen that they have difficulty making it back into their burrows. By Steve's counts, a male bee carries well over a thousand grains with him as he moves away from one flower, but he may leave half this load on the sticky stigma of the next flower he visits. After visits by several different bees during the dawn hours, the stigma of a female flower gets loaded with more than ten thousand pollen grains. Odds are that enough of those grains will reach their destination to fertilize two or three hundred ovules in the developing fruit. A wild plant that leaves behind even fifty full-sized gourds at the end of a season has had the benefit of digger bees moving more than a hundred million pollen grains into its female flowers.

Each golden female blossom shrivels as the impregnated green gourd bulges below it. In a few weeks, these fruit have grown from golfball to nearly softball size. Then fruit size peaks, and the seeds take several more weeks to "after-ripen." Fruit color seasons from green to golden, then the sun bleaches it, and rain stains it.

As the desert heat finally breaks in late October, the gourd vines have had it. Drought, coolness, or powdery mildew have taken their toll. The brittle vines shrink to the size of twine, and break with any trampling. Long after the plant's green growth has vanished from sight, the bleached gourds still wait on the edges of arroyos, or hang from the branches of desert shrubs.

Desert gourds may linger in the same place for months, shrinking in size and hollowing as the bitter flesh dries into a stringy mass around the seeds. Then, when a rain brings a torrent to their floodplain abode, they suddenly find buoyancy and ride the crest of a flashflood. As they crash into boulders, hackberry trunks and arroyo banks, the gourds' brittle shells are punctured, pounded, and pulverized into irregular pieces. Seeds are scattered by the waters and scarified as the flood bedload scours their seedcoats. They may end up in any place the water has washed over, often under several inches of rich, flood-carried silt and detritus. If temperatures are in the right range, a number of seeds may germinate while the moisture is working on them. If they've landed in a suitable place and have caught the beetles off guard, a few will survive.

For the last 9,000 years, gourds in arid America have gotten around in another way—propelled by the hand of man. Long before Fernando Valenzuela signed up with the Los Angeles Dodgers, his Mayo Indian ancestors were pitching and ducking gourds the size of baseballs. Wild gourds appear preadapted to the adolescent human hand.

For any boy living in the desert, there has hardly ever been anything so irresistible. Joe Scheerens and I learned this the hard way, one fall while working for Buffalogourd Bill Bemis. We set out to count and harvest the different kinds of gourds grown adjacent to one another in minimally irrigated field plots. Not having finished the task late one Friday afternoon, we resolved to leave the piles we had already harvested on the fieldside, and resume the following Monday.

When we returned to the field on Monday, there were no piles to be seen. Gourds were strewn everywhere—buffalos in the coyote patch, coyotes in the buffalos, and in the road, the wash, and around the lab building as well. The gourd field had turned into some boys' battlefield over the weekend, and our piles of gourds had made great ammunition to fire at the attacking forces.

The kids had made great seed dispersal agents, whether that was their aim or not.

Gourds appear to have been carried intentionally, used as small containers, long before pottery reached North America. Small, precious items could be packed inside the hollowed shells, a curved piece strapped on like a lid, and several of them could be strung together with sinew or twine around a runner's waist. Ethnobotanist Richard Ford has suggested that wild gourds were so valuable as containers that there was no selection for more palatable flesh inside the gourds in North America until after pottery had been introduced. With the advent of clay containers, selection shifted toward cucurbit consumption, and edible thick-fleshed squashes took the place of hard shelled gourds in Indian gardens.

Yet even today, in regions of Mexico, other uses take precedence over consumption of cucurbit flesh. The seeds, washed in mineral lime water to remove any bitter, adherent pulp, are shelled and prepared for use in a variety of foods. Both wild gourd and cultivated squash seeds contain twenty-five to thirty-five percent oil, and over thirty percent protein. Today, cultivated squash seeds are snacked upon, blended into nutty butters or ground with other oilseeds, condiments, and fruit to make the sauce known as *mole pipián*. Ethnobotanist Laura Merrick has found the economic value of squash seeds for *mole* so high that some Mexican farmers keep only the seeds of cushaw squash, *Cucurbita mixta,* discarding the mature fruit or feeding it to barnyard animals.

Mountains of male squash blossoms enter Mexican markets each summer day, to be blended into soups, eggs, crepes and filled with cheese, dipped in batter, and fried as *rellenos*. Ethnobotanist Hugh Cutler recorded a similar use of wild buffalogourd flowers among the Hopi Indians of northern Arizona. Cutler observed that "a cornmeal cake is dropped inside a blossom and baked," a use that possibly predates the domestication of squashes. Vorsila Bohrer has noted that the Papago have not only used fresh gourd blossoms in soups, but also once made a habit of drying and storing them in pottery vessels.

In Mexico, squash-blossom consumption is as common as cactus, and has been for thousands of years. It is perhaps excusable that most American citizens don't know this (nor do many know that zucchinis are of Mexican, not Italian, origin), but it is outrageous that some paleobotanists don't recognize this. One time ethnobiologist Amadeo Rea was talking with a botanist who was identifying plant fragments from dried human feces found in a prehistoric ruin in the U.S./Mexico borderlands. The botanist had found some pollen in some of these coprolites that he had identified as *Cucurbita,* but couldn't understand how the pollen could get in or on human stool. He had asked Dr. Rea, "Could they have used the cucurbit blossoms for toilet paper? I just can't figure out why there is so much squash pollen in these samples....the pollen should be long gone by the time the squashes are mature and ready to eat."

"Who waits to begin eating until the squashes are ripe?" Amadeo questioned. "There are several good meals on the plant before the first fruit is even set!"

Squashes. Gourds. We usually think of them as two distinct kinds of plants, the former with huge edible fruit, the latter inedible, curious but relatively worthless. Historically, however, the wild gourds have been used for a wide variety of purposes. In their native ranges, there has been a continuity of uses, as camp-following gourds were domesticated and as they evolved into what we now call squashes and pumpkins.

According to cucurbitologist Laura Merrick, gene flow has also continued between wild gourds and their domesticated progeny within northwestern Mexico. It is surprising that this phenomenon was so long overlooked by botanists, for native farmers have observed it in their fields for years. Perhaps scientists too frequently assume that when they were first domesticated, squashes were not left in contact with cross-compatible wild progenitors. Once this assumption is made, it follows that wild gourds had stopped contributing additional genes to the evolution of their cultivated counterparts long ago.

After Laura jarred me out of this assumption, I had the chance to talk with an Indian farmer named José Valenzuela, who traveled with me into Warihio Indian territory in the Río Mayo of southern Sonora. At one brief stop we made on the edge of a slash-and-burn field in the foothills of the sierras, I asked José if a particular cucurbit vine we noticed was wild or cultivated. He brought a section of the vine with fruit on it back to the truck and looked at for a while before answering. Finally, he touched a piece of leaf to his tongue, and wincing at the bitter taste, confirmed his visual identification of it:

"She is called *chichicoyota* and she is wild. If *chichicoyota* is on the edge of your fields, and if you plant squashes, you are going to lose them. Their usefulness

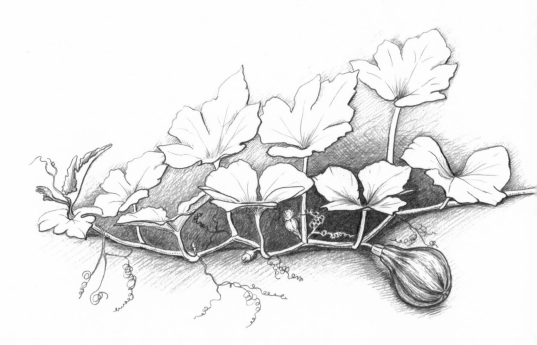

will be lost because the bad from the *chichicoyotas* will enter the good ones and spoil them."

"The bad?" I asked.

"The bitterness will go into the squashes. The trouble is that you can't tell which plants will have the bitterness just by looking at them. When the fruit begin to mature, then you know for sure, but it's too late."

"You can't eat the squash because of the bitterness?"

"Only the burros will still try to eat them after tasting such bitterness," he laughed.

José Valenzuela's comments suggested that the wild gourd in southern Sonora was not only cross-compatible with certain squashes, but that at least one wild-type gene, the Bi dominant, was occasionally showing up where it shouldn't have been—in the flesh of domesticates long ago selected to be sweet. Laura Merrick has demonstrated that by hand-pollinating cultivated *Cucurbita mixta* flowers with pollen from wild gourds of the *Cucurbita sororia* group, hybrid fruit with viable seeds could be produced. However, the bitterness infrequently shows up as a mutation in cultivated squash that are not exposed to wild gourds. How could we be sure that this was not what was occurring in southern Sonora?

The task was to find other wild traits that might be leaping into the gene pool of cultivated squashes, or domesticated traits that had flowed into wild populations. In January of 1984, I had the luck of coming across confirmation of genetic introgression that Laura expected between these two kinds of cucurbits. While driving into Onavas, Sonora, on our way to visit the few remaining Pima Indian families who live there, Amadeo Rea and I spotted some huge wild gourds hanging from trees on the edge of an Indian field. I brought one of them into the village that night and was told it was called *chicoyota*. Could the teenage boys in the family collect me a sackful in the morning, I asked. I'd be glad to pay them ten pesos a-piece, I offered just before we all retired for the evening.

The following morning the boys were off early. By nine, the first gunny sack of gourds arrived. "That's fine," I said, looking at the incredible variability within the bag. Some looked like truly wild gourds, round, golden with bristly fluted stems attached. Others looked like miniature *mixta* squashes, green-and-white-striped, with thickened, corky stems. The boys saw that I was pleased. Before I could mention to them that the one sackful would be enough, they were off again, heading for the field edges.

Unfortunately, they told their friends how pleased I was. By eleven in the morning, three more gunny sacks full of gourd-squash variants had arrived, and four boys were insisting that there were plenty more that they could find for me. I painfully forked over several thousand pesos in total, and a couple hundred pounds of cucurbit were packed into the van. Pedro Estrella, a Pima-speaking elder, looked at the fruit the day just before we drove off.

"Ahh, *chicoyotas.* They inoculate our squashes with their bitterness. *Adavi* is what we call them in Pima. We try to weed them out of our fields, but there are always some in the scrublands nearby, so we are never rid of them."

Pedro lived more than 250 kilometers away from José Valenzuela, but they told essentially the same story: Coyote gourds can spoil your squashes!

What Pedro and José had no way of knowing was that the squashes also occasionally make some of the gourds sweet. No one but a scientist would want to taste the gourds to find out. But when Thomas Whitaker saw the truckload of gourds brought back from Onavas, as we were measuring all their morphological variations, he had one suggestion: "Gary, if you're going to document introgression with the cultivated squashes, you should really taste the gourd flesh to see if any have expression of the non-bitter gene."

"But there's hundreds of them, Dr. Whitaker! I bet that most of them are bitter. I don't know if our tongues can survive that much bitterness!"

"All I'm saying is that it's the best trait you can use to confirm the flow of genes into the wild gourds. I don't think I could stomach it either, but it's just a suggestion."

Bettina Martin, a Harvard graduate who was assisting me with measuring the gourds, fortunately came up with a way to subsample for taste the gourds that looked like they had the best chance of being non-bitter. She noticed that some of the wild gourds had seeds without the fringelike margin that is characteristic of all wild gourds in the *sororia* group from central Sonora on southward. This marginless seedcoat is also known from a rare Pima Indian cushaw squash landrace of *mixta* in central Sonora and adjacent Chihuahua. It turned out that twenty-six of the twenty-eight gourds with marginless seedcoats had sweet, edible flesh. Many of them had corky stems and color patterns similar to that of the cushaw squash grown in the area by Indians for centuries.

When we reported these findings back to Laura Merrick, she felt that further study of the Onavas gourd population might give her additional perspective on several years of experimental hybridization work that she had begun with squashes and gourds. We decided to visit Onavas several times during the following growing season in an attempt to document whatever we could of the ecology of *chicoyota* and *calabasa* interactions. Did these two kinds of plants grow so close together that bees regularly cross-pollinated them? Or were the few apparently hybrid fruit collected the winter before simply flukes?

When a team of cucurbit crazies arrived in Onavas in late July, we saw wild gourds everywhere we looked near homes, dumps, fallow fields, and roadsides. Yet we were surprised and somewhat disappointed that farmers hadn't yet planted many squash. What we later realized is that the longer the farmers wait to plant squash, the less overlap there would be with flowering time of the bitter gourds. Although this late planting gave us little to do on our first visit, they weren't timing their crops for us—they were probably hoping to minimize further crossing with the bitter gourds! If farmers planted squashes at the same time that the first summer rains brought up volunteering gourds in the same field, it would be hard to know what to weed out later on. As Pedro Estrella conceded, the leaves and flowers on one look like those of the other. Immature and intermediate-sized fruit frequently fool him, he conceded. "If you go to your field and cut open one that looks like a squash, but is bitter, throw the plant away," Pedro advised us. "It will affect your others."

Returning over a month later, we saw that farmers had tried to cut the vines of most of the gourd plants that crawl towards their field edges. Nevertheless, they missed a few gourd seedlings that sprouted late in their plantings, and had not begun to reach all the wild vines sprawling around in the scrubby periphery of their fields. Although most of the gourd blossoms had already set fruit by the time the squash plants had begun to produce female flowers, there were still a few wild plants that could have been contributing pollen to these females. Were these volunteering plants within bee's reach of cultivated squashes? We were soon to find out.

Steve Buchmann had provided us with several brightly colored powders, which when placed under a black light, glowed even when small amounts were present. Late on an autumn afternoon, we found a number of wild and cultivated cucurbit blossoms in or near Pedro's field that looked as though they were to open the following day. Before leaving the field, we marked the plants, and tied their near-ready blossoms shut with yarn, so that no insects could visit them before we dusted them with the colored powder early the next day.

Early the next day was very early—four in the morning. We stumbled through the night to the marked plants, pulled off the yarn, and dusted one color of powder into each of several strategically located wild or cultivated blossoms. As the solitary bees began to stir and move from one now-open blossom to the next, a band of coyotes howled from the arroyo closest to us. "What are you doing to our plants?" I guessed they were wondering. "Are you trying to catch us in the act of tricking the squashes?"

By mid-morning we had our evidence in hand—a solitary bee which had earlier visited the wild gourd blossom marked with blue powder sixty meters away from us landed in the squash blossom nearest to where we were sitting. "What's a blue bee doing here?" our teammate Cindy Baker asked. Laura and I dove for the little fella, so laden with pollen and powder that after visiting the squash flower, she had had difficulty getting in the opening of her underground nest below the plant. We scooted her into a jar. Later in the day, with the black light in hand in a dark room, Laura checked the mixtures of colors found in dozens more flowers from all over the field and the adjacent desert. We noted that perhaps a second cultivated squash species, *Cucurbita moschata,* had been visited by these same bees. The farmers' late planting seemed to work to reduce the amount of fertilization of squashes with wild pollen, since we failed to encounter female squash blossoms tainted by "wild colors" that particular day. Yet under slightly different conditions, with a few more mornings of sampling, it was probable that the wild plants' pollen would reach a female squash flower's stigma at the right time.

Laura and I could finally visualize a limited amount of reciprocal gene flow between wild and cultivated cucurbits in Sonora—a process that botanists Edgar Anderson and Leslie Hubricht termed "introgressive hybridization" in a classic study in 1938. In special environments, two closely related plant taxa incorporate genes from one another through sporadic hybridization followed by backcrossing. In this case, the field edge brings the floodplain-dwelling wild gourds together with ancient varieties of squashes, and both become more morphologically variable than either is when found in isolation. Green, yellow, white, and striped squashes and gourds, warty or smooth-skinned, exist in Sonoran Indian fields in a greater variety of shapes and sizes that can be found anywhere else in the world.

This morphological and chemical variability makes one wonder: are the cultivated squashes picking up any genes from their wild relatives that make them any more resistant to heat, drought, or disease? What does the coyote inject into these foodstuffs besides a little bitterness now and then?

Surprisingly, bitterness itself may become the first economic product of the wild gourds that are currently being domesticated by arid lands scientists. In 1946, Larry Curtis suggested that xerophytic gourds may make excellent crop candidates for the third of earth's land surface where rainfall and irrigation water supplies are limited. He recognized the oilseed potential of buffalogourd from earlier work, but discovered a second possible product as well: the starch in the huge tuberous roots. Breaking off a buffalogourd root exposed in a five-meter-deep waterbreak in Spur, Texas, the curious Curtis put a couple of drops of iodine on the cut root surface. The vivid color change of the iodine indicated that a rich supply of starch was present, now known to make up about fifty-five percent of the root's weight. Since man-sized roots are produced by gourd plants in the matter of a few years, Curtis and followers imagined commercial production of desert gourds based on three major economic products: a cooking oil, a protein-rich seedmeal feed left after oil extraction, and an industrial starch from the root to be used in food thickeners, cleansers, and other specialized products.

Thanks to the work of Buffalogourd Bill Bemis and chemists Jim Berry and Charles Weber, Curtis lived long enough to see the first improved hybrid buffalogourds come into field trials of five hectares or more. Since Curtis's death in 1979, buffalogourd has advanced as an experimental crop in Mexico and the United States, with field trials attempted in countries such as Australia as well. It may become the first new crop for arid lands to be bred to improve nutritive quality—Allen Gathman and Bemis have demonstrated the feasibility of producing hybrids with seed oils higher in polyunsaturates. This is an important step if desert gourd oil is ever to be adopted by health-conscious consumers as a cooking oil, since coronary heart disease is negatively correlated with polyunsaturate intake. Root starch extraction, uses, and harvest techniques are being worked out to the extent that buffalogourds could have a future economic niche in semiarid areas receiving 250 millimeters of rainfall or more. In such areas, they require a little less than two acre-feet of irrigation for a commercial crop. Finger-leaved coyotegourds, capable of long-term survival in extremely arid regions receiving less than 100 millimeters of rainfall, can probably produce economic crops with less irrigation, particularly in hot coastal deserts where buffalogourd barely survives.

Despite their promise, seed and root products have not been enough to attract commercial growers to invest in plantations of these gourds in the United States or

Mexico. Instead, what may propel them into commercial cultivation is the hidden trick of their bitterness—that of attracting beetles.

The Luperini tribe includes some of the worst agricultural pests in the world—corn rootworm and cucumber beetles do millions of dollars worth of damage to crops in the United States and Mexico each year. Corn rootworm is the most serious maize pest in the upper Midwest, and cucumber beetles spread bacterial wilt to nearly all cultivated cucurbits. The economic costs of pesticides to control this damage are enormous, and hidden ecological costs—due to nonspecific chemicals' killing beneficial insects—are immeasurable.

Fortunately, a group of integrated pest management scientists at the University of Illinois realized that the beetle-attracting abilities of cucurbitacins may be useful in controlling crop damage. Through planting trap crops of wild gourds near vulnerable commercial crops, farmers can insure that nearly all the beetles will remain feeding on the wild gourds rather than in the other crops. Or by extracting the cucurbitacins and associated attractants and mixing them with a small fraction of the insect poison that would normally be used, corn crops can be sprayed with a chemical mixture that specifically attracts and kills Luperini beetles while hardly affecting beneficial insects.

Not surprisingly, these scientists have found that the hardy desert gourds of the Sonoran region are among the most ample producers of cucurbitacins with minimal economic costs. They are good to the bitter end, too, from the gourd hanging in the tree to the very tip of the swollen root two meters deep. Even Coyote couldn't predict this one— desert gourd's most disagreeable product may be the one that assures it a place in the future of American agriculture.

BIBLIOGRAPHIC ESSAY
INDEX

Bibliographic Essay

T HE following notes are of two sorts. The first set of references under any chapter are more comprehensive articles or books on the topic, which may provide a number of quotes or interpretations used throughout the chapter. Many are somewhat technical, but those of interest to the lay reader have the title marked with an asterisk. The rest pertain to specific quotes or arguments which cover only small portions of the text. These are derived from personal communications as well as technical articles. Again, any nontechnical references quoted or interpreted are marked with an asterisk. There may be particular facts in the text that are derived from unpublished data collected by the writer, or from technical reports not cited here. Serious scholars may contact me (c/o Native Seeds/SEARCH, 3950 W. New York Dr., Tucson, AZ 85745) to obtain this additional information, as well as information on availability of seeds.

Desert Plants as Calories, Cures, and Characters

In order to place the Sonoran Desert region and its native peoples in perspective, I suggest the ecological summary edited by David E. Brown, "Biotic Communities of the American Southwest: United States and Mexico," *Desert Plants*, 4(1–4): 1–382 (1982); the cultural overviews edited by Alfonso Ortiz, "Southwest," *Handbook of the North American Indians* Volume 10* (Washington, D.C., Smithsonian Institution, 1983), and the archaeological, ethnobotanical, and ethnohistorical essays in Spanish edited by Beatriz Braniff C. and Richard S. Felger, *Sonora: Antropología del Desierto* (Mexico: Instituto Nacional de Antropología e Historia, 1976).

Another part of the conversation regarding mesquite foods in the Río Bavispe appeared in my article "Mesquite: Another Great American Legume," *Organic Gardening**, April, 1984, pp. 114–115.

The extent to which the average American diet has changed in the last century is outlined in a booklet by Letitia Brewster and Michael F. Jacobson, *The Changing American Diet** (Washington D.C.: Center for Science in the Public Interest, 1978). For a perspective on dietary change within one Sonoran Desert culture, refer to "Gathering," pp. 99–109 in my book *The Desert Smells Like Rain: A Naturalist in Papago Indian Country** (San Francisco: North Point Press, 1982).

As an overview of wild food plant diversity in the Sonoran Desert, see Richard S. Felger's pioneering essay, "Nutritionally Significant New Crops for Arid Lands: A Model from the Sonoran Desert," pp. 373–403 in *Priorities in Child Nutrition in Developing Countries,* Jean Mayer and J. W. Dyer, eds. (New York: UNICEF, 1975). I have written on the little-recognized native plants independently domesticated in this binational region, summarizing recent work in the essay, "Native Crop Diversity in Aridoamerica: Conservation of Regional Gene Pools," *Advances in Economic Botany,* Volume 2 (New York: The New York Botanical Gardens, 1985).

I am serious in asking why natural history writers have not spent as much time considering the characters of plants as they have animals. The two most evocative considerations of desert animals as *personae* may be Barry Lopez's essays *Desert Notes: Reflections in the Eye of a Raven** (Kansas City: Sheed, Andrews and McMeel, 1976) and Jack Schaefer's *Conversations with a Pocket Gopher** (Santa Barbara: Capra Press, 1978).

On images of plants such as jimsonweed being common to rites of a number of Sonoran cultures, see the notes to the penetrating essay by Donald M. Bahr and J. Richard Haefer, "Song in Piman Curing," *Ethnomusicology* 22: 89–122.

The high incidence of diabetes among Southwestern Indians is discussed by K. M. West, "Diabetes in American Indians and other native populations in the New World," *Diabetes* 23: 10–18 (1974). The historic decrease in their diets of high fiber legumes such as teparies and mesquite has been well documented; see, for instance, G. P. Nabhan, C. W. Weber, and J. W. Berry, "Legumes in the Papago-Pima Indian diet and ecological niche," *The Kiva* 44: 173–190. What hasn't been made obvious is that the gumlike dietary fibers in the seed of mesquite, chia, tansy mustard, *Plantago* and other native seeds probably served to flatten post-prandial blood glucose curves to which diabetics are vulnerable, in a manner similar to the antidiabetic effects of beans described by A. R. Leeds, "Legume diets for diabetics?" *Journal of Plant Foods* 3: 219–223 (1981).

How cultures identify with and select certain foods over others is the topic of a fascinating book by Peter Farb and George Armelegos, *Consuming Passions: The Anthropology of Eating* (New York: Houghton-Mifflin, 1980). The Nicholas Hildyard quote is from his essay "There's More to Food than Eating," *The Ecologist* 5: 166–168 (1978).

The relatively greater water use of crops grown by commercial agriculture in arid zones is discussed in relation to Western water scarcity by David Pimental, S. East, W. L. Chao, E. Stuart, O. Dintzis, G. Einbender, W. Schlappi, D. Androw, and K. Broderick, "Water Resources in Food and Energy Production," *Science* 32: 861–866 (1982).

The Creosote Bush Is Our Drugstore

The creosote essay and drawing are dedicated to Kevin Dahl, who whetted our interest in this plant through his article "Creosote," *Coyote,* p. 14 (April, 1977). I drew heavily on International Biome Program creosote research results reported in two anthologies: *Creosote Bush: Biology and Chemistry of* Larrea *in New World Deserts,* Tom J. Mabry, J. H. Hunziker, and D. R. DiFeo, Jr., eds. (Stroudsberg, Pa.: Dowden, Hutchinson and Ross, 1977); and *Larrea,* Enrique Campos Lopez, Tom J. Mabry, and Salvador Hernandez Tavizon, eds. (Mexico: CONACYT, 1981).

The Pima-Papago creation story elements regarding greasewood were derived from two versions. The first was recorded by Juan Delores and published in Dean and Lucille Saxton's *O'othham Hoho'ok A'agitha: Legends and Lore of the Papago and Pima Indians* (Tucson: University of Arizona Press, 1973). The second is excerpted in Ruth Underhill's *Papago Indian Religion* (New York: Columbia University Press, 1946).

Thomas Van Devender's paleoecological studies of distribution changes in desert plants confirm that *Larrea* has been in the Sonoran Desert much longer than IBP studies understood it to be. Although he has not published this argument in its entirety, Van Devender's writings remain the finest guide to the evolution of desert flora in relation to changing weather patterns. See, for instance, T. R. Van Devender and W. G. Spaulding, "Development of vegetation and climate in the southwestern United States," *Science* 204: 701–710 (1979).

Frank Vasek's work has generated an effort by the Nature Conservancy and the California Native Plant Society to preserve the land around King Clone, as highlighted in a nationally released article by the *Los Angeles Times's* Sandy Banks, "Setting Aside a Place for the World's Oldest Living Organism," *Tucson Citizen*

Magazine, January 5, 1985, p. 1. Frank Vasek's own technical writings on the possible age of King Clone have been more reasonable, though not conservative enough for the paleoecologists such as Van Devender. See F. C. Vasek, "Creosote Bush: Long-Lived Clones in the Mohave Desert," *American Journal of Botany* 67: 246–255 (1980).

For *Larrea* chemistry and potential uses, the best summaries are CONACYT's *Larrea* book noted above; Tom J. Mabry and Charles F. Bohnstedt, "*Larrea*: A Chemical Resource," pp. 213–235; and Barbara N. Timmerman's "*Larrea*: Potential Uses," pp. 237–245. I thank Barbara for explaining to me the ecological functions of creosote resins, and for trying to temper my enthusiasm for its potential medicinal uses.

Regarding historic Sonoran ethnomedicinal documents, a new translation (into Spanish) of Ignaz Pfefferkorn's *Descripción de la Provincia de Sonora** has been accomplished by Armando Hopkins Durazo (Hermosillo: Gobernador del Estado de Sonora, 1983) and surpasses Theodore Treutlein's 1949 out-of-print translation into English published by the University of New Mexico Press. With the other essential Sonoran ethnohistory containing detailed data on plant uses, it is advisable to ignore the erroneous plant identifications in the recent translation of *Rudo Ensayo* by Alberto Pradeau and Robert R. Rasmussen (Tucson: University of Arizona Press, 1980). I prefer the more scholarly notes in Spanish by Margarita Nolasco Armas, Teresa Martinez Penaloza and America Flores accompanying *El Rudo Ensayo* (Mexico: SEP/INAH, 1977).

More recent ethnobotanical treatments of creosote ethnobotany include: David Prescott Barrows, *The Ethno-botany of the Coahuilla Indians of Southern California* (Chicago: University of Chicago Press, 1900); Lowell John Bean and Katherine Siva Saubel, *Temalpakh: Cahuilla Indian Knowledge and Usage of Plants** (Banning, Calif.: Malki Museum, 1972); Joseph G. Lee, "Papago Indian Medicine," *Arizona Medicine* 17: 87–89 (1960); Edward F. Castetter and Ruth M. Underhill, "The Ethnobiology of the Papago Indians," *The University of New Mexico Bulletin* Number 275 (1935); and Richard S. Felger and Mary Beck Moser, "Seri Indian Pharmocopoeia," *Economic Botany* 28: 414–436 (1974).

Additional creosote economic botany notes can be found in the Barbara Timmerman article noted earlier, in H. S. Colton's "Life History and Economic Possibilities of the American Lac Insect, *Tachardiella larrea*," *Plateau* 16: 20–44 (1943), and in A. Krochmal, S. Paur, and P. Duisberg, "Useful Native Plants in the American Southwestern Deserts," *Economic Botany* 8: 3–20 (1954).

Mexico's interest in creosote bush has been highlighted in Carlos Zolla's article entitled "Gobernadora," *Medicina Tradicional* 3: 1–4. Additional research has been initiated through the medicinal plants project of IMSS, a Mexican government agency.

Janice C. Beatley's original report on greasewood persistence appeared in 1965. It was subsequently confirmed and discussed in her article, "Effects of Rainfall and Temperature on the Distribution and Behavior of *Larrea tridentata* (Creosote-Bush) in the Mohave Desert of Nevada," *Ecology* 55: 245–261 (1974).

The Palms in Our Hands

The following articles are perhaps the most comprehensive articles on North American desert palm oases: R. J. Vogl and L. T. McHargue, "Vegetation of California Fan Palm Oases on the San Andreas Fault," *Ecology* 47: 532–540 (1966); James W. Cornett, "Coachella Valley's Thousand Palms," *The Nature Conservancy News** 34(5): 18–21 (1984); Reid Moran, "Palms in Baja California," *Environment Southwest* 478: 10–14 (1977); and Amadeo M. Rea, Gary Paul Nabhan, and Karen L. Reichhardt, "Sonoran Desert Oases: Plants, Birds, and Native People," *Environment Southwest** 503: 5–9 (1983). I am among those who consider *Washingtonia robusta* to be no more than an interfertile variant of *W. filifera,* and as such it does not deserve the species rank it customarily has been given. We thank Anita Alvarez Williams for palm literature and an introduction to Baja California Norte.

On the love-hate relationship that many have with the Palm Springs area, I recommend Bruce Fessier's "P.S., I Love You," *Desert Magazine* 44(1): 16 (January 1981). For landscape architects' dogma on the use of even-aged fan palms as "punctuation," and bastardization of the oasis concept, see Mary Rose Duffield and Warren Jones, *Plants for Dry Climates: How to Select, Grow and Enjoy* (Tucson: HP Books, 1981).

On the relationship between native Sonoran basketry and *huki* huts, there are several interesting references: David M. Brugge, "History, Huki and Warfare: Some Random Notes on the Lower Pima," *The Kiva* 26(4): 6–16 (1961); Timothy Dunnigan, "Lower Pima," pp. 217–229 in *Handbook of the North American Indians,* Volume 10; and Bernard L. Fontana, Edmond J. P. Faubert, and Barney T. Burns, *The Other Southwest: Indian Arts and Crafts of Northwest Mexico** (Phoenix: Heard Museum, 1977).

The ages of palms in North America and retreat of their early plant associates remain controversial. The most pertinent reference is D. I. Axelrod's "Outline History of California Vegetation," in *Terrestrial Vegetation in California,* Michael G. Barbour and Jack Major, eds. (New York: Wiley-Interscience, 1977).

Francisco Patencio's Cahuilla folklore is published as *Stories and Legends of the Palm Springs Indians** (Los Angeles: Times-Mirror Press, 1943).

The frequency of and reasons for burning palms have been discussed by several authors, most notably: S. B. Parish, "A Contribution toward a Knowledge of the Genus *Washingtonia,*" *Botanical Gazette* 44: 408–44 (1909); Victor J. Miller, "Arizona's Own Palm: *Washingtonia filifera,*" *Desert Plants* 5(3): 99–104 (1983); and the earlier-cited article by Vogl and McHargue and book by Bean and Saubel.

Miguel del Barco's *The Natural History of Baja California**, tr. Froylan Tiscareño (Los Angeles: Dawson's Book Shop, 1980) is among the finest early ethnobotanical documents available to desert enthusiasts. The introduction of this translation by Miguel Léon-Portillo is an important piece of scholarship.

Elza Iva Edwards' historical research on the Coachella Valley uncovered many of the obscure records of the demise of Palm Springs. His book *Lost Oases along the Carrizo* (Los Angeles: Westernlore, 1961) provides a chronicle of much of the destruction. His *Desert Voices: A Descriptive Bibliography* (Los Angeles: Westernlore, 1958) is a comprehensive survey of literature on this area.

For details of the prehistory and history of one California oasis, I recommend Martyn D. Tagg, *Excavations at the Oasis of Mara: Archeological Investigations at Joshua Tree National Monument* (Tucson: Western Archeological and Conservation Center, 1983). At the 1984 Palm Oasis Symposium in Palm Springs, Richard Vogl passed out a one page handout that included the quoted material here on palm oases in the absence of Native Americans. Dr. Vogl may be contacted for this fine piece of (unpublished?) writing at the Biology Department at California State University at Los Angeles.

Randall Henderson's books include *Palm Canyons of Baja California* (Glendale: La Siesta Press, 1971) taken from his numerous articles in *Desert Magazine*; and the more reflective *Sun, Sand and Solitude: Vignettes from the Notebook of a Veteran Desert Reporter* (Los Angeles: Westernlore, 1968).

The Western Yellow Bat, *Lasiurus ega,* is not an obligate of palms, but has a strong association with them north of Mexico, in southern Arizona and California at the limits of its range. See R. Mark Ryan, *Mammals of Deep Canyon: Colorado Desert, California* (Palm Springs: The Desert Museum, 1968); and Roger W. Barbour and Wayne H. Davis, *Bats of America* (Lexington: The University Press of Kentucky, 1969).

Mescal Bacanora: Drinking Away the Centuries

For an overview of agave utilization in the Americas, nothing excels Howard Scott Gentry, *Agaves of Continental North America* (Tucson: University of Arizona Press, 1982). The bacanora ecotype of *Agave angustifolia* was formerly called *A. pacifica*, and is discussed in detail as such in Gentry's earlier work, *The Agave Family in Sonora* (Washington, D.C., USDA Agricultural Handbook 399, 1972). For details regarding the making of bacanora at one site, see Conrad Bahre and David Bradbury, "Manufacture of Mescal in Sonora, Mexico," *Economic Botany* 34(4): 391–400 (1980). Yet mescal distillation technology is wonderfully improvisational, so the description here often deviates from that of Bahre and Bradbury in order to portray variants found in the Río San Miguel and Río Bavispe. For a notion of mescal bootlegging's contribution to local economies, I have relied on Thomas E. Sheridan, *Economic Inequality and Agrarian Conflict in the Municipio of Cucurpe, Sonora, Mexico* (Tucson, University of Arizona dissertation, 1983), also available from University Microfilms International in Ann Arbor.

This chapter is inspired by the work of Donna Howell, who enlisted me to learn more of wild agave depletion in Sonora while consulting on the BBC film, *The Bat, the Blossom, and the Agave.* The bat/agave symbiosis story draws upon her own fine writing, including "Bat-Loving Plants, Plant-Loving Bats," *Natural History** 85(2): 52–59 (1976); "Flock Foraging in Nectar-Feeding Bats," *American Naturalist* 114: 23–49 (1980); and several unpublished works.

The conservative water use and other aspects of agave physiology continue to be studied by Park Nobel and his students William Ehrler and Tony Burgess. Two early papers by Park Nobel are essential reading: "Water Relations of Flowering of *Agave deserti*," *Botanical Gazette* 138(1): 1–6 (1977); and "Water Relations and Photosynthesis of a Desert CAM Plant, *Agave deserti*," *Plant Physiology* 58: 576–582 (1976). For a readable account of water-saving adaptations in agaves and cacti, I recommend Mark A. Dimmitt, "The Succulent Strategy," *Sonorensis** 4(3): 5–12 (Summer 1982).

Attraction of pollinators to agaves has been discussed in relation to erection of tall inflorescences and nectar and pollen rewards by W. M. and M. V. Schaffer in two articles: "The Reproductive Biology of Agavaceae I. Pollen and Nectar Production in Four Arizona Agaves," *Southwestern Naturalist* 22: 157–167 (1977); and "The Adaptive Significance of Variations in Reproductive Habit in Agavaceae II. Pollinator Foraging Behavior and Selection for Increased Reproductive Expenditure," *Ecology* 60: 1051–1069 (1979).

At the international conference held in Los Angeles, I presented data indicating that wild agaves suitable for mescal production are being rapidly depleted from Sonora. The proceedings from this meeting, *Bioresources and Environmental Hazards of the United States-Mexico Borderlands,* will appear under another (undetermined) title. My provisional estimate was based on multiplying an active bootlegger's annual harvest of mature rosettes by the average number of active bootleggers in two municipalities; I then extrapolated to include all municipalities in Sonora where *Agave angustifolia, A. palmeri,* and *A. shrevei* are being actively harvested today by Sonora's rapidly growing population.

Agave remains in coprolites have been discussed by E. O. Callen in several articles, including "Food Habits of Some Pre-Columbian Mexican Indians," *Economic Botany* 19: 335–343 (1965).

The discovery of extensive agave cultivation in south-central Arizona is discussed by Suzanne Fish, Paul Fish, Charles Miksicek, and John Madsen, "Prehistoric Agave Cultivation in Southern Arizona," a paper submitted to *Desert Plants.*

Native agave cultivation in the protohistoric period can be documented through the seventeenth-century observations of Andrés Pérez de Ribas, *My Life among the Savage Nations of New Spain,* tr. Tomas Antonio Robertson (Los Angeles: The Ward Ritchie Press, 1968). Baja California agave cultivation cannot be ruled out; see the intriguing journal note by Junipero Serra, *Diario: The Journal of Padre Serra (1769),* tr. Ben F. Dixon (San Diego: Don Diego's Libreria/Associated Historians of San Diego, 1967).

Sandfood and the Sand Papago: A Wild Kind of Mutualism

For overviews on sandfood, see my earlier review, "*Ammobroma sonorae,* an Endangered Parasitic Plant in Extremely Arid North America," *Desert Plants* 2(3): 188–196 (1980); and Franklin A. Thackery and M. French Gilman, "A Rare Parasitic Food Plant of the Southwest," *Annual Report of the Smithsonian Institution* 3094: 409–416 (1931). Recently, George Yatskievych has taxonomically revised the Lennoaceae, and this plant should now be properly called *Pholisma sonorae.* See his "A Conspectus of the *Lennoaceae,*" *Phytologia* 52: 73–74 (1982).

Colonel Andrew Belcher Gray and party left several kinds of documents which form a mosaic regarding sandfood's "discovery" by modern science. First, there is the "Letter Addressed to Dr. John Torrey, on the *Ammobroma sonorae* (Communicated to the Association by Dr. Torrey)," *Proceedings of the American Association for the Advancement of Science* 9: 233–236 (1855). More important, perhaps, is the *Report of Colonel Gray to the Texas Western Railroad Company* (Cincinnati: Texas Western Railroad Company, 1856) reprinted by Westernlore Press, Los Angeles, with reminiscences by Pete Brady, who accompanied Gray.

The actual first report of people eating sandfood is that of Juan Mateo Manje, *Luz de Tierra Incognita**, ed. and tr. Harry Karns (Tucson: Arizona Silhouettes, 1954).

Regarding the dismal results of germination research on sandfood, see David Jackson Cothrun, *Some Aspects of the Germination and Attachment of* Ammobroma sonorae, *a Root Parasite of Desert Shrubs* (Stillwater: Oklahoma State University, 1969), also available from University Microfilms International, Ann Arbor.

For background on environment and vegetation in the dunes area, I recommend Richard S. Felger, "Vegetation and Flora of the Gran Desierto," *Desert Plants* 2(2): 87–114 (1980); and a forthcoming natural history of dune fields in North America by Janice Bowers.

Carl Lumholtz is most often quoted regarding Sand Papago subsistence, but he failed to meet any of these people who were still making their living in the Gran Desierto. See his *New Trails in Mexico** (New York: Charles Scribner's Sons, 1912, reprinted by Rio Grande Press, Glorieta, New Mexico). More detailed are the notes left by Thomas Childs, who actually fished and gathered with the Sand Papago: "Sketch of the Sand Indians," *The Kiva* 19(2–4): 27–39 (1955); and unpublished interviews in the Amerind Foundation archives, Dragoon, Arizona. Recent interviews with the elders quoted here, done for the National Park Service by Childs' daughter Fillman Bell and Ofelia Zepeda, give an even richer perspective on Sand Papago life. So far, only part of these documents has been published: Fillman Bell, Keith M. Anderson and Yvonne G. Stewart, *The Quitobaquito Cemetery and Its History* (Tucson: Western Archaeological and Conservation Center, 1980).

For confirmation that off-road vehicles are a serious threat to dune and desert plant life, I recommend Roger A. Luckenbach and R. Bruce Bury, "Effects of Off-Road Vehicles on the Biota of the Algodones Dunes, Imperial County, California," *Journal of Applied Ecology* 20: 265–286 (1983). See also Richard M. Iverson, Bern S. Hinckley, and Robert M. Webb, "Physical Effects of Vehicular Disturbances on Arid Landscapes," *Science* 212: 915–916 (1981); and Harold Koopowitz and Hilary Kaye, *Plant Extinction: A Global Crisis** (Washington, D.C.: Stonewall Press, 1983).

Mesquite as a Mirror, Mesquite as a Harbor

This chapter is dedicated to journalist Jane Kay, whose articles on mesquite in the *Arizona Daily Star* have sensitized many to the value of this tree and the side effects of control programs aimed at it. Most of the time, I will be referring to the velvet mesquite (*Prosopis velutina*) of the northern Sonoran Desert. When speaking of the Southwest in general, however, the range and uses of *Prosopis glandulosa* will also be included. Both taxa were formerly considered varieties of *Prosopis juliflora*, a name which actually refers to a species far to the south of the Sonoran Desert. I have drawn heavily upon the IBP synthesis, *Mesquite: Its Biology in Two Desert Ecosystems,* B. B. Simpson, ed. (Stroudsburg, Pa.,: Dowden, Hutchinson and Ross, 1977), and especially to Richard Felger's chapter, "Mesquite in Indian Cultures of Southwestern North America," pp. 150–175.

For a history of the San Ignacio church just a few kilometers north of Magdalena, Sonora, I have relied on the help of Dr. Charles Polzer and on the book by Paul M. Roca, *Paths of the Padres through Sonora: An Illustrated History and Guide to Its Spanish Churches* (Tucson: Arizona Pioneers' Historical Society, 1967).

Most of the early historic accounts I have quoted are discussed in Richard Felger's "Mesquite in Indian Cultures," or in Anita Alvarez Williams, *Travelers Among the Cucapa* (Los Angeles: Dawson's Book Shop, 1975).

For a history of criollo-derived longhorn, corriente, and chinampo cattle, see the fine book by John E. Rouse, *Criollo: Spanish Cattle in the Americas* (Norman: University of Oklahoma Press, 1977). On the hardiness of these desert-evolved cattle ecotypes, see Aurelio Martínez Balboa, *La Ganaderia en Baja California Sur* Vol. 1 (La Paz, B.C.S.: Editorial J. B., 1981).

Paul Martin's views on large herbivores and mesquite are most eloquently presented in his essay "Vanishings, and Future, of the Prairie," *Geosciences and Man* 10: 30–49 (1975). It appears that one reason that mesquite seeds are aided by large herbivores is that vertebrate gut juices kill bruchids. See O. T. Solbrig and B. B. Simpson, pp. 38–40 in B. Simpson, ed., *Mesquite.* Ecologist Dennis Cornejo is quoted in Bil Gilbert's fine essay, "A Tree Too Tough To Kill," *Audubon** 87(1): 84–97 (1985).

Bill Doelle's work on mesquite replacement by wheat and subsequent Pima population growth remains unpublished. However, his dissertation contains fascinating caloric estimates on mesquite harvesting investments and rewards. See

William H. Doelle, *Nonriverine Resource Use: An Archaeological Study in Western Papaguería* (Tucson: University of Arizona, 1980). For mesquite in Pima and Papago country, see also Amadeo Rea, "Velvet Mesquite," *Environment Southwest** 486: 3–7 (1979); and G.P. Nabhan, C. W. Weber, and J. W. Berry, "Legumes in the Papago-Pima Diet and Ecological Niche," *The Kiva* 44 (2–3): 173–190 (1979).

For the historic woodcutting story, the best synthesis is a recent manuscript by Conrad J. Bahre and Charles F. Hutchinson, "Impact of Historic Fuelwood Cutting on the Semidesert Woodlands of Southeastern Arizona," available from the authors.

Mesquite as a phreatophytic indicator of groundwater is discussed by O. E. Meinzer, "Plants as Indicators of Groundwater," *Washington Academy of Sciences Journal* 16: 553–564 (1926); and Kirk Bryan, "Change in Plant Associations by Change in Groundwater Level," *Ecology* 9: 474–478 (1928). See also B. I. Judd, "The Lethal Decline of Mesquite on the Casa Grande National Monument," *Great Basin Naturalist* 31: 153–159 (1971).

Mesquite bosque wildlife is discussed by several authors: L. W. Arnold, *An Ecological Study of the Vertebrate Animals of the Mesquite Forest* (Tucson: University of Arizona Master's Thesis, 1940); Alan Phillips, Joe Marshall, and Gale Monson, *The Birds of Arizona* (Tucson: University of Arizona Press, 1964); and Thomas E. Gavin, *An Ecological Study of a Mesquite Bosque* (Tucson: University of Arizona Master's Thesis, 1973). I thank Julio Betancourt for discussion of mesquite bosque declines on the Santa Cruz River.

A review of mesquite scrubland conversion costs are in Bill E. Dahl's "Mesquite as a Rangeland Plant," pp. A-1–A-20, in *Mesquite Utilization*, Harry Parker, ed. (Lubbock: Texas Tech University College of Agricultural Sciences, 1982). Several articles by Jane Kay cover the mesquite conversion controversy in southern Arizona, as does Bil Gilbert's article mentioned earlier. See Jane Kay, "Mesquites Yielding to Grass, and Controversy," *The Arizona Daily Star,* p. E–1 (September 23, 1979); and "Papagos May Try to Kill Mesquites with Herbicides," *The Arizona Daily Star,* p. B–1 (June 4, 1980). A more positive view of mesquite's value is found in John R. Lacey, Phil R. Odgen, and Kennith E. Foster, *Southern Arizona Riparian Habitat: Spatial Distribution and Analysis* (Tucson: University of Arizona School of Renewable Natural Resources and Office of Arid Lands Studies, 1975).

Prosopis seed persistence is discussed by S. Clark Martin, "Mesquite Seeds Remain Viable After 44 Years," *Ecology* 29: 393 (1948).

Mesquite insect users are surveyed in three chapters of B. B. Simpson, ed., *Mesquite:* R. Gates and D. F. Rhoades, *"Prosopis* Leaves as a Resource for Insects," pp. 61–82; B. B. Simpson, J. L. Neff, and A. R. Moldenke, *"Prosopis* Flowers as a Resource," pp. 84–106; and J. M. Kingsolver, C. D. Johnson, S. R. Swier, and A. L. Teran, *"Prosopis* Fruits as a Resource for Invertebrates," pp. 108–121. B. B. Simpson and J. L. Neff also discuss mesquite's influence on other plants in "Vascular Plants," pp. 122–132.

Mesquite's role in nitrogen cycling is not understood in its entirety. See Peter Felker and P. R. Clark, "Nitrogen Fixation (Acetylene Reduction) and Cross Inoculation in 12 *Prosopis* (Mesquite) Species," *Plant and Soil 57*: 177–186 (1980). Also of interest is R. C. Barth and J. O. Klemmedson, "Amount and Distribution of Dry Matter, Nitrogen, and Organic Carbon in Soil-Plant Systems of Mesquite and Palo Verde," *Journal of Range Management* 35(4): 412–418 (1981).

For a discussion of mesquite's benefits on desert field crops, see Wendell Berry's wonderfully observant essay, "Three Ways of Farming in the Southwest," pp. 47–76 of *The Gift of Good Land: Further Essays Cultural and Agricultural** (San Francisco: North Point Press, 1981); and my dissertation, *Papago Fields: Arid Lands Ethnobotany and Agricultural Ecology* (Tucson: University of Arizona Press, 1983), also available from University Microfilms International, Ann Arbor.

For discussions of packrats and their mesquite caches, see Richard S. Felger and Mary Beck Moser, "Seri Indian Food Plants: Desert Subsistence Without Agriculture," *Ecology of Food and Nutrition* 5: 13–27 (1976); and Edward F. Castetter and Willis H. Bell, *Yuman Indian Agriculture* (Albuquerque: University of New Mexico Press, 1951).

Organpipe Cactus: Bringing in the Rainfeast

This cactus is known as *Lemairocereus thurberi* in all but the most recent literature. It is now recognized as a species in the larger genus, *Stenocereus,* a relationship which holds up anatomically, as discussed by Arthur C. Gibson and K. E. Horak, "Systematic anatomy and phylogeny of Mexican columnar cacti," *Annals of the Missouri Botanical Gardens* 65: 999–1057 (1978). For the single best ethnobotanical study of cacti, I recommend an article which first attracted me to this field: Richard Stephen Felger and Mary Beck Moser, "Columnar Cacti and Seri Indian Culture," *The Kiva* 39 (3–4): 257–275 (1974). I quote and paraphrase extensively from this article and related material in a new book by the same two authors, *People of the Desert and Sea: Ethnobotany of the Seri Indians* (Tucson: University of Arizona Press, 1985).

For Papago use of cactus wine in their Vi'igita ceremony, see E. H. Davis, *The Papago Ceremony of the Vikita* (New York: Museum of the American Indian, Indian Notes and Monographs, 1920). An update on Quitovac plant use indicates that organpipe jam continues to be made and sold there. See Gary P. Nabhan, Amadeo M. Rea, Karen L. Reichhardt, Eric Mellink, and Charles F. Hutchinson, "Papago Influences on Habitat and Biotic Diversity: Quitovac Oasis Ethnoecology," *Journal of Ethnobiology* 2 (2): 124–143 (1982).

For bat/organpipe relationships, there are several references: Stanley M. Alcorn, S. E. McGregor, and George Olin, "Pollination Requirements of the Organ-pipe Cactus," *Cactus and Succulent Journal* 34: 134–137 (1962); Donna Howell, "Adaptive Variation in Diets of Desert Bats Has Implications for Evolution of Feeding Strategies," *Journal of Mammalogy* 61 (4): 730–733 (1980); and E. Lendell Cockrum, *Bat Populations and Habitats at the Organ Pipe Cactus Monument* (Tucson: National Park Service/University of Arizona, 1981).

For plant associates of organpipes in the north, see T. W. Mulroy, *Perennial Vegetation Associated With the Organ Pipe Cactus in Organ Pipe Cactus National Monument* (Tucson: University of Arizona Master's Thesis, 1971). For columnar cacti shape and freezing at the northern edges of their ranges, see Richard S. Felger and Charles H. Lowe, "Clinal Variation in the Surface-Volume Relationship of the Columnar Cactus *Lophocereus schottii* in Northwestern Mexico," *Ecology* 48: 530–536 (1967); and Park S. Nobel, "Morphology, Surface Temperatures, and Northern Limits of Columnar Cacti in the Sonoran Desert," *Ecology* 61(1): 1–7 (1980).

For the Pérez de Ribas quote, see *My Life Among the Savage Nations*. It is not clear where organpipe's southern limits are, but their distribution in Baja California Sur may be nearly as far south as that on the mainland. See Ann Zwinger's *A Desert Country Near the Sea* (New York: Harper and Row, 1984) for comments on its natural history in the Cape Region. Miguel del Barco's *Natural History* and Homer Aschmann's "The Central Desert of Baja California: Demography and Ecology," *Ibero-Americana* 42 (1959) include the quotations on pitahaya in Baja California. Richard Felger, however, feels that *Pachycereus* seeds, rather than those of *Stenocereus,* were most frequently rescued off rocks.

Carl Lumholtz wrote the unforgettable *Unknown Mexico** (Charles Scribner's Sons, 1902) after five years in the Sierra Madre. Campbell Pennington is his spiritual descendant, further exploring the ethnobiology and material culture of several Sierran cultures over three decades' time, as he reports in several books: *The Tarahumara of Mexico: Their Environment and Material Culture* (Salt Lake City: University of Utah Press, 1963); *The Pima Bajo of Central Sonora,* Volumes One and Two (Salt Lake City: University of Utah Press, 1979–1980).

Felger and Moser were preceded in Seri country by several interesting ethnologists, each with his own idiosyncrasy. See, for instance, Gilg's Seri encounters, edited and translated by Charles Di Peso and Daniel Matson as "The Seri Indians in 1692 as Described by Adamo Gilg, S. J.," *Arizona and the West* 7 (1): 33–56 (1965); W. J. McGee, *The Seri Indians of Bahía Kino, Sonora, Mexico* (Glorieta, N. M.: Rio Grande Press, 1971), reprinted from his earlier Bureau of American Ethnology report, with notes by Dr. Bernard Fontana; and Edward Davis and E. Yale Dawson, "The Savage Seris of Sonora," *Scientific Monthly* 3 (4): 158–178 (1945). Work in process on Seri ethnohistory by Thomas Sheridan will, I hope, put to rest once and for all the view that the Seri were savage, mystical cannibals.

Amaranth Greens: The Meat of the Poor People

For the technical background upon which much of this chapter is based, see Chapter Five of my dissertation, *"Oidag C-ed I:waki:* Vegetation Diversity and Plant Use in Fields." I also coordinated the writing of a booklet for the Papago on wild greens: Meals for Millions Foundation and Save the Children, *O'odham I:waki: Wild Greens of the Desert People** (Tucson: Meals for Millions Southwest Program, 1980). The use of wild *Amaranthus palmeri* and related species should not be confused with the cultivation of domesticated grain amaranths, which in the Southwest dates back to the time of Christ. For a summary of historic grain amaranth growing in the Greater Southwest, see my "Amaranth Cultivation in the U.S. Southwest and Northwest Mexico," pp. 129–133 in *Second Amaranth Conference Proceedings** (Emmaus, Pa.: Rodale Press, 1979). More recent archaeological analyses by Vorsila Bohrer and Charles Miksicek suggest that both *A. hypochondriacus* and *A. cruentus* were cultivated prehistorically north of the present-day international boundary.

Miguel del Barco was more open-minded than other Jesuits, as his *Natural History* reminds us, but Dr. Spicer's rather severe generalization about the frontier Jesuits may still be pertinent. See Spicer's *Cycles of Conquest: The Impact of Spain,*

Mexico, and the United States on the Indians of the Southwest, 1533–1960 (Tucson: University of Arizona Press, 1962).

Tom Sheridan's quote from a Cucurpeño is from his dissertation *Agrarian Conflict...in Cucurpe,* and the Lumholtz quote is from his *New Trails in Mexico.*

On fluctuations in amaranth pollen contributions to the Tanque Verde Wash area, see R. J. O'Neal and G. D. Waller, "On the Pollen Harvest by the Honey Bee (*Apis mellifera* L.) near Tucson, Arizona (1976–1981)," *Desert Plants* 6(2): 81–128 (1984).

James Ehleringer and colleagues have been studying *Amaranthus palmeri* and its desert adaptations for several years now. See his "Ecophysiology of *Amaranthus palmeri,* a Sonoran Desert Summer Ephemeral," *Oecologia* 57: 107–112 (1983); his review article with R. W. Pearcy as senior author, "Comparative Ecophysiology of C3 and C4 Plants," *Plant, Cell and Environment* 7: 1–13 (1984); and his synthesis, with I. N. Forseth as junior author, "Solar Tracking by Plants," *Science* 210: 1094–1098 (1980).

For *Amaranthus palmeri's* nutritive value, see Ruth Greenhouse, *The Iron and Calcium Content of Some Traditional Pima Foods and the Effects of Preparation Methods* (Tempe: Arizona State University Master's Thesis, 1979); and Edith M. Lantz, Helen W. Gough, and Mae Martha Johnson, "Nutritive Values of Some New Mexico Foods," *New Mexico Agricultural Experiment Station Bulletin* 379 (1947). These are summarized and compared with other greens in the MFM/SCF *O'odham I:waki.*

An analysis of potential nitrate and oxalate poisoning from amaranths was published by Ara Der Marderosian and seven colleagues as "Nitrate and Oxalate Content of Vegetable Amaranth," pp. 31–41, *Proceedings of the Second Amaranth Conference* (Emmaus, Pa.: Rodale Press, 1980). My desert amaranth nitrate and oxalate data remain unpublished.

Recent archaeobotanical analyses are finally clarifying or debunking the somewhat whacky interpretations of amaranth evidence that certain Americanists have developed in the past, such as Henry Dobyns's "Altitudinal Sorting of Ethnic Groups in the Southwest," *Plateau* 47 (2): 42–48 (1974). Amaranth cultivation by Lowland Pima and Mayo, and by the prehistoric Hohokam, as well as many "montane cultures," proves that there was no elevational sorting—amaranths were grown in several environmental zones. Bohrer's ongoing ethnobotanical studies of pollen and macrofossils continue to shed light on the amaranth weeds and cultigens.

Dick Marsh's observations appeared as "Two Contemporary Papago Recipes of Indigenous Plants and the American Southwest Botanical Implications," *The Kiva* 34 (4): 242–246.

Tepary Beans and Human Beings at Agriculture's Arid Limits

Tepary beans are the subject of a special symposium volume which I edited, "The Desert Tepary as a Food Source," *Desert Plants** 5 (1): 1–64 (1983). The bibliographies prepared by the several authors in this volume cumulatively comprise the most complete reference source on this bean.

The Pinacate tepary story is derived from an ill-fated technical manuscript written by myself and Charles Hutchinson, "Native American Runoff Agriculture at Its Most Arid Margins," still unpublished. Sneak previews of its results have been included in my dissertation, in a soon-to-be-published book by Julian Hayden, and in journalistic pieces by Charles Bowden in *The Tucson Citizen* and by Exequiel Escurra in *Uno Mas Uno* and *El Imparcial*. See also Noel Vietmeyer's "Saving the Bounty of a Harsh and Meager Land," *Audubon* 87 (1): 100–107 (1985).

The Lumholtz quote is from *New Trails in Mexico*. The best climatic summary of the Pinacate vicinity is in Exequial Escurra and Valdemar Rodrigues, "Rainfall Patterns in the Gran Desierto, Sonora, Mexico," *Journal of Arid Environments* (in press).

The Opata derivation of the word tepary is suggested in Jean B. Johnson, *The Opata: An Inland Tribe of Sonora* (Albuquerque: University of New Mexico Publications in Anthropology 6, 1950). The Papago story is in Saxton and Saxton's *Legends and Lore*.

Phaseolus filiformis is placed in perspective in R. Buhrow's "The Wild Beans of Southwestern North America," *Desert Plants* 5(2): 67–72, 82–88. Neil Ackerly's archaeological find remains unpublished, but will appear in his Arizona State University dissertation. Other wild bean uses are discussed in G. P. Nabhan, J. W. Berry, and C. W. Weber, "Wild Beans of the Greater Southwest. *Phaseolus metcalfei* and *P. ritensis*," *Economic Botany* 34(1): 68–85 (1980).

Wild tepary harvests are discussed in G. P. Nabhan and R. S. Felger, "Tepary Beans in Southwestern North America: A Biogeographical and Ethnohistorical Study," *Economic Botany* 32(1): 2–19 (1978). The Sara Villalobos quote and other Seri Indian data are from Felger and Moser's *People of the Desert and Sea*.

Relating beans to diabetes and the nutritional needs of Southwestern Indians are G. P. Nabhan, C. W. Weber, and J. W. Berry, "Variation in the Composition of Hopi Indian Beans," *The Ecology of Food and Nutrition* 16: 135–152 (1985); Leeds, "Legume Diets for Diabetics?"; Mary Petrie Greene, *A Diet of the Prenatal Papago* (Tucson: University of Arizona Master's Thesis, 1972), and J. C. Scheerens, A. M. Tinsley, I. R. Abbas, C. W. Weber, and J. W. Berry, "The Nutritional Significance of Tepary Bean Consumption," *Desert Plants* 5(1): 11–14, 50–56 (1983).

For the Birds: The Red-Hot Mother of Chiles

The primary references for chiltepines and native chiles in the Greater Southwest are Bill Bridges, *The Great American Chili Book* (New York: Rawson and Wade, 1981); J. A. LaBorde and colleagues, *Presente y pasado de chile en Mexico* (Mexico: Instituto Nacional de Investigaciones Agricolas, 1982); and my article, "Chiltepines! Wild Spice of the American Southwest," *El Palacio* 8 (2): 1–5. Jean Andrews' new book, *Peppers: The Domesticated Capsicums** (Austin: University of Texas Press, 1984) and Cynthia Baker's University of Arizona research on chiltepines, now in process, eclipse all these in technical detail. Although taxonomists have called the wild variety of *Capsicum annuum* many names, we follow Hardy Eshbaugh, whose systematic and evolutionary works on this genus are exemplary. See, for instance, W. Hardy Eshbaugh, Sheldon I. Guttman, and Michael J. McLeod, "The Origin and Evolution of the Domesticated *Capsicum* Species," *Journal of Ethnobiology* 3(1): 49–54.

The ethnological note from Wendell C. Bennett is from his book with Robert M. Zingg, *The Tarahumara: An Indian Tribe of Northern Mexico* (Chicago: University of Chicago Press, 1935). The Pfeffercorn quote is in Theodore Treutlein's translation of *Descripción de Sonora*. The Cora creation story was translated by Daniel Matson, and introduced by Kieran McCarty, "Franciscan Report on the Indians of Nayarit," *Ethnohistory* 22(3): 193–222 (Summer 1975).

Chile chemistry is reviewed by Joseph A. Maga, "Capsicum," *Critical Reviews in Food Science and Nutrition* 6(2): 177–196 (July 1975). Their location of most pungent compounds in the crosswall of the chile is discussed by V. L. Huffman, E. R. Shadle, B. Villalon, and E. E. Burns, "Volatile Components and Pungency in Fresh and Processed Jalapeño Peppers," *Journal of Food Science* 43: 1809–1811 (1982). Capsaicin as a pain-reliever and anti-irritant is discussed in an article by

Claudia Wallis, "Pain," *Time,* pp. 64–66 (June 11, 1984); and more technically by Jan M. Lunberg and Alois Saria, "Capsaicin-Induced Desensitization of Airway Mucosa to Cigarette Smoke, Mechanical and Chemical Irritants," *Nature* 302: 251–253 (1983).

Cowboy Milton is the subject of James Evetts Haley's *Jeff Milton: A Good Man with a Gun* (Norman: University of Oklahoma Press, 1948).

Capsaicin appears to function differently from the alkaloids associated with other solanaceous plants in terms of repelling predators. For chile/potato beetle interactions, see Ting H. Hsiao and G. Fraenkel's two papers, "The Role of Secondary Plant Substances in the Food Specificity of the Colorado Potato Beetle," pp. 485–493; and "Selection and Specificity of the Colorado Potato Beetle for Solanaceous and Nonsolanaceous Plants," pp. 493–503, *Annals of the Entomological Society of America,* 61: 493–503 (1968).

Barbara Pickersgill discussed bird dispersal of wild chiles in her article, "The domestication of chili peppers," pp. 433–450, *The Domestication and Exploitation of Plants and Animals,* P. J. Ucko and G. W. Dimbleby, eds. (London: Gerald Duckworth, 1969).

Howard Scott Gentry discusses chiltepines in both of his early books, *Río Mayo Plants* (Washington, D.C.: Carnegie Institution of Washington Publication 527, 1942); and *The Warihio Indians of Sonora-Chihuahua: An Ethnographic Survey* (Washington, D.C.: Bureau of Ethnology Bulletin 186, 1963).

Alfredo Noriego's chile planting is placed in another perspective in my chapter, "Replenishing Desert Agriculture with Native Plants and Their Symbionts," pp. 172–182 in *Meeting the Expectations of the Land,* Wes Jackson, Bruce Colman, and Wendell Berry, eds. (San Francisco: North Point Press, 1985). The plant has also been brought into cultivation in the Río Moctezuma, with only limited success.

Devil's Claw: Designing Baskets, Designing Plants

Devil's-claw domestication has been discussed in several papers: Peter Bretting, "Morphological Differentiation of *Proboscidea parviflora* subsp. *parviflora* (Martyniaceae) Under Domestication," *American Journal of Botany* 69: 1531–1537 (1982); G. P. Nabhan, A. Whiting, H. Dobyns, R. Hevly, and R. Euler, "Devil's Claw Domestication: Evidence from Southwestern Indian Fields," *Journal of Ethnobiology,* 1(1): 135–164 (1978); and G. P. Nabhan and A. M. Rea, "Plant Domestication and Folk Biological Change: The Upper Piman/Devil's Claw Example," *American An-*

thropologist (in press). This chapter is dedicated to Peter Bretting, whose dissertation and more recent devil's claw publications in *Southwestern Naturalist* and *American Journal of Botany* continue to enrich our knowledge of these plants. Note that the Southwestern *Proboscidea* species are called *Martynia* in many older publications.

Harry H. Dunn's "Rootless Cactus of California," *Technical World* 9(5): 564–565 (July 1908), is something that only a rootless Californian could dream up. It was harshly criticized by Forrest Shreve, "Botany in the Magazines," *Plant World* 11(9): 186–187 (September, 1908), whose daughter later did her master's thesis work on devil's claw in Papago Indian basketry. Do these sound like obscure journals? *Technical World* was later renamed *Popular Mechanics,* and *Plant World* became *Ecology!*

Seri use of perennial devil's claw is discussed in Felger and Moser's *People of the Desert and Sea.*

Devil's claw archaeology is summarized by Nabhan and colleagues in "Devil's Claw Domestication."

Mrs. Kitt told Harold Bell Wright many of the "Papago" stories in his *Long Ago Told: Legends of the Papago Indians* (New York: D. Appleton, 1929). I include another Papago legend about devil's claw's encounter with coyote in *The Desert Smells Like Rain.*

Paul D. Hurd, Jr., and E. Gorton Linsley's sexual encounter of a floral kind was entitled, "Pollination of the Unicorn Plant (Martyniaceae) by an Oligolectic, Corolla-Cutting Bee (Hymenoptera: Apoidea)," *Journal of the Kansas Entomological Society* 36(4): 248–251 (1963).

Richard Yarnell's suggestion of devil's claw as one of the few North American domesticates is in his chapter, "Native Plant Husbandry North of Mexico," *The Origins of Agriculture,* Charles A. Reed, ed. (The Hague: Mouton, 1977). Since then, Sonoran panicgrass and wild desert barley have been added to the list of possible domesticates.

Edward Palmer's "Notes and Observations on the Pimo Indians of Arizona," a looseleaf of notes predating 1885, on file in the Arizona State Museum Archives, may be the first to note devil's-claw trade between tribes. Edward Jaeger's *Desert Wild Flowers* (Stanford: Stanford University Press, 1941) is an interesting source on devil's-claw diffusion and many other topics. Other diffusion data are summarized in Nabhan and colleagues, "Devil's Claw Domestication," and in a forthcoming article by Peter Bretting and myself.

The key references on Sonoran panicgrass are Castetter and Bell's *Yuman Indian Agriculture,* and Gary Nabhan and J. M. J. de Wet, *"Panicum sonorum* in Sonoran Desert Agriculture," *Economic Botany* 38(1): 65–82 (1984). Dr. Alan Beetle's suggestion that *Panicum sonorum* should be considered a variety of *P. milliaceum* lacks genetic data to support it and is ungrounded morphologically and biogeographically. Key references on the Cocopa include Anita Alvarez de Williams' "Cocopa," pp. 99–112, *Handbook of North American Indians* Volume 10, and William H. Kelly's *Cocopa Ethnography* (Tucson: Anthropological Papers of the University of Arizona, 1977).

The story of the cave cache of panicgrass is adapted from Arizona State Museum notes, a telephone interview with Mrs. Yowell, and from Wilma Kaemlein's "A Prehistoric Twined-Woven Bag from the Trigo Mountains, Arizona," *The Kiva* 28: 1–13 (1963).

Robert Forbes' interesting article on Chemehuevi Indian agriculture in the Parker-Fort Mohave vicinity is "The Colorado River West," *University of Arizona Monthly* 6: 119–126 (1904).

Aldo Leopold wrote of the Colorado River delta in *A Sand County Almanac* (New York: Oxford University Press, 1949). For other Colorado River history, see Philip L. Fradkin, *A River No More* (New York: Knopf, 1981, also available in paperback from the University of Arizona Press); and Godfrey G. Sykes, *The Colorado Delta* (New York, Kennikat Press, 1970), and his earlier "End of a Great Delta," *Pan-Pacific Geologist* 69: 241–248 (1938).

United States Cocopa communities' nutritional, medical, social, and economic strifes are reported in D. H. Calloway and J. C. Gibbs, "Food Patterns and Food Assistance Programs in the Cocopah Indian Community," *Ecology of Food and Nutrition* 5: 183–196 (1976); and in Charles Mangel's "Sometimes We Feel We're Already Dead," *Look,* pp. 38–43 (June 2, 1970).

Dr. Howard Scott Gentry's writings on panicgrass appear in *Río Mayo Plants* and in *Warihio Indians.* A note on the rediscovery of Sierra Madre panicgrass cultigens first appeared in G. Nabhan, "Grain Amaranths and Other Rare Crops of Northern Mexico," *Dry Country News* 3: 20–22 (1979). In addition to returning seed of panicgrass to other Warihio, Mayo, Mountain Pima, and Cocopa communities, Native Seeds/SEARCH has petitioned that it be listed as a threatened species in the United States. The Office of Endangered Species response in January, 1985, was that it may now be extirpated in Arizona, but the office considered its status too unknown in Mexico to list the plant formally. This may be the first agriculturally associated plant to be nominated for threatened or endangered species status in the United States, and it is still under investigation.

Good to the Bitter End: Wild Desert Gourds

The key references for this chapter are: W. P. Bemis and T. W. Whitaker, "The Xerophytic *Cucurbita* of Northwestern Mexico and Southwestern United States," *Madrono* 20: 33–41; Gary Nabhan and Jill Thompson, *Wild* Cucurbita *of Arid America: An Annotated Bibliography of Ethnic Uses, Chemistry, and Geography** (Tucson, Native Seeds/SEARCH, 1985); and work in process by Laura Merrick of Cornell University for her dissertation. This chapter is dedicated to Laura Merrick, who demonstrated to me that ethnobotany is a key to cucurbit genetic diversity.

The name *chichicoyota* is a direct Hispanization of Nahuatl: "chichi," meaning breasts; and "coyotl," meaning coyote. For another coyote/cucurbit story, see my chapter, "Plants Which Coyote Steals, Spoils, and Shits On," pp. 75–86 in *The Desert Smells Like Rain*.

For a review of cucurbitacin bitterness, see Robert L. Metcalf, Robert A. Metcalf, and A. M. Rhoades, "Cucurbitacins as Kairomones for Diabroticite Beetles," *Proceedings of the National Academy of Sciences* 77(7): 3769–3772 (1980).

Vorsila Bohrer's "Plants that Have Become Extinct in the Southwest," *Symposium on Threatened and Endangered Plants* (Albuquerque: Society of Range Management, 1973) suggests that buffalogourds have been locally extirpated in the highly desertified areas of the Colorado Plateau.

The possible medicinal value of wild *Cucurbita* remains unconfirmed. See preliminary studies: Simon Gitter, Ruth Gallily, Batia Shohat, and David Lavie, "Studies on the Antitumor Effect of Cucurbitacins," *Cancer Research* 21: 516–521 (May 1960); and H. C. Ferguson's "The Preliminary Investigation of an Extract from the Root of *Cucurbita foetidissima*," *Journal of the American Pharmaceutical Association* 44: 440–442 (1955).

Ethnobotanical references, including Curtin for the Rio Grande, Bean and Saubel for the Cahuilla, Swank for the Acoma and Laguna, Pennington for the Nevome Pima, and many others, are discussed and cited in Nabhan and Thompson's *Wild* Cucurbita *in Arid America*.

For results of the geographic analysis of various *C. foetidissima* collections made by the University of Arizona team, see Joseph Scheerens, W. P. Bemis, M. L. Dreher, and J. W. Berry, "Phenotypic Variation in Fruit and Seed Characteristics of Buffalo Gourd," *Journal of the American Oil Seed Chemists Society* 55: 523–525 (1978).

Steve Buchmann's gourd pollination ecology work is soon to be published in several papers, including one with Ellen Ordway, "Activity of Bees (*Apis, Peponapis, Xenoglossa*) on Flowers of *Cucurbita foetidissima* as a Function of Nectar and Pollen Standing Crops," and "Anthecology of Buffalo Gourd *Cucurbita foetidissima* in Arizona," both in press. An earlier paper by Paul Hurd, Jr., E. Gorton Linsley, and Thomas Whitaker, "Squash and Gourd Bees (*Peponapis, Xenoglossa*) and the Origin of the Cultivated *Cucurbita*," *Evolution* 25(1): 218–234 (1971), discusses the significance of these bees to cucurbit biogeography.

The earliest (cultivated?) cucurbit remains in association with human cultures in North America are discussed by Nicholas Conrad and nine coauthors, "Accelerator Radiocarbon Dating for Evidence of Prehistoric Horticulture in Illinois," *Nature* 308: 443–446 (March 1984).

The nutritive value of gourd seeds is the topic of an article by W. P. Bemis and five coauthors, "Oil Composition of *Cucurbita*," *Journal of the American Oil Chemists Society* 64: 429–430 (1967).

Hugh Cutler's comments on Hopi gourdblossom cornmeal cakes are in his *Corn, Cucurbits, and Cotton from Glen Canyon* (Salt Lake City: University of Utah Anthropological Papers 80, 1966).

Laura Merrick and I have published a progress report on the gourd/squash introgression in Sonora as "Natural Hybridization of Wild *Cucurbita sororia* Group with Domesticated *Cucurbita mixta* in Southern Sonora, Mexico," *Cucurbit Genetics Cooperative* 6: 74–75. I added a note on the Pima field situation as "Evidence of Gene Flow Between *Cucurbita mixta* and a Field Edge Population of Wild *Cucurbita* at Onavas, Sonora," pp. 76–77, in the same volume. Campbell Pennington's background work in Onavas is in his two *Pima Bajo* volumes.

Edgar Anderson and Leslie Hubricht first discussed "Evidence for Introgressive Hybridization," in *American Journal of Botany* 25: 396–402 (1938).

I discuss Larry Curtis and his pioneering work with buffalogourd in "New Crops for Desert Farming," *New Farm* 1(3): 52–60 (1979). A more thorough history has been written by A. C. Gathman and W. P. Bemis, "The History, Biology and Chemistry of the Buffalo Gourd, *Cucurbita foetidissima* HBK," *Biology and Chemistry of the Cucurbitaceae* (Ithaca, Cornell University Press, in press).

The new uses of cucurbits for biological control are discussed by Robert Metcalf and five coauthors, "Cucurbitacin Contents and Diabroticite (Coleoptera: Chrysomelidae) Feeding Upon *Cucurbita* Spp.," *Environmental Entomology* 11(4): 931–938 (1982).

Index

207